# UNQUITTABLE

## Finding and Keeping the Talent You Need

**Jim Bitterle**

**Society for Human Resource Management**
Alexandria, Virginia | shrm.org
**Society for Human Resource Management, India Office**
Mumbai, India | shrmindia.org
**Society for Human Resource Management, Middle East and Africa Office**
Dubai, UAE | shrm.org/pages/mena.aspx

SHRM®
BETTER WORKPLACES
BETTER WORLD™

The Society for Human Resource Management is the world's largest HR professional society, representing 285,000 members in more than 165 countries. For nearly seven decades, the society has been the leading provider of resources serving the needs of HR professionals and advancing the practice of human resource management. SHRM has more than 575 affiliated chapters within the United States and subsidiary offices in China, India, and United Arab Emirates. Please visit us at www.shrm.org.

Library of Congress Cataloging-in-Publication Data

Names: Bitterle, Jim, author.
Title: Unquittable : finding & keeping the right talent / Jim Bitterle.
Description: First edition. | Alexandria, VA : Society for Human Resource Management, [2020] | Includes bibliographical references and index. | Identifiers: LCCN 2020010672 (print) | LCCN 2020010673 (ebook) | ISBN 9781586446598 (paperback) | ISBN 9781586446604 (pdf) | ISBN 9781586446611 (epub) | ISBN 9781586446628 (mobi)
Subjects: LCSH: Employee selection. | Employee retention.
Classification: LCC HF5549.5.S38 B53 2020 (print) | LCC HF5549.5.S38 (ebook) | DDC 658.3/11--dc23

Printed in the United States of America

FIRST EDITION

PB Printing 10 9 8 7 6 5 4 3 2 1                                    61.15204

# UNQUITTABLE

*This book is dedicated to each and every employee at EDSI. I've never seen a group that is so devoted to helping clients, all while supporting each other at a level I never dreamed possible.*

# Contents

Acknowledgments   ix
About the Author   xi
Introduction   xiii

Chapter 1
Talent Is All We've Got. . . . . . . . . . . . . . . . . . . . . . . . . . . . . . . . . . . . . . . . . . 1

Chapter 2
Employer Branding: Attracting Talent . . . . . . . . . . . . . . . . . . . . . . . . . . . . 11

Chapter 3
Highly Desirable Internships . . . . . . . . . . . . . . . . . . . . . . . . . . . . . . . . . . . 27

Chapter 4
Onboarding . . . . . . . . . . . . . . . . . . . . . . . . . . . . . . . . . . . . . . . . . . . . . . . . . 41

Chapter 5
Incentive Systems . . . . . . . . . . . . . . . . . . . . . . . . . . . . . . . . . . . . . . . . . . . 55

Chapter 6
Career Paths . . . . . . . . . . . . . . . . . . . . . . . . . . . . . . . . . . . . . . . . . . . . . . . 69

Chapter 7
Career Sculpting . . . . . . . . . . . . . . . . . . . . . . . . . . . . . . . . . . . . . . . . . . . . 83

Chapter 8
Exit Interviews . . . . . . . . . . . . . . . . . . . . . . . . . . . . . . . . . . . . . . . . . . . . . 97

Chapter 9
Corporate Universities . . . . . . . . . . . . . . . . . . . . . . . . . . . . . . . . . . . . . . 113

Chapter 10
Flexibility . . . . . . . . . . . . . . . . . . . . . . . . . . . . . . . . . . . . . . . . . . . . . . . . 125

Chapter 11
Performance Management. . . . . . . . . . . . . . . . . . . . . . . . . . . . . . . . . . . . 137

Chapter 12
Mentoring. . . . . . . . . . . . . . . . . . . . . . . . . . . . . . . . . . . . . . . . . . . . . . . . 153

Chapter 13
Strategic Workforce Planning . . . . . . . . . . . . . . . . . . . . . . . . . . . . . . . . . 167

Chapter 14
People Analytics and Talent Dashboards . . . . . . . . . . . . . . . . . . . . . . . . 179

Chapter 15
**Compensation Systems** . . . . . . . . . . . . . . . . . . . . . . . . . . . . . . . . . . . . . . . . . 189

Chapter 16
**Continuous Improvement** . . . . . . . . . . . . . . . . . . . . . . . . . . . . . . . . . . . . . . . . 205

Chapter 17
**Leadership Buy-In** . . . . . . . . . . . . . . . . . . . . . . . . . . . . . . . . . . . . . . . . . . . . . . 223

**Conclusion   237**
**Endnotes   241**
**Index   243**
**Additional SHRM-Published Books   255**
**SHRMStore Books Approved for Recertification Credit   257**

# Acknowledgments

I'd like to thank Kevin Schnieders, EDSI's owner and Chief Servant Leader, for consistently encouraging the design and implementation of an amazing corporate culture. This book would never have materialized without his support. I'd also like to acknowledge Kathy Wilson Peacock; her assistance with storytelling, writing, editing, and moral support were fundamental to ensuring this book is not only informational but also fun to read.

# About the Author

Jim Bitterle, managing partner of EDSI Consulting, spent ten years as an executive in the specialty chemical business and has led both domestic and international businesses. He also brings more than twenty-four years of management consulting experience to his insights into talent attraction, development, and retention. Jim's experience in a variety of general management, operational, organizational improvement, and strategic consulting engagements, as well as direct experience as a corporate leader, gives him great perspective in understanding the universal need for all organizations to find, develop, and retain great people. Jim has an MBA in finance and marketing, with honors, from the Kellogg School at Northwestern University. He also holds a BA degree in operational management from the Broad School of Management at Michigan State University.

# Introduction

Has this ever happened to you? You spend over a month recruiting, interviewing, hiring, and onboarding someone for a long-vacant position, only to have the individual resign after a short time on the job. Sometimes they're polite and resign properly; other times they walk out the door at the end of the day and never come back. Either way, you're back to square one.

It's tempting to blame the individual for wasting the company's time and money, but you also wonder how the whole debacle could have been prevented. The good news is that, yes, there are ways to make such woeful occurrences as rare as a hassle-free software update on your laptop. However, like most good things in life, it will take hard work. Plus, leaders must be willing to adopt and follow through with new ways of doing things.

## LESSONS LEARNED FROM THE FOUR FAILWAVES

For the past thirty years, I've witnessed some colossal business train wrecks, first as a manager and later as a consultant. You've probably seen some train wrecks too, and maybe you've even been a victim of one. The casualties of bad business decisions include once-iconic American brands: Pontiac, Howard Johnson's, Blockbuster, Sears. Nothing lasts forever, but bad business decisions can kill a company quicker than you can say Toys "R" Us.

Businesses fail for all kinds of reasons, many of which can be traced back to the issue of talent. Notice the semantics: The term *talent* recognizes that people are the heart and soul of a business in a way terms like *workers, staff,* or *employees* do not. *Talent* needs to be recognized and developed; *workers* and *employees* need to be managed and controlled.

The transition from *workers* to *talent* was a happy watershed and marks a new era. In fact, I call this new epoch the Talent Failwave because companies and organizations that fail will most likely trace their downfall to disrespecting and neglecting to develop the talents of those who work for them. The Talent Failwave will affect the business world as significantly as the previous three failwaves of quality, cost, and technology. Each of these failwaves holds a lesson for us, and each is studded with timely case studies. Smart organizations are led by those who understand this history and know how to change with the times. A good leader will know where we've been and where we're going. To understand how we arrived at the Talent Failwave, let's take a look at the previous three.

## The First Failwave: Quality

In the 1970s, global manufacturing quality left a lot to be desired. This created an opportunity for companies that could create high-quality, reliable products. They positioned their goods and services as being more reliable than the other guys'. That's how the Toyota Corolla eventually became the best-selling passenger car in the world.[1] It wasn't flashy and it wasn't particularly fun to drive. But it cost $2,700 and it didn't burst into flames in a rear-end collision (like the Ford Pinto) or break down without warning.[2] Many European and American cars simply weren't dependable. While Ford was busy maximizing profits by cutting corners on design and functionality, Toyota was building a quality product via the Toyota Production System. This well-defined management system led to many more innovations, including modern lean manufacturing concepts, which incorporated continuous improvement and respect for people. Ironically, Toyota pulled from the Ford Motor Company's earlier efforts when establishing the basics of their own early production systems. During the Quality Failwave, companies adapted to new demands, systems, and procedures. If they didn't, they fell behind, failed, and went the way of the dinosaur.

## The Second Failwave: Cost Competition

Next, rampant consumerism changed the business landscape as companies began a "race to the bottom." The winners were the companies that could manufacture or sell products cheaper than their competitors. Main Street, USA, became a ghost town while big-box retailers set up shop over yonder, surrounded by acres of parking lots. Waves of general stores, hardware stores, machine shops, and a myriad of other businesses went bust. They just couldn't stay competitive with their low-cost rivals. Quality was no longer the primary concern, and neither was employee training or job satisfaction. However, savvy companies that couldn't compete on price survived by creating a meaningful point of difference. For example, although Volvos were ugly, expensive, and not particularly luxurious or reliable,[3] they were built like tanks and kept you and your family safe, so their awkward design became a geeky status symbol. In the service industry, mid-priced, ho-hum hotel chains failed to derail luxury brands such as the Ritz-Carlton because the company capitalized on its commitment to excellence in service through the Ritz-Carlton Learning Institute and Ritz-Carlton Leadership Center. The company is the only one in the hospitality industry to date that has received two Malcolm Baldrige National Quality Awards.[4] Mediocrity was everywhere, but smart companies learned how to set themselves apart from the low-cost competition. Those that didn't have a point of difference and couldn't compete on price failed.

## The Third Failwave: Technology

The Technology Failwave defines the digital era, but its roots go further back. The Singer Corporation, for example, began manufacturing sewing machines in 1851. Within a few years, the pedal-powered marvel was indispensable in thousands of American homes.[5] Instead of fading into the dust heap of bygone technology along with Dictaphones, trebuchets, and bloodletting, the Singer sewing machine remains an iconic and vibrant brand with a product line of electronic, computerized, and programmable machines trusted by hobbyists and professionals alike. How has a company like Singer stayed relevant for over 150 years whereas a similar company like Kodak, founded in 1888 and also a household name, filed for bankruptcy in 2012? The answer: by keeping up with technology. When sewing machines changed, Singer changed with them. For Kodak, as long as cameras needed film, they were golden. But in the world of digital cameras, they were also-rans. Singer embraced the mechanical-digital divide; Kodak did not.

More recently, many of us can relate to the Blockbuster versus Netflix fight to the death. Blockbuster successfully transitioned to DVDs when VHS tapes fell by the wayside, but the company completely missed the boat to the twenty-first century. Blockbuster passed up the chance to buy

Netflix and canceled a video-on-demand deal. Its efforts to launch its own DVD mail-order and online service were too little, too late.[6] Since 1990, scores of companies have failed because they didn't stay current with new technology or because they backed the wrong developments. Hence we've been living through the Technology Failwave. Hard to believe, but chances are that Google, Amazon, Apple, and Microsoft may follow in Blockbuster's footsteps someday.

## The Fourth Failwave: Talent

The fourth wave—the Talent Failwave—is powered by historically low unemployment, mass baby boomer retirements, and a significant skills gap between open jobs and available people. Today, we have more job openings than qualified people to fill them.[7] To make matters worse, job growth is projected to outstrip the growth in the workforce, leaving companies fighting for talent.[8] Combine this fundamental shortage with school systems that are not preparing today's students for tomorrow's jobs, and you have a talent crisis unlike anything we've seen in the past.

Don't like your job? Quit! Better benefits and pay are right around the corner. We've already seen some winners and losers: Costco pays good wages and provides defined career pathways for their talent. Down the street, Sam's Club claims they can't afford to pay those same wages to their employees. McDonald's understands that growth requires reducing barriers to employment for young people around the world. Team members can receive pre-employment readiness training, apprenticeships, career pathways programs, free GED training, and tuition assistance.[9] McDonald's understands what it means to be unquittable.

The scary thing about the Talent Failwave is that it may not look like talent is the issue on the surface. Many failing companies believe that quality and service issues are behind their decline. These may contribute to a company's failure, but they could also indicate deeper problems with attracting, hiring, and retaining quality employees. First, the company stagnates. It cannot grow because it cannot attract and retain the talent it needs for development. The company loses some employees and struggles to fill open positions, often resorting to hiring untrained, less capable employees. Service and quality levels degrade to the point that the company loses customers. The cycle continues until, in some cases, the company fails. This is the new Talent Failwave!

## THE SMARTEST GUY IN THE ROOM SYNDROME, OR THE BABY BOOMER LIKE ME

People often ask me, "Jim, how could these companies be so stupid? Everyone knows that to retain employees you have to pay them appropriately, provide reasonable benefits, and treat them well." It does seem simple, doesn't it? But the answer is that the companies on the brink of failure are often those run by one of two types of leaders. The first is the Smartest Guy in the Room. He (and it's almost always a "he") has got confidence and ego to spare, and he's an expert on numerous topics. He's got a great track record of success and he doesn't listen to the advice of others. The problem is that what worked twenty or thirty years ago isn't necessarily what works now. If he really was the smartest guy in the room, he'd quit and enjoy a fruitful retirement rather than run a once-successful business into the ground.

The second type, sadly, is a baby boomer like me. These individuals have spent most of their careers in a traditional environment that formed their opinions on work, workers, and workplace culture. Boomers often believed they were lucky to have a job at the start of their careers, so they tolerated the dysfunctional attributes of companies and their cultures. This strategy led to success for millions of people, but that doesn't mean it was right or that it will continue to work. Too often, we cast millennials as having a poor work ethic, little company loyalty, and a high need for attention. The reality is that older bosses like me need to change. Younger workers thrive when we place them in the right environment. In many cases, they can be as productive (if not more) as we thought we were at their age.

I hope you never work for the Smartest Guy in the Room or a baby boomer who is unwilling to change. More importantly—don't become one. Your goal is to understand how to attract, retain, and develop talent in an ever-changing business landscape. That means you can never stop growing, learning, or listening. This book is a good place to start.

## HOW TO USE THIS BOOK

The companies and people in this book are fictional and illustrate key concepts of talent management. Each chapter contains a "good" story, in which a talent technique is introduced to the workplace with a positive result. The counterpoint "bad" story demonstrates what happens when a technique is either ignored or implemented incorrectly. Good intentions aren't enough. Success requires conviction, investment, confidence, and time.

You may think that some of these "bad" scenarios are exaggerated. I assure you, they are not. I've witnessed enough in my long manufacturing management career to, well, write a book. Factories where the cops are routinely called to break up fistfights. Drug rings run out of stockrooms. Company officers sent to jail for embezzlement. Managers unwilling to pay workers more than minimum wage. Racism. Sexism. Ageism. All types of discrimination. The good news is that these practices will inevitably sink an organization.

Each chapter discusses a technique in the talent toolbox. Taken together, they are a veritable workshop of choices to address common issues in the workplace. The tool to attract quality candidates? Employer branding and desirable internships. How to develop skills and loyalty? Career sculpting, corporate universities, and mentoring. Measuring employee satisfaction? Talent dashboards and continuous improvement. These techniques aren't solely for large companies; they can be scaled for any size organization. In fact, smaller and midsize companies could benefit the most. Small changes can have great effects!

Finally, the talent concepts in this book are universal, no matter your business, industry, product, or service. It doesn't matter whether you work in the public, private, for-profit, or nonprofit sector. Each time you value human ingenuity, you are one step closer to becoming unquittable. Fly-by-night new hires will be a distant memory.

## COVID-19: A SWIFTLY CHANGING LANDSCAPE

This book went to press just as the world began grappling with a once-in-a-lifetime pandemic. Within weeks of COVID-19 hotspots erupting throughout the country—and the world—it was clear that the economic fallout would be devastating. Virtually overnight, the U.S. unemployment rate leaped from historic lows to historic highs. Entire industries were gutted, and people's lives were upended in almost unimaginable ways. The steam is out of the kettle on the longest economic expansion in U.S. history.

Yet, I stand by the information in this book. You'll need to look past the now-outdated statistics about how there are more jobs than people to fill them. That's no longer true, at least in the short term. But even a pandemic can't stop the larger demographic shift: the largest generation in U.S. history—those born between 1946 and 1964—is beginning to retire en masse and will continue to do so for the next six to ten years. The Millennials are now the largest living adult generation, and this has huge ramifications for how businesses should attract and nurture talent. As employers face unprecedented uncertainty, they can gain a foothold in this shifting economy by recruiting, training, and retaining talented individuals. The techniques in this book require leadership, stamina, and vision. In the aftermath of this world-changing scenario, success will be a byproduct not of an economic tide that lifts all boats, but rather of a very deliberate process.

This recession, like every other, will eventually end. In the meantime, implementing some of the talent tools discussed in this book is a smart move. Most of them don't take gobs of capital to get started. Being intentional about your employer brand while millions are looking for work can pay off handsomely. Being able to explain your career paths to job candidates may make your offer more attractive than your competitor's when you're in a position to hire again. Reassessing flexibility after millions of people have learned how to work efficiently from home will position you as forward thinking. Take the longer view here. With a few new processes in place, you'll be well positioned when the economy comes roaring back.

# CHAPTER 1

# Talent Is All We've Got

It's harder than ever for people to find their dream job, yet the reality is that every day, over seven million positions go unfilled in the United States—way more than the number of people looking for jobs.[1] This is good news for job seekers, but employers have the hard task of finding the right people for their organizations and getting them to stay. The American workforce will continue to grow for the foreseeable future, but it won't be fast enough. To make matters worse, many new workers aren't being trained for positions or industries where they're desperately needed. We're churning out too many history majors and not enough plumbers. Regardless, your organization may not need either. Thriving in the current marketplace requires understanding what skills those history majors have that could translate to your business—might they sync up with your organization's need for detail-oriented individuals who can write policy manuals? The stakes are high and mutually beneficial; workers need employers, employers need workers, and everyone deserves respect and happiness.

Workers no longer pledge their allegiance and loyalty to their employers like they once did. There's no earthly reason why they should. The secret to attracting and retaining talent boils down to that holiday chestnut: "Give them everything they need and some of what they want." But what's a want and what's a need? It's an inexact science. It varies for everyone and across industries. You'll make headway as long as you take the issue seriously and really listen to what people are saying.

In the following scenario, Ashley and Odette represent the alpha and omega of the talent landscape: an eager acolyte and an ossified but capable workforce veteran. Their experiences have differed dramatically and shaped them uniquely, but they both listen to reason.

1

## THE BELIEVERS AND THE DOUBTERS

Even with the lights shining in her eyes, obscuring much of the audience, Cherilynn could gauge the audience's reaction from her vantage point onstage. It was an important part of public speaking—assessing your audience, knowing when they are rapt and when their attention is wandering. Cherilynn was practically in love with the young woman in the first row, who was attempting to film the whole presentation on her phone and take notes at the same time. She must not know that both the video and the PowerPoint deck would be posted on the conference website.

The woman's eyes were trained on Cherilynn as she traversed the stage. It was a real ego boost; Cherilynn didn't have a fan club at the office unless you counted the CEO's dog, which occasionally roamed the halls looking for treats and snuggles. Now, with an HR enthusiast watching her every move, Cherilynn's confidence soared as she glided through her presentation.

And then her clicker malfunctioned. She jabbed at it, trying to change the slide, but the presentation was stuck on a photo of a plumber with a large wrench gazing confidently at a dripping pipe. A snicker erupted from somewhere to the left of the young woman in the front. Cherilynn scanned the crowd. The offender looked to be an older woman in a dark outfit that did not fit the humid Orlando weather. Her arms were crossed and her glasses reflected the light from the stage. Cherilynn knew the type—a nonbeliever. An old-school "back in my day we didn't have any EEO laws, and we liked it like that" type. Cherilynn whacked the clicker with the side of her hand, but the slide didn't budge.

The ill-natured woman in the audience muttered something about technology, loud enough for everyone to hear. Cherilynn figured she was probably only here to take advantage of a free trip to Orlando, quite possibly smuggling three grandchildren and a daughter-in-law into her company-provided hotel room. She'd seen it before. If anyone were to check the woman's giant handbag on her way out of the conference room, they'd probably find half a dozen granola bars and a fruit cup from the buffet.

A third whack of the clicker did the trick. The next slide popped up, and Cherilynn moved on to the war for talent and work-life balance.

Ashley owned up to being an HR geek. She thought of it as the compassionate side of business, where you got to know and work with the people who made a company successful. It made her somewhat unusual at school. Her college friends were busy making short documentaries about the uncontacted tribes of the Amazon and finding summer internships at hot tech start-ups, while she spent a significant portion of her time coordinating her school's Business Student Association. Her latest project, apart from attending this conference, was lining up guest speakers for the group's annual symposium. Cherilynn Fenton would be perfect! She was a futurist prepping a whole new generation on what the workplace would look like twenty years from now. Just like everything else, the HR field had trends and people had to stay on top of them. But Cherilynn's fee was probably outrageous, and Ashley had no clue how to approach her.

The trip to the conference was the top prize of her university's annual essay contest, and she wanted to make the most of it. Her ultimate goal was to be the CHRO for a *Fortune* 500 company. She loved the idea of helping a business find qualified people and encouraging them to live up to their potential. Engineers, software developers, accountants, or sous chefs. It didn't matter. She would get to meet new people every day.

How does a 20-year-old college junior decide her fate lies in HR? It began for Ashley when she was 17. She had a part-time summer job in the office of a landscaping company. She was only supposed to answer phones and fill out stuff on the computer, but the employees' schedules proved to be so erratic that she ended up doing whatever was needed. One particularly awful Thursday, a whole crew just up and left at the end of the day. The crew leader, Joe, claimed they were insubordinate and that he fired them. But everyone knew Joe had a temper, so he was no doubt partly to blame. It didn't really matter. They had a packed schedule the next day, and they needed four guys, fast.

The office manager usually did the hiring (and firing), but she had jury duty. Ashley called the company owner, Phil, and he told her to place an ad online and start interviewing people at 6:00 a.m. the next morning. The idea was to find four people capable of operating a lawnmower and get them on the crew by 8:00 a.m. Phil said he'd come in and sign the paperwork.

The prospect of interviewing people both terrified and thrilled Ashley. She felt a little like an unprepared understudy who has to go onstage when the lead dancer twists an ankle. She had the ad placed by 7:00 p.m., got six responses by 10:00 p.m., and told them all to be at the office for an interview by 6:30 a.m. She stayed up until midnight googling "how to interview people for a job."

The next morning, only four of the six interviewees showed up. Of those four, only two brought resumes and only two could start that day. She hired the pair that could start immediately, but she felt only semiconfident about one of them.

All her preparation from the online research—asking where they saw themselves in five years and describing a situation in which they had overcome adversity—was moot. The real issues were: Do you have a driver's license? Can you operate a lawnmower and hedge clipper? Can you get through the workday without committing a felony?

The two new hires went out with Joe, who appeared that morning looking more contrite than usual. By 9:00 a.m., five more people responded to the ad and Ashley told them to get to the office ASAP. She hired two more people by noon. Phil strolled in at about 1:00 p.m. and signed the papers.

It was an object lesson in flying by the seat of her pants. Ashley was hooked.

Odette started working at Big John's in the spring of 1983, when the ink on her divorce papers was barely dry. She was a secretary—the term *admin* was still over the horizon—with two young children at home. Her job involved answering the phone, scheduling meetings, and typing memos on an IBM Selectric. She was John Griskow's "girl" at Big John's, and she was pretty sure she got the job based on how she looked in a tight skirt, because her shorthand skills left something to be desired.

Odette put up with a lot from "Big John" over the years, all for the sake of her kids. Mr. Griskow—it was never John—was a typical boss: oblivious, chauvinistic, and condescending. Odette never exactly approved of his behavior, but what could she do? She needed the job. Griskow was fairly flexible—or at least he was out of the office so much he didn't really know what was going on. She rolled her eyes at him behind his back when he told dumb-blonde jokes, and she bought his wife thoughtful birthday gifts and signed the cards "Love always, John."

But 1983 was well over thirty years ago. She could have left or gone back to school once the kids were grown and gotten herself a better paying job. Truth was, she kind of liked the little fiefdom she had established at Big John's. She was an efficient gatekeeper to the CEO, and Griskow trusted her. It would have been a pain to start over somewhere else.

Her job had evolved as the company grew. She was good with numbers, so she was in charge of payroll by the mid-1990s. Just as important as the actual checks was her tight lock on information. Griskow was adamant that no employee was ever to know what anyone else made. The reason was clear—he played favorites. Fortunately for Odette, she was one of them. She might have made more elsewhere, but she was frugal and lived within her means. She had paid her house off by the time she was 40, her car was old but reliable, and she seldom took vacations. Her only vice was a weekly trip with her kids to the neighborhood pizza joint. Her frugality was matched by Griskow's. The administrative offices sported threadbare carpet, and the employee bathrooms were a time capsule from the 1960s.

By the turn of the millennium, she was Big John's HR manager. She recruited employees, hired them, fired them, and oversaw compliance issues. She had three people working under her. Never in all those years did she take a class in HR management.

That she had convinced Griskow to foot the bill for this conference in Orlando was proof that she had enormous influence over him. The years hadn't softened him at all; if anything, he had become even more creative in finding ways to pinch pennies.

Odette was using the trip as an excuse to take her granddaughters to Disney World. She wanted to make up for the fact that she hadn't been able to take her own children when they were young. So she pitched the Orlando conference to Griskow as a way to stay abreast of legal issues in HR. His fear of expensive and time-consuming lawsuits was well known.

All she had to do was sit through the keynote address and a workshop on new EEO regulations, then it would be off to Magic Kingdom. She juggled a muffin while trying to pull her buzzing phone out of her purse, thinking it was a granddaughter telling her to hurry up.

Instead, it was Griskow telling her that two plant supervisors had just quit. Lovely. As she took her seat and the lights dimmed, she was suddenly overwhelmed with finding not one, but two plant supervisors before production nosedived. Odette knew why they had quit. They might have withstood the long hours and low salary if there had been other benefits—a great work environment, safe and modern facilities, a 401(k) plan that might have made retirement a reality someday. But Big John's had none of those things. Her tenure as the HR manager had been one long stretch of lackluster candidates and high turnover. She assumed it was like that everywhere.

Cherilynn Fenton was exactly what Odette expected. Her suit was a strange shade of purple and her hairstyle smacked of Texas. She strutted across the stage firing off a barrage of facts intended to shock and awe the crowd:

- "If you think finding and keeping talent is hard now, just wait—it's going to get worse. Much worse."
- "As a country, we want our GDP to grow by over 2 percent annually. How can we do that if the workforce only grows by 0.5 percent?"
- "Every year, over four million baby boomers retire. Leaving with them is a wealth of institutional knowledge and a strong work ethic."
- "In 2019, the number of open positions climbed to a new record: 7.2 million."

Each doomsday statement was matched by a vivid image on the giant screen behind her: charts with choppy red lines zooming into the stratosphere. A photo of a revolving door with a happy, fit, gray-haired man waltzing out and a stoop-shouldered millennial in a hoodie grimly shuffling in. A young woman staring at a computer spreadsheet with a horrified expression on her face, as though she couldn't understand the difference between the red and black numbers.

Odette rolled her eyes. The HR industry was built on fear; it funded shindigs like this one and perpetuated steep annual dues for professional organizations that claimed to "keep you on top of the latest developments in the industry." Fear sold magazines, workshops, and books.

The reality was quite different in Odette's eyes. People needed jobs, and Big John's had positions to give. It was a workplace, not a nursery school, and if you couldn't be there on time and do your job, that was your problem and no one else's. She was living proof, having gone from penniless divorcee to owning her own home in less than twenty years—without spending a minute in college, no less.

Cherilynn Fenton cased the stage, as confident as a newly minted Dale Carnegie graduate. A young woman in the front row was actually filming the presentation on her phone. Odette would have bet her day pass to Disney World that the girl was majoring in HR management at an outrageously overpriced college, going into debt to learn something that she could learn on the job. Millennials had a weird fixation on education.

Odette had no idea where she would find two plant supervisors, or how Big John's would make its quotas until she did.

The purple-suited speaker launched into a tirade about how few young people were choosing to be plumbers and electricians and how the skilled trades needed to do a better job of recruiting them into apprenticeships. The slide showed a grinning young man, grease artfully smeared on his cheek, happily hoisting a big wrench toward a leaky pipe.

The slide stuck. The woman on stage jabbed her clicker at it. Odette laughed—louder than she meant to. People nearby turned and scowled. "Technology, am I right?" she commented, snickering again. No one smiled. Honestly, people took these conferences so seriously.

On stage, the speaker got the picture to change and all went back to normal. There was more talk about "the war for talent" and employees' desire for "work-life balance." The photo showed a bunch of office workers doing yoga in a conference room. Please.

Herb, one of the former plant managers, hadn't even been at the company for a year. What was his deal?

Odette's phone buzzed with another text. Hourly absenteeism was at 8 percent for the day. That was high—even for a Monday. But it's not like she could do anything about it from five states away. Nevertheless, the news put a damper on her mood. Griskow would expect a call at her earliest convenience.

Only one year until retirement; that was the plan. Twelve more months until she sailed through the office doors for the last time, like the man in the photo.

"Six million people are looking for jobs. Their skills don't match those employers require. But companies still think they'll find a needle in a haystack."

Odette had to admit the purple woman had a point. Finding two plant supervisors would be like finding two needles in a haystack. And it *was* true—job applicants did not have the skills Big John's needed. People applying for work in the office didn't know how to create a spreadsheet, people applying for work in the warehouse had never seen a hi-lo, and people wanting the better-paying jobs in manufacturing had never even heard of a CNC machine.

Young people with no work history thought they could demand a job starting at $15 an hour. No one could deny the huge disconnect between what employers wanted and what job seekers expected.

Odette became more uncomfortable the longer the woman talked. She had given thirty-five years to Big John's, more than half her life. She'd spent more time with Griskow than anyone else, and the company meant something to her—she had helped build it. Maybe it was wrong to think of it as only a job, a means to an end.

She knew that turnover was a huge problem at the company; it was expensive and it affected productivity. Sales had declined in the last few years. It was easy to dismiss as a cyclical phenomenon, but the truth was that "talent" (they used to call them "workers") was hard to find. She wasn't sure how to fix it. She didn't want the company to go out of business because then it would be like she had given it her best years for nothing. Kind of like her marriage. Darn that speaker, stirring up feelings Odette had worked hard to tamp down.

Ashley loved the concept of employer branding. In fact, it would be a perfect topic for the symposium. She could create an employer branding program at the Lawnmore Landscaping Company and crush the competition. They could earn a reputation as the region's best landscaping company to work for, and they could facilitate employee growth by expanding into patio installation, pond design, and deck building. It could be the subject of her senior thesis.

The memory on her phone was full, so she was forced to watch Cherilynn directly. Their connection was undeniable! Cherilynn looked her in the eye more than once. She wondered where she could get a suit in that same shade of purple. It really made a statement.

Cherilynn was invigorated by the applause following her presentation. Thankfully, the stuck slide was the only glitch. This was definitely one of the largest crowds she'd spoken to, and now that her keynote was over, she could relax for the rest of the conference. She'd be chairing a few smaller workshops, nothing more.

A small group gathered around her in the hubbub following her address. She wasn't surprised to see the young woman approach her, but she was surprised to see the older woman in the dark clothing also come forward.

The first woman introduced herself as Ashley, an HR management major. She was adorably nervous and Cherilynn recognized in her a sense of engagement that would lead to success in her life.

"I really connected with what you said, especially the part about employer branding," Ashley said. "It would make a fabulous topic for the symposium my school's Business Association is hosting in September. Is there any way you might be interested in participating? I'm not really sure about the right way to ask."

Cherilynn was impressed by Ashley's firm handshake. "Let me give you my card. Shoot me an email next week and I'll check my calendar."

"Really? Okay!" Ashley was equal parts delighted and surprised.

Cherilynn turned to the other woman, who introduced herself as Odette. "I have to admit, your talk took me by surprise," Odette said.

"Really?"

Odette considered her words carefully. "Two of my production supervisors quit this morning."

"I'm sorry to hear that."

"I'm afraid my company is in real trouble. The way we used to do things isn't working anymore."

Cherilynn sensed a lot of history behind the statement.

"These are hard times for small manufacturing companies," Odette said. She paused, distracted by a new thought. "When did 'workers' become 'talent'?"

Cherilynn chuckled. "It's a way of reminding ourselves that people are more than employees, that they're individuals who bring unique assets to the table, assets that should be cultivated and used."

Odette raised an eyebrow. "I'm not looking for a circus performer. I just need someone who can get the job done."

"Tell you what," Cherilynn said. "Come to my workshop on practical talent solutions this afternoon. I'd like to hear more about your situation."

That would put a kink in Odette's vacation plans. "I'll see if I can fit it in my schedule," she said. Griskow was texting her furiously, and she was wavering between putting him at ease and ignoring him. Truth is, they were both old dogs. She wasn't sure she could change after so many years, and she wasn't sure that Griskow would let her if she tried. Maybe it was time for something new, or maybe the heat was just getting to her. The enthusiasm that permeated the crowd at the conference—would she be able to bottle it up and take it home with her? It may take a little while, Odette knew, but eventually Mr. Griskow would come around. After all these years, she knew him best, and she knew he wanted his company to survive.

# CHAPTER 2

# Employer Branding: Attracting Talent

Having a strong, positive employer brand means that job seekers want to work for you. They've heard that yours is a fabulous company and they want in. Think GM in the 1950s, IBM in the 1960s, and Google in the 2010s. Eager go-getters regularly check your job postings online, hoping for an opening that meshes with their skills.

Employer branding is a crucial part of an organization's reputation, the flip side of which is product branding. After all, can you think of a company with a lousy product or service that people really want to work for? On the other hand, some companies have a great reputation for their product or service but are known to have less-than-ideal working conditions (a certain e-tailer's warehouse practices come to mind). In an economic climate where people have *choices,* you need to give them a *reason* to want to work for you. Why will a qualified individual choose you over your competitor?

Employer branding encompasses everything from free coffee to high-end bonus packages, from the physical space to the culture that exists within a company's walls. Smaller companies can find a way to enter the employer branding game without the clout of a swoosh logo. News of perks will spread like wildfire among your prospective talent pool. Signing bonuses, holiday bonuses, birthdays off, sports tickets, team lunches—these all help. However, some of the most useful techniques are less costly: a robust onboarding program, advancement opportunities, a bright and clean workspace, a culture of optimism and understanding, flexible scheduling, and true dedication to work-life balance.

As seen in the scenarios below, Elevate Mortgage was founded on respect for all individuals, a principle extending throughout the company from the top. The CEO views each employee as an internal customer. This technique can't be faked; just saying it doesn't make it true. At Accord Insurance, conversely, the head honcho's ego affects everything he chooses to do. He gives lip service to an ambitious team player who recognizes the problem and suggests improvements. But shortsightedness wins the day, and a diamond in the rough decamps for another company.

## THE RESUME AVALANCHE AT ELEVATE MORTGAGE

Will Taliferro had a vision in mind when he founded Elevate Mortgage in 1995. His parents were Realtors, so he knew all about hard work and the ins and outs of real estate. The sky's-the-limit payday appealed to him, too, unlike the uniform. The oppressive suit and tie, the stiff dress shoes, the industry's reputation for conformity and lack of humor. Will wanted to do things his own way. He played the balalaika in a Russian folk band and was well known in his college fraternity for his cake decorating skills. He stood out at business school with his dreadlocks, scruffy beard, and tendency to quote Albert Camus.

Will knew a bit about the mortgage business from watching his parents and decided to create a mortgage company for people like him—people who wanted to break free from the stuffy confines of such a traditional industry. He conveyed a grand vision and was intelligent, hardworking, and charismatic, making his business attractive to investors early in his career.

Within twenty-five years, Elevate Mortgage had become the biggest mortgage and real estate company in the state and a major sponsor of local events and charitable causes. Will had cultivated a high-profile, enviable employer brand with over five thousand employees. The headquarter's campus attracted millennials with flexible scheduling, an on-site wellness center, development opportunities, and napping pods.

Job seekers looking for a range of work, from cleaning and landscaping to senior leadership positions, flooded the HR offices with resumes each week. The bounty was the direct result of Will designing the company around his core values: "Citizenship, Community, Shared Prosperity." It was short, simple, and a great tool. Most of all, he believed it and hired others who did too.

Kelsey's favorite job as an HR associate for Elevate Mortgage was prescreening applicants to determine whether they would be a good fit for the company. She would have a five- to ten-minute phone conversation that often stretched to fifteen minutes or more if she hit it off with someone talkative. Kelsey enjoyed meeting such a variety of people, and she could usually tell right away whether the candidate should move on to an in-person interview—and vice versa.

It was an otherwise unremarkable Tuesday, and Kelsey had four prescreening phone calls. Elena, who was applying for the fitness coach position in the company's wellness center, was first. Kelsey started off with her basic prompt: "Tell me a little about why you want to work for Elevate Mortgage." Like the first page of a novel or bite of an entrée, an applicant's response gave Kelsey a good idea of whether or not it was going to work.

"I love the idea of helping a company develop a wellness program that can benefit so many people," Elena said. "As a certified personal trainer, I enjoy the one-on-one connection I have with my clients, but it would be great to have a broader impact."

Kelsey thought that was a good answer. "What's your impression of Elevate?"

"They've sponsored a number of events that I've participated in as a triathlete, so I admire their commitment to the community and also to events that promote health and well-being."

"You're a triathlete?"

"Yes! So far I've completed a Half Ironman, and my goal is to do the Ironman in Cozumel in two years."

"That must take a lot of commitment."

"I have a passion for training. My goals keep me focused."

"What would your ideal wellness program look like?"

"It would be customized to meet each employee's fitness level. Diet and exercise will always be twin components, but it's imperative to offer as many options as possible. Some people love spinning; others would prefer a nature walk. Elevate's size would allow me to organize people into groups that could reinforce good habits. I imagine groups for yoga, runners, softball, maybe even bowling! Groups are great not only for wellness, but also for team-building and achieving a work-life balance."

Employer branding had done its job and attracted a good candidate to Elevate. Kelsey liked what she heard, and Elena easily passed the prescreen interview.

The next prescreen was with a graphic designer, Sophie. Kelsey was attracted to her application because it included a portfolio of both cutting-edge work and more restrained designs for her job in the city communications department.

"Tell me a little bit about why you'd like to work for Elevate," Kelsey said, getting ready to type notes into the candidate database.

"I'm looking for a change of pace. I've been at my current position for over ten years, and it no longer offers much of a challenge. I've heard that Elevate encourages its employees to innovate and think outside the box, and that's not really the city's goal. Mortgage banking may not be the most avant-garde industry, but Elevate is involved in so many different events that I hope I could help them maintain their brand across various markets. Plus, it seems like a really great place to work—one of my friends works in the PR department and loves it."

Once again, Elevate's brand was attracting job candidates.

"What's your impression of Elevate as an employer?"

"Benevolent. Fair. Stable, but open to new ideas. Exactly what I'm looking for."

Kelsey made the notes in the system for Sophie to move on in the process.

Kelsey's third prescreen of the day was with Shawn, a newly minted mortgage loan officer with only a year's experience at a local credit union. She opened with the usual: "Tell me a little about why you want to work with Elevate."

"You guys are the best, and I want to work for the best. It's as simple as that."

"What makes Elevate the best?"

"Reputation. All my friends want to work here."

"Why?"

"The perks are sick. Free NBA tickets and food. That's what I've heard."

"What can you contribute to Elevate as a mortgage loan officer?"

"I graduated at the top of my class. I also would have done an internship with you guys, but I chose Wells Fargo instead; Elevate was my second choice. I'm competitive, and I meet or beat all my goals. You won't regret hiring me."

The alarm went off in her head. The downside to an exceptional employer brand was attracting many job seekers who didn't fit the company's core values. Somehow she doubted that Shawn would embrace the values of citizenship and community. He was more likely to end up on Wall Street, ordering expensive bottles of champagne each time the market reached new heights. She made the note and passed.

Alan was Kelsey's final prescreen. He was applying to be a customer service representative, a call center job.

"I'm attracted to Elevate Mortgage because of their commitment to customer service. At many companies, the call center is the lowest rung on the ladder and the team is treated unfairly. But the call center reps are on the front lines. They interact with the customer more than anyone else."

"How did you hear about Elevate?"

"A buddy of mine works there now and he says the call center isn't a forgotten outpost like at most companies. It pays decent, the facilities are nice, and they treat their reps like partners with valid opinions."

So much of Elevate's employer branding took the form of referrals to friends and family.

"What can you contribute to Elevate as a customer service rep?" Kelsey asked.

"Experience. I actually like customer service and see it as a valid profession, not just as a stepping stone to something else. But ultimately I would like to be a manager."

Kelsey nodded. It was a perfectly reasonable goal, perhaps even a bit too modest. "I see your current position is at a car dealership. What attracts you to the mortgage business?"

"As much as I love cars, I'm looking for a different environment. Elevate seems like a place that has more room for upward movement. I'm serious about establishing a career now that I'm almost out of college. I'll admit I don't know much about the mortgage industry, but I do understand that good customer service is good customer service regardless of the industry."

Even if Alan's answer hadn't been so solid, he still would have sailed through the process simply for using the proper form of the word *regardless.* The call lasted a few more minutes, and Kelsey found out that Alan played in a band and had two Siberian Huskies. She scheduled his in-person interview for the following week.

Elevate's reputation as one of the best companies to work for in the area entailed processing an incredible amount of paperwork and resumes, an influx so large it required its own server. Kelsey found it overwhelming at times, and the volume of phone calls from people inquiring about their status could try her patience.

Will Taliferro spent considerable time in the HR area. He liked to roam and chat with people in person rather than cycle through phone calls behind closed doors. Kelsey wondered how many other people at her age and lowly status could joke around with their company's CEO.

Will sailed through the door one afternoon. "How's it going?"

"We could use a DDOS attack just to catch up on this paperwork," Kelsey joked.

"Perhaps I need to make more enemies," Will said, knowing full well the enormous amount of resources that went into maintaining a secure network for the company.

"I could start a rumor that you're in cahoots with a team of oligarchs who are trying to overthrow the US banks and return to a feudal patronage system," Kelsey said.

"You've put some thought into this, haven't you?" Will said.

"I read a lot."

"If I ever trace any malfeasance back to you," Will threatened, "I'm going to insist that the entire HR team wear gold blazers and plaid pants to work every day. It's the worst punishment I can think of."

Kelsey didn't doubt him. Even though he had long since traded his college-era dreads for a banker's haircut, he maintained a nose for mischief.

"I don't think even bad fashion could put a dent in Elevate's employer brand."

## SQUASHING HOPES AND KILLING DREAMS

Jessica sipped her merlot. "What I need is a job applicant who can pass a drug test and fog a mirror."

Andrea laughed. "Is that in the job description?"

"No one wants to work for Accord. Even the stray cats avoid us."

"You guys are toxic. It's common knowledge." Andrea speared an olive in her martini glass.

"Is it really that bad? It's a good place to start, get some experience."

"They don't call it Discord Insurance Company for nothing."

"They don't—"

"They do. You've been there five years and you make what? Fifteen bucks an hour?"

"Sixteen fifty."

"Jess, you need a new job."

Jessica knew her big sister loved her, but she was trying to unwind and didn't need unsolicited advice from a woman whose idea of a struggle was coordinating her handbag with her weekend outfit. Andrea worked at an advertising agency with a shark tank in the lobby and a café stocked with an enviable selection of granola bars. She didn't understand Jessica's predicament.

"Accord seems to attract the weirdos. This one guy brought his mom to his interview."

"Wow." Andrea seemed duly impressed. She thought for a second. "What you've got is an employer branding problem," she said.

"Or just an idiot problem," Jessica countered. She checked her phone and signaled the bartender for another round.

"Accord has a bad reputation," Andrea said. "Helmut Schmidt is a piece of work. Everybody knows it."

"He leaves us alone. He golfs a lot."

"That car he drives around town is obnoxious."

"The Tesla? He mentions it in his company-wide emails. Like he's saving the environment single-handedly by driving an expensive sports car."

"He should care more about his company's reputation than his car." Andrea said.

Jessica shrugged, a gesture halfway between anger and defeat. "Why should he? Daddy left him a trust fund."

"That Tesla is not going to solve Schmidt's problems. The whole company is circling the drain. You could be the one to do something about it."

"How? I'm just an HR rep."

Andrea sighed. Her little sister's lack of confidence overshadowed her untapped talent and ambition. "That company suffers from a vacuum of leadership. You could make a bold power play and come out on top."

The bartender set down two fresh drinks.

"That's ridiculous. At best nobody would care. At worst I would get fired."

"So you want to keep interviewing potheads and Burger Magic rejects?"

Jessica considered this for a while. "If I could fill openings in less than thirty days, the annoying director of underwriting might leave me alone."

Andrea nodded. "Think about it. Turn that company around and you'd have a prize resume. It could be a real jumping off point for your career."

Jessica rested her head in her hands. "Maybe I could get a condo with a fireplace and a balcony."

"Employer branding," Andrea reiterated, lifting her drink for a toast. "It's a tonic for your soulless job."

Jessica sighed. It seemed like a lot of work.

One week later, the final straw was Mac. He was twenty-three minutes late for his interview for an entry-level customer service representative position. He was dressed in a dingy T-shirt and flip-flops. The oddest part was that he sauntered into the room arm in arm with an unusual looking woman. She was wearing a frilly top and miniskirt, but the coup de grace was a giant, curled wig. It was rubber duck yellow with ringlets resembling octopus tentacles. She took a seat, demurely crossing her legs as Mac made his way to the counter. "Are you Jessica?" he drawled, his gaze failing to land on her face. Jessica reached for her phone to text Andrea as soon he shuffled back to his seat with a clipboard of paperwork.

The swanky hotel ballroom was more appropriate for a wedding reception than a conference on employer branding. Jessica selected a muffin from a bountiful continental spread and made her way to a table of strangers. Attendees were dressed in conservative business attire, so Jessica had worn her trusty black suit. Everyone exuded confidence despite the large name tags on lanyards around their necks, which made them look like kindergarten students on a field trip.

Jessica still thought employer branding sounded like a buzzword that could disappear like last week's garbage, but nevertheless, she was happy to be here. Accord didn't have a habit of dropping money on conferences for anyone but the top echelon. As it was, Jessica's manager only approved her request because the event was within driving distance.

Jessica feigned interest in her phone until the first speaker bounced up on the dais to warm applause. She was from a well-known company with a well-known logo. Jessica owned several pairs of their shoes and loved them. The company had succeeded with product branding—nobody could argue with that—but employer branding? She needed proof of its usefulness. In Jessica's eyes, when people need a job, they need a job. You just apply for what's available, right?

The woman was an engaging speaker; Jessica admired her ease on stage and even conceded that she made several good points. However, she couldn't help but think that Company Wonderful's success was due almost solely to the fact that they paid great salaries. Their starting salary for someone commensurate with Jessica's experience was way above the point she had spent five years climbing to reach. How hard can it be to attract talent when you pay living wages?

The next presenter was from a beverage conglomerate and spoke about things Jessica had never heard of, like eNPS scores and continuous improvement teams. She nearly laughed when he talked about employee recognition awards. The recognition program at Accord consisted of Star Awards: You could nominate someone each month for going above and beyond the call of duty, and the randomly chosen winner received a gift card to a frozen yogurt shop. Jessica had never received one, nor did she know anyone who had. Ultimately, Jessica felt that Accord had little in common with these other companies. Maybe there was such a thing as "corporate culture," but it was obvious that instituting even a rudimentary employer branding initiative was going to require executive buy-in on a scale that she didn't have the power to budge. Even the company's mission statement skewed in the wrong direction: "Accord provides superior insurance products that stand out in a competitive marketplace." Helmut Schmidt came up with this, or at least the consultant he hired did, and the most notable thing about it was that the company's employees didn't figure in it at all.

Nevertheless, as much as she was a creature of habit, it had been nice to spend the day out of the office. Jessica stuck around for the wine and cheese reception after a long day of taking notes and attending roundtable talks. It turned out to be one of the smartest career moves she ever made, apart from quitting her job at an ice cream parlor after discovering a cockroach in the milkshake machine.

She was standing in a corner of the ballroom when a stately woman in a red power suit, bedecked with immaculate accessories, approached her. Her name was Jan, and she worked for a place called Elevate, Inc.

"I see you're with Accord," Jan said, nodding toward Jessica's comically large lanyard.

Jessica nodded. "Five years."

"I worked there after high school and had a blast. One time we had this great picnic in the parking lot. Someone dumped a load of sand in the middle and three guys brought in kiddie pools. Everyone wore shorts and T-shirts. We played volleyball and Gerhard Schmidt grilled hot dogs." Jan was lost in a reverie of decades ago.

Jessica blinked, unable to comprehend someone harboring a fond memory of the place.

"It was the reason I decided to go into HR." Jan's smile held firm.

Jessica blinked again. "Things have really changed."

"I heard Gerhard passed away some years ago. Is Helmut running things now?"

Jessica cleared her throat. "In a manner of speaking."

Jan laughed. "I suppose he's settled down by now. At least he has the good sense to invest in employer branding."

"Well, that's really my idea."

"Really?" Jan seemed intrigued.

"I had to convince my boss to let me come. We don't really have the capacity to invest in an employer branding program right now."

Jan almost choked on her Triscuit. "Tell me, how many applicants are you getting for each opening?"

Jessica looked at the floor. She didn't know, and she didn't know she was supposed to know.

"I thought so."

"It's more about the quality of the applicants than quantity," Jessica responded.

"How's the quality?"

"Okay, I get your point," Jessica conceded. "But we're a local insurance provider, not Geico or Prudential."

"You can't afford not to invest in employer branding. You guys are burning money just looking for people. And let me guess—your turnover rate is at least 20 percent."

Jessica's eyes widened. "Twenty-two, actually."

"You know what else I know? You don't pay people enough."

Jessica sighed. "It's really frustrating. I'm constantly hiring for the same positions, and the same rejects keep applying. It would almost be funny if it weren't so sad."

Jan nodded sympathetically. "You deserve better. The good news is that it can be fixed. Let me give you the name and number of a consultant who could really help."

Jessica spent several weeks meticulously reading articles and crafting a plan. Stage one included a redesigned web site with employee testimonials and new job positions. The biggest battle she faced was creating a career path for new hires by re-tooling positions and job descriptions, corresponding with reconfigured salaries across the board. She wanted to propose ninety-day, 180-day, and 365-day bonuses to reduce turnover, and a one-time bonus based on tenure for the current employees. Each idea was phrased in a roundabout way to make it palatable to higher-up, stressing at every point that it was just a starting point for a conversation.

Her actual conversation with Don, her manager, went about how she expected. "I'm glad you're taking the initiative with new ideas, but I'm afraid my hands are tied. What you're talking about is a huge commitment at nearly every level of the company. Frankly, our bottom line is fine."

Jessica surprised herself at how passionate she had become about employer branding. Jan blew her mind with that story of the beach party—Accord was once a fun place to work, and it could be that way again. She was energized enough to call the consultant Jan had recommended, but Don put a stop on scheduling a meeting.

Undeterred, Jessica crunched some numbers on turnover rate, cost per hire, and even the company's reviews on Glassdoor, and presented her data to Don.

"Glassdoor is a scam," he said.

She settled in for a fight. Andrea suggested she go over Don's head, straight to the head of HR, Aidan Cooley. It was a risky move, but while Don had both an ego and a temper, he was also lazy, so any repercussion would likely be temporary and toothless.

"What's up, Jennifer?"

"Jessica." It had taken her several weeks to pin Aidan Cooley down and she was determined to make the best of her time with him. "I wanted to share some ideas on how to improve our hiring process. I've written out a plan. Here." She slid a folder across the desk to him. It was an action plan based on her research and her conversations with Jan and Andrea. She'd worked on it over the weekend in an uncharacteristic burst of enthusiasm for her career, fortified by dreams of one day being able to afford a condo with a balcony.

Cooley glanced at the folder, opened it up, shuffled through the papers, and set it down again. "Give me the elevator pitch."

Jessica tried to raise her sinking hopes. "It's about incorporating employer branding into our marketing and human resources efforts. The goal is to attract a different class of candidates to our open positions—people with experience and long-term prospects, which will ultimately lower our turnover rates and hiring costs."

Long pause. "Sounds expensive."

"Actually, in the long run—"

Aidan cut her off with a particularly vociferous and phlegmatic cough. "I'm just messing with you. It sounds like a good idea," he said. "I know things have been a bit stale around here. I think you're right—it's time to try something new."

Jessica was dumbstruck. She had wholly expected more of a fight. She grasped to find the right words. "Wow. That's great. If you take a look at my plan—"

"I'll read it later. What do you need right now?"

Jessica filled him in on Jan and the consultant she recommended.

"Don's going to hate this."

She couldn't agree more, but she said nothing.

Cooley was correct, Don did hate it—and so did Helmut Schmidt. He even paid a visit to the HR department on an otherwise regular Tuesday afternoon. Jessica was stunned to look up and find herself eye-to-eye with the CEO. "Are you the one causing all the trouble with this employer branding business?"

She felt like a puppy who got caught eating a slipper. "I was under the impression that—"

"We will not be pursuing the matter."

Dazed, it took her a moment to respond. "If you look at some of the research, we could improve key metrics by developing a campaign—"

"I'm touched by your enthusiasm, but efforts like this require expertise beyond your position."

"I was really looking forward to using this as a learning experience."

"If we are interested in pursuing employer branding, it will be a decision made by the directors. Right now our business model doesn't require it."

Jessica felt defeated. "I understand."

"Perhaps you can recruit good candidates by other means."

"I just thought we'd try something new."

Schmidt's round glasses reflected the fluorescent light, lending him an unnecessarily sinister air. "New is good. Expensive is not."

It was incredibly short-sighted. "I understand."

"Good. Long-term business decisions are not made at this level. I don't know why Don and Aidan encouraged you."

"I apologize." Her face burned with shame. She just wanted him to go away.

Within two months, Jessica had a new job at Elevate working under Jan. She considered it a narrow escape from Accord. Had Andrea not convinced her to look into employer branding, she would still be toiling away, her dream of a condo ever receding over the horizon. She was grateful to be part of a new team; the pace was still frenetic, but in a good way. She didn't stay in touch with too many people from Accord, but she wasn't surprised to learn that both Don and Aidan Cooley had departed as well. Meanwhile, Helmut Schmidt became the proud owner of the town's first driverless car, inspiring even more eye-rolling than the Tesla.

## UNQUITTABLE

- Employer branding is the best attraction tool in your toolbox.
- Employer branding should be a reflection of your company's culture. Intentionally building a great culture is a fundamental step in building a great employer brand.
- The employee experience, from recruiting through retirement, must be in alignment with the employer brand you're promoting. If it isn't, focus on the experience first, then focus on the employer brand and its promotion.
- Research is critical: Conduct internal and external research to ascertain how employees perceive the company and how the company is perceived

in relation to other employers. Obtain input relative to an aspirational (desired) employer brand; i.e., what would employees like to say about their employer?

- Promote your employer brand through social media, website content, and ongoing communications in the community and within your organization.
- Use a continuous improvement program to fix behaviors, policies, benefits, and facilities that are not consistent with your desired employer brand and aspirational culture.
- Employer branding is a long-term investment. Create a plan and stick with it. It won't happen overnight!
- Most importantly, make sure your culture, physical environment, benefits, and policies match the employer brand you're trying to build (i.e., aspirational employer brand).

## QUITTABLE

- Having a poor employer brand, and worse yet—not knowing it's bad.
- Promoting an employer brand that does not match reality.
- Focusing entirely on financial results with no appreciation for how a great culture and employer brand can help improve growth.

# CHAPTER 3

# Highly Desirable Internships

First things first: If you want talented, engaged interns, you have to pay them. It's as simple as that. Young people are spending too much money on college to spend their summers or semesters gaining nothing but experience. Secondly, interns aren't there to make your coffee and shred your documents. Yes, they need to pay their dues, but hopefully you're paying them too much to make grunt work worth their while. A highly desirable internship offers talented young people meaningful experiences and the chance to participate in tasks that contribute to the company's or organization's well-being and bottom line. This two-way street is a win–win situation. You can help align a young person's work ethic in a way that benefits the company and create a pipeline of job-ready professionals in the process. This is all part of your employer brand, because someone who has already had a good experience with your company will find it an ideal place at which to launch their careers. In a word, the highly desirable internship is the one that makes your company a highly desirable employer to both interns and their peers at school. Highly desirable internships are invaluable in developing your talent pipeline and a key element of an unquittable organization.

Over the course of two internships, Thom learns what he does and doesn't want. Captain Dave is a buffoon as a boss, and his small company's inability to utilize Thom's skills is a lost opportunity. But Thom flourishes when he's given a chance, proving that being a self-starter and having a little bit of gumption are valuable traits when launching a career.

## CAPTAIN DAVE'S SHIP OF FOOLS

Thom had been meaning to apply for a summer internship, but his sopho-more year at Southeastern Minnesota University had been wildly busy. First, there was his class load, which could only be described as aggressive. After the big adjustment of freshman year—in which he became distracted by the dining hall's bottomless french fries and overall lack of supervision—he had settled into the groove, joined the school's Student Marketing Association, and learned to balance his responsibilities and extracurricular activities. Weirdly enough, the busier he got, the higher his GPA climbed. He'd been a solid student in high school, and his test scores reflected his capability of even greater things. Here he was in college, thriving academically and learning to enjoy new challenges.

Most fun of all was his rising reputation due to the Torrie the Tornado incident. It began as a lark but had become an object lesson in the power of social media. He created a joke Twitter account for the school mascot—Torrie the Tornado—during the football season his freshman year, poking fun at the school's Class B status. His tweets went viral during the tragic homecoming game when the Tornadoes lost in a 24-21 heartbreaker to their cross-state rival, Northwestern Minnesota University. Thom created a GIF of Torrie the Tornado doing a hilariously half-hearted dance on the side-lines and tweeted it with #sadtornado. The account grew from twenty-seven followers to 375 that night, and now hovered in the 5,000 range, with many faculty and administrators following him and using the hashtag on tweets for everything from students sleeping in class to fender benders in the parking lot. A "sad tornado" was now the university's buzzword for an unfortunate event.

So, yes, Thom had every intention of finding a summer internship, but he had missed a crucial deadline over spring break with everything going on. By late April, Thom's only recourse was to consult the job board in the Marketing Department office. There were lots of unpaid opportunities that touted "exposure" and "experience" as if they were commensurate with cold, hard cash. Given the debt his degree would earn him—even with his partial scholarship—Thom needed to sock away some serious cash over the summer. He followed up on the posting for a full-time internship at

Mainsheet Sailing Equipment. The pay wasn't fantastic—$10 an hour—but it was on the right side of zero and the company was owned by the father of a friend. Best of all, he could commute from home.

It was a Skype interview, and it was weird.

"Call me Captain Dave," Mr. Gustafson said by way of greeting. He was dressed in a striped sweatshirt and sported a white beard—a parrot and an eye patch would really have completed the look. He appeared to be sitting in a lawn chair on a dock, sailboats bobbing in the water behind him. The wind made it hard to hear him talk as it whistled through the computer's speakers.

"Good afternoon," Thom replied from the comfort of his dorm room. He was wearing a proper shirt and tie, had reviewed a list of possible questions, and drummed up answers to inquiries about adversity and teamwork. He felt Boy Scout prepared.

"I hear you know my Johnny." Captain Dave took a swig from a coffee cup in a manner that suggested the drink inside wasn't coffee.

Thom knew the son as John and had last seen him passed out on the common room sofa wrapped in a Star Wars sheet with some very expressive eyebrows inked onto his forehead. "He seems to be enjoying his time at SMU."

Captain Dave erupted into a phlegmatic chortle that ended with a coughing spasm. "He's a chip off the old block, that's for sure. Won't be home for the summer to help me out. Got a chance to go backpacking in Thailand with his buddies and I suppose I can't stop him."

Thom was pretty sure Captain Dave could stop his errant son by repossessing his Visa card. "I would appreciate the opportunity to help your company grow."

"I don't know about growth, Tommy, but we sure could use another set of hands around here. We're gearing up for our busy season. I spend most days chartering fishing trips, so someone needs to hold down the fort."

Thom liked the idea of the Captain being far away for most of the day—it was probably for the best. "Can you tell me what the intern's duties will be?"

"We need a jack of all trades to step in wherever help is needed. You'll be fine if you know your bow from your aft and your port from your starboard. And how to run a cash register."

"The cash register I've got covered, but I admit that I don't know much about sailing, other than some basic boater safety. But I'm willing to learn."

"Great. When can you start?"

Thom was taken aback, figuring that the interview process might be a little more involved than this. In fact, its very brevity gave him pause. "I don't know exactly. I wanted to ask you if there would be a chance for the intern to participate in any marketing activities. That's my major."

"What'd you have in mind?"

"I'm not sure exactly. Maybe you could tell me a bit about your marketing department."

"I filmed a commercial once. Hired a helicopter to shoot me in the crow's nest aboard the *Superior Siren*. Nowadays you do it all with drones. Hell of a lot cheaper."

Thom's heart sank, but time was running out. Finals would be over in a week and he needed a plan. He didn't have any other options.

"I can start May 20th. It would be a pleasure joining the company for the summer." He tried to look happy about it. What's three months?

Captain Dave seemed pleasantly surprised. "Welcome aboard, mate." He raised his coffee cup to the computer screen in a long-distance toast.

Thom pulled into the parking lot at 9:49 a.m. on Monday, May 20, and, despite the sign over the building, wondered if he had the wrong place. The parking lot was empty; the building was locked and dark.

At 10:05 a.m. two things happened simultaneously: A fishing boat taxied in to the dock adjacent to the building, and an old station wagon pulled into the gravel lot. Captain Dave was on the boat; a woman was driving the car. She got out, seemingly oblivious to Thom's car, unlocked the building, flipped on the lights, and disappeared inside.

Thom made his way around the side of the building to the dock after a couple minutes. Captain Dave was tying up the boat.

"Hi. I'm Thom Bosworth." He held out his hand.

Captain Dave finished his task, stood up, and looked at him as if trying to remember who he was and what he was doing here. Finally, a smile spread across his face. "Of course." He slapped him on the shoulder. "Glad to meet you, son. Go see Tina inside. She'll set you up."

Captain Dave stepped back into the boat, preoccupied with an assortment of fishing tackle. Thom had been excused.

The day was less than a whirlwind. Tina was Captain Dave's sister-in-law; they ran the business together, selling sailing supplies to local residents and other vendors. A substantial portion of their business was online, so Thom got a crash course in packing boxes and printing out shipping labels and invoices. The store didn't have much foot traffic and it got kind of lonely, especially with Tina's son, Ron, packing boxes with his headphones preventing any sort of conversation. The Captain, as everyone called him, seldom stepped inside the building. He was always on his phone when he did, and he never stopped to talk to Thom, or anyone else for that matter. A few other people came and went, but Thom wasn't introduced and they tended to sequester themselves in a back office. Presumably taking care of the financial end of things.

By the end of the first week, Thom had done a fair share of packaging and light boat maintenance. The cash register didn't seem too important. Tina perched herself at the counter and completed those transactions herself, mostly local boaters popping in for ropes and extra life jackets. But other than that, she surfed the web, and half the packages UPS delivered each day were from Amazon and addressed to her.

The second week, Thom decided he would be proactive. He asked Ron who took care of the Mainsheet Sailing website.

"Dunno. Johnny maybe?" He stuck his earbud back in.

The website was too professional to be managed by a college junior of questionable work ethic. He asked Tina.

"We outsource it," she said, without looking up from her phone.

"Any chance I could learn the ropes? I have some ideas about SEO that could really increase traffic."

Tina looked at him, somewhat puzzled. "You'll have to ask the Captain."

He got the chance the next day when the Captain wandered through the warehouse on his way to the back room, where the maybe-possibly-accountants were gathered.

"Hey, Captain. Got a moment?"

The Captain stopped. "What's up, sport?"

"I was wondering if I could help out the marketing team with some strategies for increasing your web traffic."

The Captain clasped Thom's shoulder. "It's nice to see some gumption in you young people. I'll have Carol get in touch with you. She handles all that stuff."

"Thanks. I appreciate it." Thom had no idea who Carol was.

It took a few more days to solve the Carol mystery. Turns out she was a local freelance web developer, and Thom made her acquaintance when she stormed into the building on Thursday afternoon demanding to see the Captain.

Tina looked up from her phone. "What can I help you with, Carol?"

"Where's Dave?"

"Did you try calling him?"

"I want my money."

"Talk to the bookkeeper."

"I invoiced two months ago, Tina. I can't wait any longer."

Thom just happened to be passing through at that moment and felt like he was eavesdropping on private business, but it was also his opportunity to do more than pack boxes and pick up the slack from Ron. He froze in place, waiting for the right time to include himself in the conversation.

It never came. He quietly backed away after a few minutes as Carol and Tina descended into name-calling and Tina lunged over the counter in an attempt to punch Carol in the face. Carol dodged the blow and retaliated by swinging her purse and connecting with Tina's shoulder. Thom didn't know what to do—try to break it up, call someone? Ron peeked out of the mail room; the noise was enough to infiltrate his sonic bubble. Thom looked at him, silently beseeching him for help. Ron shrugged. Finally, Carol threatened to call the police, involve a lawyer, and Tina threatened the same thing. Carol stomped out, got into her truck, and peeled out of the parking lot.

It was four weeks later and Thom had lost hope. His proactive efforts had gone belly up and he was bored. More often than not, he felt invisible, like if he failed to show up in the morning no one would care—or even notice. He got an evening job as a barback at a place close to home, and the pay turned out to be better than what he was making at Mainsheet Sailing Equipment. Plus, the people were a heck of a lot more fun. Most nights after the bar had closed and been cleaned up, the staff played darts. Thom started going in to his day job later, at either 10:30 or 11:00 a.m. No one seemed to mind.

By the end of the summer, Thom had created quite a social media presence for the bar and even brought in more business by hosting a trivia night. He drew up some statistics on the sales increases during trivia hours and put it on his resume. He reasoned that the data would also come in handy as a class project in the future.

The Captain left Thom a parting gift on his last day at Mainsheet Sailing Equipment. It was a striped sweater identical to the Captain's. The accompanying note read, "Thanks for the great work, Tom. You'll make a fine sailor someday. Say 'hi' to Johnny for me when you see him." Thom was surprised at his sense of relief when he pulled out of the gravel lot for the last time.

He went straight to the bar and worked a final shift. Several of his friends from high school showed up to say goodbye, and his new work friends presented him with a parting gift: a pair of custom-made Chuck Taylor high tops with the bar's logo on the side. He wore them proudly nearly every day the following school year. He sincerely missed the place and considered working there again next summer if nothing else panned out.

## TRIUMPH OF THE SAD TORNADO

Thom had a successful junior year. He was elected vice president of the Student Marketing Association, worked his GPA up to an impressive 3.75, and even took on a weekend job at a bar near campus. He not only made extra bank, but also new friends to match the old ones. In addition to maintaining his Torrie the Tornado Twitter account, in which #sadtornado trended locally with every losing football game, he created a new Twitter account for the bar. It quickly gained followers with his artistic photos and friendly quips about the staff and clientele, turning them into some semblance of local celebrities.

This year, however, he vowed not to miss the boat on internships. He followed the proper channels, did his research, and ended up interviewing with his first choice: LongStar, a marketing and communications firm in Indianapolis. They tended to recruit from top tier colleges, but he heard through the grapevine that SMU was included in their rounds because the HR director was a former Tornado herself.

Visions of Captain Dave still fresh in his mind, Thom prepared for his interview, this time wearing a complete suit for an on-campus interview. He traded out his now-worn Chuck Taylors for a pair of dress shoes he had made peace with.

Sharice met Thom in the conference room of the Student Marketing Association, introduced herself, and shook his hand. She asked him a few basic questions and got a wealth of information in response. He was prepared with his answers, shared his goals, and even told her the story of #sadtornado, which made her laugh and take notes. She was even more impressed when he described relaying that first social media success into additional hits at the two bars where he had worked.

Thom was well-spoken, enthusiastic, academically successful, and showed strong leadership potential. He emailed Sharice a prompt thank you after the interview, reiterating his desire for the internship. Sharice checked the various social media accounts Thom ran and was impressed with their playful positivity and lack of offensive material—a real hazard for his age group. Of course, competition for the eight spots in the LongStar program was intense. Sharice had interviewed thirty candidates at the four colleges she had visited, all of whom had been recommended by their professors or counselors. Part of the reason LongStar was able to attract such competitive students to their program was because they paid $18 an hour—a total of $7,200 over the ten-week program. Sharice wished she had been lucky enough to nab a spot back in her undergrad days.

LongStar had been founded by CEO Kevin Trainor twenty years earlier, and the internship program had gained a solid reputation since its inauguration five years later. It arose from Trainor's belief that internship programs are a cost-effective and proven method of attracting vibrant young talent in the industry. Students loved the program because it gave them real-life, hands-on experience that resulted in deliverables, and it paid decent money—it had to in order to attract top talent. The students came from a variety of majors and collaborated on a different project each year, presenting their results to the partners on the last day. The program was a microcosm of the work world, and students gained valuable experience in project and time management, team work, presentations, budgets, and client relations.

Thom eagerly accepted the internship when Sharice called with the good news. In fact, he was so thrilled he immediately started searching for a place to live. He barely said goodbye when his mom dropped him off at a questionable-looking house near Indiana University. He had two suitcases: one full of shorts and t-shirts, the other full of newly purchased business casual attire. Swaddled in a messenger bag slung over his shoulder was his gaming console.

Sharice was waiting for Thom when he made it to LongStar by 7:52 the following morning. The new interns were already getting to know each other. Most of the morning consisted of an "onboarding" process, a term unfamiliar to Thom but that smacked of sensibility. They filled out paperwork and watched a video presentation about the history of the company, then an IT analyst set them up with laptops and passwords. Sharice gave them a tour of the entire building, where they met everyone from the admins to the partners; even Kevin Trainor excused himself from a meeting and came out of a conference room to shake each intern's hand. Thom was nearly star struck—he'd never met a CEO before. But then he realized—yes, he actually had. Kevin Trainor bore no resemblance to Captain Dave at all, even though they appeared to be the same age.

Lunch was catered in the cafeteria and was definitely a step above the typical college fare that Thom had come to regard as acceptable. The intern team enjoyed a round of Two Truths and a Lie as an ice breaker. Thom's truths were that he could ride a unicycle and had once won $500 playing blackjack; his lie was that he'd met Oprah. Nobody got it right. He learned a lot about his colleagues, all of whom were bound for their senior year of college. They were a talented bunch: One girl could waterski and another could solve a Rubik's Cube in under three minutes. One person was from New York, another from California. Two, including him, were from

Minnesota. Some of them were majoring in marketing, some in business, one in advertising art, two in communications, and one was majoring in something called American culture studies. All eight seemed like a good match, as if they fit a profile specific to LongStar. Thom wondered if that was by coincidence or design.

The final presentation of the first day was from Ali, an account manager, who gathered them in a conference room to introduce the project they would be working on for the summer: the marketing plan for a new product, a dog collar with a chip that tracks location and health data, tentatively called WiFido. Thom's ears perked up, as did everyone else's. This wasn't some fake project. It was real work, and they would be pitching their campaign directly to the client in August. Ideas swirled in Thom's head.

"This bloodhound is boss!" Thom was flipping through images online. He spent a considerable amount of time looking at pictures of cute puppies and imagining unlikely scenarios for them, something that would sell the product.

"Aww," Caitlyn fawned. She had become his strongest ally on the team. They were working together to coordinate print and social media, but she had her heart set on a rather plucky Dalmatian as the face of the campaign.

"Cute puppies are for memes." Tonya, the intern from New York, loved to play devil's advocate. "We need to show a bunch of stranded pets. Strike at people's worst fears." She wanted to structure the project around how useful WiFido would be during natural disasters like hurricanes or floods, when people got separated from their pets. It was a sticking point with the rest of the group, but she wouldn't budge.

They scheduled a meeting with Ali, who was serving as their mentor. She sided with the majority. Tonya folded her arms and stared at the ground. The chill in the room was slightly unpleasant, but it sure beat the scuffle Thom had witnessed at Mainsheet Sailing the previous summer.

They were slightly behind schedule. Half of the team was worried about the delay, and the other still felt pretty comfortable. Thom was sure they could get back on track by putting in a couple late nights. He'd developed quite a hankering for Jockamo pizza, and he'd be happy to stay late if a large pie with ham and pineapple was part of the deal.

Sharice played a vital role in the internship program throughout its duration. She lined up three lunch-and-learn sessions that proved to be a hit with the whole company, not just the interns. The first speaker was Kevin Trainor himself. The interns and a cross section of the general office population gathered in the cafeteria amidst a spread of Indian food.

"The goal of an internship program is to benefit the company, not the interns." He paused for effect. "The goal of everything we do is to make the business stronger and more profitable. The fact that the program *does* help the interns is an awesome byproduct."

Thom couldn't help wondering, were they not the prized unicorns they imagined themselves to be?

"But experienced interns make great employees—especially if we start out with the best and give them the experience they need to hit the ground running. We believe that interns—even those who are 20 or 21 years old—have valuable qualities to bring to the table.

"I worked on a farm for the summer when I was 19. I was happy to work on my tan and have some time to think about what I really wanted out of life. It turns out what I really wanted was to not work so hard." Polite laughter from the audience. "Unless it involved climbing up a mountain.

"I earned enough money that summer to travel to Devil's Tower in Wyoming. I used all my equipment and all my muscle to make it to the top. That's where I had my first epiphany.

"My epiphany was: God, that was hard.

"But it was also exhilarating. I felt alive and I felt connected to this great natural sculpture that the Native Americans had held sacred for hundreds of years. I wanted that feeling of exhilaration to last, so when I rappelled down and returned to school, the first thing I did was change my major from economics to marketing. I wanted to tell everyone how great our National Parks were."

Thom was enraptured. He'd never been to Devil's Tower, but he understood the feeling Kevin was describing. He'd felt it himself when he gained followers on the social media accounts he managed—he was parlaying his enthusiasm for the places he worked and the people he worked with to others. He was connecting people to each other. Even if it was just on behalf of a local business.

By the time Thom had finished his plate of chicken vindaloo, he felt a kinship with Kevin Trainor and understood something about his own wants and desires. He had a clear vision of what he wanted to do with his life, and he was already doing it. Marketing, public relations—the whole field— might be messy and fraught with conflicts, but it was also fun.

The second lunch-and-learn Sharice scheduled a couple weeks later was with the executive director of the Indy Chamber of Commerce. Thom tucked into a big plate of Chengdu chicken as the speaker talked about the difference between marketing a city and marketing a physical product. She also gave them a sneak peek at a new campaign. It made Thom want to explore the city even more.

The third lunch-and-learn was a field trip to meet with the director of communications for the massive Indianapolis Motor Speedway complex. Turns out the communications director was an old friend of Kevin Trainor's. Suddenly, Thom understood the value of networking, of maintaining contacts and friends over the years. He felt a holistic sense of everything he'd learned coming together into a comprehensive worldview, and he wondered if he was becoming an adult. The thought scared him enough that when he got back to his flat that evening, he enjoyed four solid hours of gaming.

All the interns took turns during the final presentation to the client. Thom presented his social media campaign, featuring a wayward cat and dog having a night on the town as their respective owners chase after them. When they finally catch up and the pets are safe, the owners realize that fate—and WiFido—has brought them together.

Nine months later, Thom walked through the doors of LongStar once again, having tossed his graduation cap in the air several weeks earlier. It was summer in Indianapolis again, and he had found a new flat. This time he had his bike with him as well as his gaming console. He shook Sharice's hand as she welcomed him as LongStar's newest employee and led him to his new desk, right next to Caitlyn's.

## UNQUITTABLE

- View interns as high-potential individuals capable of meaningful work that contributes to a company's goals.
- Make interns, as well as those with whom they communicate, a critical element of the talent pipeline.
- Involve interns in meaningful projects and tasks that are associated with their chosen field of study.
- Integrate interns into the workflow of a given department or team.
- Provide a mentor for all interns. Make sure the mentor gives the interns quality interaction time.
- Treat interns as equal members of the team during their tenure.
- Pay interns well! Money attracts interns.
- Impress the interns with the employment experience. They will share their perceptions with other young people.

## QUITTABLE

- Hire interns, then ignore them.
- Fail to take advantage of an intern's ability to contribute meaningfully to projects and ongoing work.
- Assign grunt work and busy work to interns.
- Focus assignments on work that is unrelated to a student's major or interests.
- Segregate interns into their own teams and prevent them from getting to know others in the company.

# CHAPTER 4

# Onboarding

Onboarding is more than filling out a W-4 and setting up a computer login—the first ninety days of employment set the tone for an individual's career with the company. It's the sole opportunity for an organization to convey its culture and values. Done properly, the process is welcoming and celebratory but also structured and thorough. Needless to say, it should be standardized across all departments.

A good onboarding program is both formal and informal. It involves many departments and people, and presents a clear roadmap of what achievements an individual needs to become a high-functioning employee. Team members train the individual on specific tasks, while those from other departments walk them through benefits, recording hours, invoicing, booking travel, etc. Onboarding begins before an employee's start date and can continue through the first year. It closes the deal that began with recruiting and continued with a job offer.

## THESE PICKLES AIN'T SOUR: MEGAN MERGES INTO FARMBERRY

Fifty jars of pickles were lined up like soldiers on Megan's kitchen counter, all ready for the finishing touches of gingham ribbons and custom labels. An afternoon well spent, and now she was ready for the holiday season. She'd been making and selling pickles since she was 16—even growing her own cucumbers. Of course, there was no shortage of pickle purveyors in Wisconsin, but Megan's edge was her dedication to quality control and consistency. Each of her varieties, from chili pepper to Bloody Mary, always had consistent taste, texture, and color. She had even experimented with making her own vinegar, and her next step was to market her products to local restaurants.

Megan grew up around farms, and what she found most fascinating about agriculture was the science behind the food. In fact, as much as she enjoyed her pickle business, it was going on hiatus while she started her new job with FarmBerry, Inc. as a quality technician. She was trading in her countertop cucumber assembly line for the mass production of fruit-based foods.

Megan's job as a quality technician was to make sure that every package of every product the company shipped met stringent quality metrics, even stiffer than those mandated by the USDA. As a recently minted college graduate, Megan was excited to have landed such a great job and hoped she could live up to the company's expectations.

Her first day was a whirlwind of paperwork, new faces, computer logins, and passwords. Her work station was waiting for her, complete with a welcome card signed by the Quality Team. She received an extended tour of the administrative offices and onsite manufacturing facilities from her new manager, the operations director. This was all part of the meticulously scheduled onboarding process mapped out in her online calendar. The first two weeks included lots of tutorials for company systems—time tracking, expenses, reporting, and the like. The schedule eased off quite a bit after that, but there were still sessions about quarterly reports, vendor relations, and a trip to FarmBerry's actual farm where they grew new varieties of fruits and vegetables.

After lunch, the new hires attended an hour-long presentation by CEO Sharon McGillroy. Sharon was young for her position, and had started out in FarmBerry's Sales & Marketing division fifteen years ago. She was confident, outgoing, intelligent, and passionate about FarmBerry's two-fold mission: creating and selling high-quality fruit products and fostering a corporate culture that invested in its employees and engaged them in all facets of the business. Sharon referred to this process as "harvesting happiness." It was hokey but harmless.

"Onboarding lasts six months," Sharon explained to the five new hires during the lunchtime presentation. "And it's more than just on-the-job training. It's our promise to you that everyone at FarmBerry will support you as you learn our company and values. Some companies have a 'sink or swim' mentality, but we don't believe that will help us remain a forward-thinking, innovative workforce."

Megan was impressed. Sharon McGillroy could have phoned in with a pre-recorded video presentation, but here she was in person, getting to know the new hires' names and job titles, giving the spiel of the company's founding. Sharon walked everyone through the FarmBerry product line after her presentation and gave a brief overview of their competition.

"My job, as I see it," Sharon said, "is to make sure everyone has the resources they need to do their jobs correctly. I encourage each of you to reach out to me to share your triumphs and travails. I believe that flattening the hierarchy makes us more efficient and accountable. It is this sense of empowerment that collectively makes us a great company."

Megan nearly applauded with enthusiasm. In a crowded consumer marketplace, the margin between survival and defeat was razor thin. Everyone had to know how to adapt to change, and good leadership was crucial.

Sharon explained the concept of the Functional Improvement Team (FIT): small groups of volunteers throughout the company who came together to innovate or find a solution to a business need. After about eight weeks, they presented their outcome to the executive leadership team. The idea of FITs appealed to Megan's penchant for teamwork, employee recognition programs, and career ladders.

Sharon then introduced Corrine, a marketing specialist, but whose unofficial title was Minister of Culture. Corrine passed out swag bags that constituted a starter kit for becoming a full-fledged member of the FarmBerry family. Everyone got a t-shirt with the company logo, a keychain, a variety of sample-sized products (including the sought-after mint jelly) a packet of brochures advertising local attractions, and, best of all, three gift cards to local restaurants. The rest of Corrine's presentation included recommendations for everything from the best novel about the area to the enrichment courses at the local community college.

Megan raised her hand. "Where's the nearest yoga studio?"

Sharon, who was still in the room, piped up. "Yogi Pose, over on Tillson Road. A bunch of us go every Thursday at 5:00 p.m. You're welcome to join us."

Wow! Her first day and already an invitation to do yoga with the CEO.

As Megan soon learned, part of the onboarding process was two weeks of one-on-one training with the outgoing quality technician. She had been particularly anxious about her learning curve, as this was her first full-time job in her new career, but the job shadowing allayed many of her fears. Ted, the outgoing quality technician, was leaving the company to move closer to his aging parents. Megan took copious notes as he meticulously explained each process she'd be responsible for. Clearly, Ted took pride in his work.

But it wasn't only Ted. As they walked the plant together, each station was clean and well-functioning. The machines were in good repair; the produce that served as their raw material was top quality, stored impeccably. Nothing escaped Ted's eye. He constantly noted machine temperatures, the cleanliness of each nook and cranny of the equipment, storage conditions, and more.

"Do you ever get tired of the smell of berries?" Megan asked.

Ted chuckled. "I'm nose blind to it now, but I know it'll come flooding back the first time I have a slice of cherry pie after I leave."

One of the most surprising things Megan learned during her shadowing was that quality control was just as much about maintaining great relationships with the production staff as it was about handling the chemistry and mechanics of the manufacturing process. Everyone at FarmBerry understood why it was important to maintain high quality standards; they bought into quality control and recognized it as vital to the company's success.

Megan was worried about flying solo without Ted. But when a window closes, a door opens. The day after Ted left for good, Megan's manager introduced her to her new mentor, Ben. He was the plant manager—several levels above Megan—but the hierarchy at FarmBerry wasn't all that important, as Megan's meeting with Sharon on her first day indicated. Megan's manager strongly believed in the company mentor program, and people were not matched by age, job title, or gender. Instead, they were matched via working style as measured through a personality assessment. Both were outgoing individuals in a division with a lot of introspective types, and they met for lunch every other week to talk about general quality control and how to apply major concepts to specific situations at FarmBerry. Megan found that

Ben's personal anecdotes illustrated ideas that might have otherwise taken her years to learn.

Two weeks after her start date, Megan's first paycheck landed in her checking account without a hitch. Six months later, when the onboarding process was officially complete, Megan barely noticed, except for the fact that her 401(k) contributions kicked in automatically. She felt fully integrated into the company, and every day her confidence grew. She was particularly drawn to the work being done in the company's test kitchen. By the time she hit her one-year mark at FarmBerry, she had joined a FIT to streamline the test kitchen's product development flow.

Megan's first real test as a quality technician came at the thirteen-month mark. One of the cookers began registering funky temperatures. She and the production team suspected that the temperature was fine, but the gauge was malfunctioning. The only way to know for sure was to get a manufacturer's technician in to look at it, necessitating dumping the batch of half-cooked raspberries, a significant loss of money and time.

Ben urged her to finish cooking the batch, get it pumped to the next step of production, and then have the machine inspected. "We've got a delivery deadline to make," he said.

"If there's even a million to one chance that the cooker malfunctioned and the pasteurization process was compromised," Megan said, "we have to scrap the batch."

"Do you realize the repercussions if we can't make this shipment date?"

"We can't risk people getting sick!"

Ben sighed. "The temperature is fine. This will have a huge ripple effect all the way down the line, and I'll get blamed for it. This could put us days behind schedule."

Megan couldn't believe her ears. This man was her mentor; he had taught her most of what she knew about the company. "If I don't have the authority to shut this cooker down, why am I even here?"

Ben crossed his arms, looked at the ground. "I know you're trying to do the right thing. But I think you're being overly cautious."

"The word *quality* is right there on every jar. It means something."

Ben threw his hands up. "This is really going to screw up the production schedule. We'll have to reload the bottle machine. That will cause additional delays."

"We need to do this, Ben. I'll call the manufacturer, and then I'll call the inspector. We'll be offline for seventy-two hours at most."

He walked away. She had won the argument, made the right decision, but she'd have to smooth his feathers later on. She'd wholly embraced the company's mission of quality, which had been ingrained in her since day one.

If she'd had time to stop and think about it—impossible, under the circumstances—she would have realized that FarmBerry's thorough onboarding process had served her well. It gave her the confidence to stand up to her superiors when she knew she was right. Compromising on product safety and quality was not what the company was about, and she felt secure enough in her position to stick to her guns.

## WELCOME TO THE MCELROY GROUP: FIX EVERYTHING NOW

Justin had been a banquet captain at the Wellington Inn since he was in high school. He liked dressing up and working in a ballroom on weekends, listening to live music and watching people have a good time even as he served dinner and bussed tables. During the summer, the schedule let him sleep in and game to his heart's content. After six years, however, what was good money as a teenager wasn't enough to start a family. So, at 24, he cut back his hours, dipped into his savings, and went back to school to study hospitality. His goal was to become an event manager, or even a hotel manager. A degree would allow him to climb the career ladder and attain financial security for himself and the family he hoped to raise with his partner, Stephanie. Luckily, her salary as a nurse went a long way and allowed him to focus on his studies for four years.

He had been an indifferent student in high school, but college was different. After suffering through some truly tiresome supervisors in the real world, he appreciated what the instructors had to offer. He graduated in four years with a 3.8 GPA.

Justin reluctantly left the Wellington Inn for a new position at the McElroy Group, a hotel chain with 133 resorts under several brand names.

He was starting out as a banquet manager at one of McElroy's older properties in St. Louis. While he was sad to leave his old haunt, with its dedicated staff and do-what-works ethos, Justin was excited to join an organization with lots of growth potential.

On the first day of his new job, he showed up at 3:10 p.m. for his 3:30 p.m. start time. The HR department was dark and locked. He wandered the hallway with the flickering light, but it remained empty until 3:35 p.m., when a sallow-complexioned man trudged in, unlocked the door, and disappeared inside without so much as acknowledging Justin's presence.

Justin followed him in. "Hi. I'm Justin Bissell, the new Banquet Manager. I'm starting today."

The man looked up at him indifferently. "Have a seat. Tara will be with you when she gets back at 4:00."

"Thanks," Justin replied, taking a seat in a row of three chairs along the wall. The man disappeared behind another door, leaving only the sound of a ticking clock behind.

At 4:01 p.m., a woman whom Justin could only presume was Tara breezed into the office and disappeared behind the other door without glancing at him. Was he supposed to follow her?

Ten minutes later the door opened; she was holding a clipboard. "Justin? Pleased to meet you. I'm Tara. Could you please fill out this paperwork and we'll get started."

Justin rose from the wobbly chair and grabbed the clipboard. Tara disappeared behind the door again. As he was filling out the forms with the proper numbers and dates, a couple more people strolled into the office. One appeared to be a receptionist. She sat at the desk kitty-corner to Justin but didn't say anything.

Where had everyone been that they were just now sauntering into work like a bunch of hungover cooks?

He finished the forms and brought them up to the receptionist. "Should I give these to you?"

"Tara will be with you in a minute. Have a seat."

Tara finally returned, and he handed back the clipboard. "Did you meet Tim during your interview? He's the food and beverage director, your boss."

"Yes," Justin replied. "He interviewed me. I'm looking forward to working with him."

"I've already called him down. He'll be with you in just a minute."

And that was the last Justin saw of Tara until their paths crossed at the holiday potluck three months later.

Tim strode through the door at 4:17 p.m., and was still as tall, thin, and harried as he had been at the interview. Justin rose and shook his hand.

"Great to have you onboard. You'll just have to bear with me today, things are a little crazy," Tim said.

Justin followed Tim as they headed out the door and down a series of back hallways to the banquet kitchen. "Here we are. You'll have to jump right in. As I told you, our previous banquet manager quit three weeks ago, so things are a little chaotic. I know you can handle it."

Their time together was brief, the tour incomplete. Tim got a call on his cell phone and ran off to address a crisis in the restaurant kitchen, leaving Justin to introduce himself to the banquet staff, a number of familiar types who were wandering in to prep for the evening's event. A disconcerting first day, to say the least. He looked around uneasily, wondering where to start. Luckily, there were enough experienced people on the staff that the event, an awards banquet for a local hospital, went smoothly. Justin stayed busy meeting people and observing the buffet preparation, service, and clean-up. It was less than efficient, which he suspected was due to high turnover.

The differences between The Lilac by McElroy and the Wellington and were more stark than he was expecting. Among them:

1. The absence of doors on the staff bathroom stalls. To ward off drug use, according to management.
2. Dismal conditions in the back of house. Stairwells were dark, doors didn't lock, and the vending machine in the employee break room was broken.
3. Constantly flickering lights in the hallway, which gave the place the ambiance of a horror movie.

While these were just distressing cosmetic issues, Justin soon realized that they were harbingers of deeper problems. He had taken a pay cut to get in at

McElroy. At the Wellington, he had worked his way up to $18 an hour, and here he was down to $17.25. He told himself it was worth it in the long run because he would move up the ladder quickly with his degree.

The next day, shortly after Justin had discovered the unappealing banquet office on his own, Tim reappeared with a vein bulging in his neck. "Bissell, we've got five openings for banquet servers. When are they going to get filled? We can't afford to pay overtime to the other crew members."

Justin stood at attention, wondering what he had missed. He didn't even know he had five openings, much less how to go about filling them. He found himself apologizing for something he hadn't even known was a problem. "I'll get right on that." Even so, he knew the hiring process would take time. He'd have to study the schedule to figure out a way to redistribute hours.

"Is there an official policy on overtime?"

Tim didn't give the impression he had time to sit down and walk through company policies. "It's more unofficial, but there's no way to make your budget if you're paying overtime, especially for a crew that sits around twiddling its thumbs all day."

"Has the position been posted anywhere?"

"Have no idea. Check with HR. And ask if any of your part-timers can pick up a few extra shifts. Half of these idiots will tell you they're in school, but they're just playing video games in their parents' basement all day. Not one of them has completed a math problem in years that didn't require weighing an illicit substance." Tim's vein was still bulging.

Justin had been one of those "idiots" as recently as a month ago, and that's not at all how he would characterize the staff at either the Wellington or The Lilac. There will always be those who underperform at entry level positions like this, but there were also going to be diamonds in the rough. However, Justin was a little surprised that a large organization like McElroy paid minimum wage—it wasn't the way to get the best people, especially in this labor market. That said, he was surprised at one difference between the Wellington and The Lilac. The Wellington was family owned, and the camaraderie of the staff had a real warmth to it. The managers were always willing to work around people's school schedules and family obligations. At The Lilac, Tim's gruffness seemed to be endemic. The air was thick with surliness.

By the end of the second day, Justin had a fuller picture of who he was dealing with, and it wasn't motivated hospitality professionals. Half the banquet staff was stoned; their gazes were hollow and resigned. Clearly, eliminating stall doors in the bathrooms had failed to solve the problem.

It took half an hour for an HR representative to get back to Justin when he called to find out if the open banquet positions had been posted. It turned out they always accepted applications for banquet servers, and it was up to him to request the latest batch from HR. He also inquired about the process for dealing with employees suspected of substance abuse, and she said she would forward him a copy of the employee handbook. "You should have received that on your first day, anyhow," the representative said.

Justin was pleased to have so much autonomy, but he would have preferred more structure and guidance. On his third day, the event director notified him that they had just booked a funeral luncheon for the next day. Justin scrambled to find the minimum coverage—five servers. He could only round up four, and there was a good chance at least one would not show up.

"Bissell!"

Justin's head snapped up. Tim was on the war path.

"Get your staff in here tomorrow! Go to their houses and tie their shoes on yourself if you have to."

"I've exhausted my resources. Can I ask some of the restaurant servers if they want extra time?"

Tim looked at him like he had antlers sprouting out of his head. "What? No! That's not how we do things."

"I'm short two people. It would easily solve the problem." At the Wellington, Justin would have been praised for his quick thinking.

"That would be a nightmare for payroll to figure out. You need to get your department together, Bissell. Time to turn things around." Tim turned on his heel and left. Justin was no closer to a solution and was feeling more and more isolated.

In the end, Justin donned a uniform and lent a hand, lugging trays of roast chicken and potatoes to and from the kitchen, filling water glasses, and bussing tables. It felt good to do something familiar, something he was good at. But he knew that if Tim caught him, there'd be hell to pay for violating the unwritten rule that the managers steer clear from helping out the hourly staff.

Meanwhile, he poured over resumes and booked interviews, something he'd never done before. He asked HR about the process, what kind of questions to ask—something to make sure he was doing things right. The HR representative—it was someone different each time—just shrugged. Finally, he asked Tim.

"How does anyone hire anyone?" Tim asked, shrugging. "Ask if they can hold a tray without dumping soup down an old lady's dress. Ask if they can work until 1:00 a.m. on weekends. Ask if they can show up on time with their shirt buttoned."

During the interviews, Justin felt more unprepared than the interviewees. They asked the valid question, "What's the next step?," and he had to fake it. "You'll hear back from us within a week," he said. He had no idea if HR had to do a background check or what.

To top off his unspectacular first two weeks with McElroy, Justin's paycheck never made it into his bank account. He called payroll. "You were supposed to fill out a direct deposit form and give us a cancelled check on your first day," the woman said, accusingly.

"Did I miss a welcome packet when I started? I feel a little lost with all these procedures."

"McElroy is a competitive, fast-paced environment. We hire people who enjoy the challenge. I'm sure Tim felt you could jump right in."

Justin felt like a failure. His team was in turmoil and he didn't know who to turn to for help. Tim was too busy dealing with his own crises to care about the banquet staff. He couldn't believe he'd spent four years in college for this when he could have stayed at the Wellington, where the owners knew everyone by name and the staff were allowed to take leftovers home.

By the end of the following week, he had filled only three of the five openings. He dreaded asking Tim a question, but he had to know if it was possible to pay above minimum wage.

"No can do, amigo," Tim said. "The wages are set by the bozos at corporate."

"I'm having trouble filling these openings."

"Yeah. It's always a problem."

"Is there a way to change the process?"

"That's not really your job."

"Whose job is it?"

"The bozos at corporate."

"Are we allowed to talk to them?"

Tim shrugged. "They won't want to hear that you can't fill openings. It'll make us look like we don't know what we're doing."

"I don't understand what the company expects from me. What do I and don't I have the authority to do?"

"You just do what you have to do."

That didn't satisfy Justin. Was he crazy to consider asking for his old job back at the Wellington? At the very least, he could quit and get a job as a waiter. Then he would know what was expected of him and get a good night's sleep after a hard day's work.

## UNQUITTABLE

- Onboarding programs are standardized and welcoming.
- Employees' work spaces and required equipment are ready to go on the start date.
- In the short-term, onboarding is training oriented; in the long-term, it includes elements of mentoring, corporate culture, and career pathways information.
- New employees are recognized and welcomed as individuals on day one. They make personal connections with others.
- Modern onboarding programs take the time to promote the company's values and culture in a meaningful way. They also help employees understand the company, its products and/or services, and its customers.
- While the intense portion of an onboarding program may be one to two weeks, it should last longer—ideally, a few months to a year.

## QUITTABLE

- Onboarding is largely administrative.
- New employees encounter an environment that doesn't make them feel special or included; instead, it leaves them feeling alienated and regretful.
- Disorganization during onboarding conveys company-wide disarray. First impressions are poor.
- A lack of standardized onboarding leads to lack of productivity and longer learning curves.

# CHAPTER 5

# Incentive Systems

As you learned in Psychology 101, introducing a stimulus following a desirable behavior makes the desirable behavior more likely to occur in the future. To put it bluntly, what works with lab rats also works in the office. In fact, incentives are a time-honored component of capitalism and free market economics. Stimulus responses, incentives, rewards—technically they are different things, but unless you're wearing a white coat and conducting an experiment at a prestigious university, no one cares. In the workplace, rewards work well. Many organizations offer referral bonuses and tuition reimbursement as a way to attract, develop, and retain talent. Sales-driven organizations offer commission. Some places award top performers with vacations or extra time off. Use your imagination! Company parking spots, an unexpected gift card, concert tickets—all incentives.

Keep in mind, however, that people who expect a reward for their work sometimes do not perform as well as those who expect no reward at all. As you may also remember from Psych 101, intermittent reinforcement works the best. That's when an incentive follows a desired behavior randomly, not every time the task is performed. But don't take it too far. It's bad practice to offer something essential to doing a job well as an incentive rather than as a common courtesy. All thriving workplaces provide livable wages, a comfortable work environment, positive feedback, self-determination, and respect.

Incentive systems should be part of a larger recognition program for top performers. A good program has various rewards/awards from various levels—coworker to coworker, manager to team member, director to manager or department. Talent should be empowered to recognize each other on a regular basis, and the top echelon should recognize performance and talent regularly. And let's be clear: When we talk about performance, it's not just about financial performance. Performance can be related to desired behaviors, core values, superior service or quality, etc. Recognition and incentives are two sides of a coin, and having a strong plan for both will have a positive impact on your employer branding efforts.

In the first scenario below, Thom has come a long way from his college days. He thrives in an environment that gives him autonomy and incentives that are win–win propositions for both him and the company. While LongStar's incentives may not motivate everyone, they motivate enough individuals that the return on investment is worth it.

In the second story, Steve reluctantly takes a sales position that is partly based on commission and appears to give him significant autonomy. The people who run the company believe they are doing Steve a favor by letting him work for them. This mindset benefits no one, and their constant turnover is the result of treating talent as expendable. An intrinsically unsexy industry like office cleaning requires a strong incentive program to attract people who are looking for a future and career in the business.

## THE CATMAN'S COMMISSION

By his first year at LongStar, Thom had become known as Catman, a term of endearment that was both literal and figurative. There were his two tabby cats, Diego and Frida, and his constant stream of social media posts about their feline antics. But perhaps more importantly, he was a rising star associate account executive, a tiger when it came to pitching clients. His internship success with the Wifido project led to more work with a new client, Whiskereens, a gourmet cat food and snack company. The nickname became an excuse for coworkers to bestow upon him cat-themed items, and his desk area now contained half a dozen cat puppets (both hand and finger) and a six-foot inflatable Siamese cat that could star in a Japanese horror movie.

His love of cats aside, this particular Thursday Thom had a meeting with Torrie the Tornado (or rather, his friend who had worn the costume during the height of his #sadtornado days) to discuss an important business venture: working at LongStar. As was his specialty, Thom planned on killing two birds with one stone—find LongStar a great new media buyer and line his pockets with another $1,000. Thom loved maximizing his fringe benefits.

"That outfit made me look like a purple carrot," Rob said.

Thom laughed at the memory of the Torrie the Tornado get-up. "From what I recall, it smelled pretty ripe by the end of the season."

"It was so hard to move around in. I kept ripping the damn thing right up the middle."

"Whose idea was it anyhow?"

"Not a clue. Did you hear the engineering students made a new costume with synchronized flashing lights? Makes it look like it's rotating, like a real funnel cloud."

"I hope the new guy doesn't get electrocuted."

They laughed and reminisced about mutual acquaintances until Rob cut to the chase: "What can you tell me about LongStar? It's got to beat dancing on the football field in a foam rubber costume in the November snow."

"I love it," Thom replied. "The environment is energizing. I do different things every day. I'm never bored."

Rob nodded to the car parked outside. "It must pay pretty good, too."

"I made the down payment with the two bonuses I earned by recruiting my friends to come work for the company. You could have one, too."

Rob leaned back in his seat, smirking. "So I'm just a car payment for you, is that it?"

"I'm telling you, it's a great gig. The benefits alone," Thom clasped his hands together and reached to the sky.

"This customer service gig is getting old. They made me a manager last fall but gave me a stupid small raise considering all the stuff I have to put up with now. I thought I'd have more control over things, but instead I'm just caught between the guys below me and the guys above me."

"I hear you and Liz are engaged."

"You heard right. We'll be engaged at least two years to save up for the wedding."

"Seems like a long wait if you've already made the decision."

"Well, it just happened so nothing's set yet."

"Think about LongStar. You'd be a great media buyer. You earn commission, so the sky's the limit."

Rob paused, considered it. "What about base pay? I need to know there's a bottom."

"It's above twenty, but I'm not sure of the specifics. It's not a lot, but I guarantee you won't have trouble making a decent commission. Plus, you could always dress up as Torrie and dance in the street for tips."

"I'm afraid my foam latex days are behind me." Rob slurped the rest of his latte. "Two questions. How does the company treat their media buyers, and what kind of control do I have on price?"

Thom leaned back. It was just a matter of reeling him in now. "LongStar has an insanely high retention rate. That alone speaks volumes about people's loyalty to the company. During my internship, we had this electronic dog collar project and we got to work with all the departments in the agency. Then when I was hired, I did rotations in four departments and ended up choosing Accounts. I did a stint in media buying. I think you'd like it."

"My degree is in journalism."

"It doesn't matter. LongStar likes smart, industrious people. They hire the individual and teach you what you need to know."

"What about the money? I've never negotiated prices before."

"LongStar attracts high-end clients willing to pay to get the coverage they need. Negotiating is something you pick up during your training. Kevin Trainor wants everyone to feel like they have control over their own accounts, so the buyers have a lot of leeway. It creates a deeper bond with our clients as well."

"You make it sound like Oz. Where are the flying monkeys?"

"Honestly—the worst thing I've seen is a bad kombucha habit from some of the creative types. The hippies can be annoying, but they always come up with great pitches."

A sizable group gathered in the café commons to celebrate the semi-annual LongStar Meteor awards. Terence Williams, the head of HR, presented a number of gift cards and raffle items to employees who had been submitted for exceptional performance on a project and winners of the company's other incentive programs, including top sales.

The aggregation of various subcultures was anthropological in nature. The creative types wore rumpled t-shirts and sandals, the account executives tailored suits and tasteful accessories, and the marketing folks wore bright colors and designer glasses. The lunch buffet was catered by one of Kevin's old friends, who ran a regional chain of restaurants but still liked to drive a food truck on the side. Everyone helped themselves to an assortment of sliders and sides while the production team set up the presentation.

In addition to the sales leaders, they celebrated "goodwill ambassadors," those who upheld the company's core values and excelled at customer service. It wasn't just about revenue. Their rewards were customized, so Ali received a round of golf at the swanky Isle Blanc Golf Club and Carly got a weekend at the Turnberry Bed-and-Breakfast. Some people did grumble that so-and-so should have been recognized instead of Ali and Carly, but the undercurrent of jealousy soon petered out. The majority of people understood that the recognition was deserved and that someday their turn would come.

Finally, it was time for the award Rob had been waiting for. "I'm delighted to offer our latest $1,000 referral bonus to Rob Houseman," said Terence. "Rob has been with the company for less than a year and has already managed to nab one of these oversized checks."

His colleagues gave him an appropriate round of applause.

"Many of you also know that Rob himself was recruited through the referral program by Thom Bosworth. We are proud that this program has met with so much success. You know what it's like to work at LongStar, and you impart that enthusiasm to your friends and family. Now that Rob's fiancée, Liz, has made it past the four-month mark, we are happy to present this check for $1,000 for making her part of the LongStar family."

Rob felt compelled to say a few words. "I know I'm preaching to the choir right now, but I also know that Terence never minds effusive praise."

Terrence laughed along with the others from the sidelines.

"I may still be in the infancy of my career, but I already know the two elements that separate LongStar from its competitors. First, the mentorship program. Without Doug's guidance these past ten months, I wouldn't have made it as far as I have. Instead of inventing my own wheel, Doug let me borrow his, and the ride was pretty smooth."

Doug raised his glass of iced tea in acknowledgement.

"Secondly, LongStar has come up with an incentive system for its media buying staff that makes everybody happy. Happy buyers, happy clients. Upper management trusts us to make pricing decisions that work for everyone. I'm in the driver's seat of my own job. That's a powerful feeling, and there's no question that it begets loyalty to the company."

Terence pulled out his phone. "Can you say that again? I need to get it on video for the company intranet."

## GOLDEN SPOON STEVE

Years ago, a human resources assistant at Super Cleaning Services printed out a thick stack of papers, secured them with a heavy-duty binder clip, and disposed of them in the third drawer of a four-drawer file cabinet that later got relocated to an off-site storage unit. That was the last anyone ever heard or saw of anything regarding the company's employee referral system. Had an interested party undertaken the adventure required to unearth the document, he or she would have been underwhelmed to discover that the award for jumping through multiple hoops to secure a referral award was a whopping $100.

In another time and place, an unsuspecting recent college graduate had the following heart-to-heart with his father:

"Dad, you don't honestly expect me to take the first job I find, do you?"

Steven Tillson, Sr., rested his fork on his plate. "You graduated eight months ago. What's the holdup?"

"I was in Nepal for two of those months."

"And it cost me $4,000 more than it should have."

"You can't expect me to travel halfway round the world and then skimp on the experience."

"I suspect many of your experiences were pharmaceutical. But that's not the point. The point is that you need a job."

The server stealthily refilled his wine glass. She'd been waiting tables at the club for years and didn't need to ask.

"I have a business degree. I'm not going to settle for some stupid job that anyone off the street can get. Finding a good job takes time."

The server gave him a slight side-eye, but due to his general lack of interest in his current situation, he didn't catch it.

"I offered you a perfectly good job at my company."

"Widgets are boring."

"Those widgets paid for you to attend one of the finest private colleges in the country. Those widgets are floating your entire lifestyle!"

Steve tossed his napkin on the table. He'd lost his appetite. "I'm going to Silicon Valley next week. Take meetings with venture capital firms."

Steven, Sr.'s face twisted into angry perplexity. "That's not how business works. You don't just waltz into a venture capital firm and demand a job."

Steve pushed back his chair and stood up. "We'll see about that."

It would have to be temporary. No way he was going to stay at Super Cleaning Services (SCS) a moment longer than he had to. As soon as those Silicon Valley guys got back to him on his innovative Airbnb for boathouses plan, funding would come pouring in. Until then, however, his father had blocked his credit card and strong-armed him into accepting a position in sales. For a cleaning company. Absolutely mortifying.

Terry was his dad's old fraternity brother, one of six partners of SCS in Boston. Five of the partners—including Steven Tillson, Sr.—were silent. Terry ran the company day-to-day, and his vociferous opinions more than made up for the silence of the other five.

Steve Jr. met Clarence, one of the silent owners, at his father's club for an interview. It was unclear if Clarence even knew where their company's office was. Clarence was dressed in a suit, reading an actual, physical newspaper as if it were 1999. The men shook hands.

"Would you like a drink?" Clarence asked.

It was 11:00 a.m. Steve didn't know if he was talking about orange juice or whiskey, so he just said no.

"How's your mother doing these days, Steve?"

"She's in Gstaad with her third husband."

Clarence dispensed with the pleasantries. "Taking this position is the right move. Sales is the beginning and end of everything in business. A young man such as yourself needs to know how to close a deal."

Steve wondered if Clarence had ever gotten any closer to the sales process than getting a great deal on his waterfront home.

"How much did your father tell you about the position?"

"Not much, but I'm eager to start." And eager to quit.

"We need a salesperson for the west Boston area. The previous guy was unreliable, and that doesn't work for us. You won't have a lot of supervision, Steve. I hope we can trust you to be a self-starter."

"Of course." Steve considered himself an excellent self-starter. That's what he did with the venture capital firms on the West Coast. Just showed up and shook some hands. Crashed a few events—acted like he belonged there.

"Base salary is $30,000. Commission is 3 percent of all sales."

His father sure was trying to teach him a lesson.

"If you sign three $10,000 contracts your first month, for example, you'll make $900 in commission. If you sign an average of five contracts a month, you'll take home something like $48,000 a year."

It still didn't seem like a lot. His college had been $60,000 per year. "Seems pretty straightforward."

"Best of all, we have very attractive incentives."

Steve's ears perked up.

"Apart from our commission system."

Steve's ears wilted.

"This club maybe isn't the most exciting place for you. You young folks are always on the go. But it's important to have a special space to woo clients, so you'll have use of my suite for select Celtics games."

Steve would have preferred courtside seats, but whatever. "Anything else?"

Clarence sensed his disappointment. "It's fully catered."

"How about a company car?"

Clarence was a little taken aback. "Let's take one thing at a time. One of SCS's other incentives is a trip for two to Turks and Caicos for the salesperson with the highest customer service rating for the year."

Steve considered this. The possibility to tilt things in his favor was promising.

"We have other awards for the person who brings in the most new customers, the person who upsells an existing client the most. Stuff like that. In sales, you can write your own ticket."

"How hard could it be? Every business needs their office cleaned," Steve said.

"That's the spirit. You're allowed some control over pricing, but we have a price card for a reason. Our rates are what work best for the company, but we know that each territory has particular market demands."

Steve nodded.

"Our top salespeople make about $75,000 a year. You're not going to find many offers like this right out of college."

Steve wasn't so sure about that; it's just that he wasn't going to try to find anything else while he was trying to land his Silicon Valley deal. The two men rose and shook hands.

"I intend to make the most of this opportunity," Steve said, hoping that he'd get a call from California before Monday.

No calls from Silicon Valley ever materialized, and Steve quickly became familiar with what $30,000 a year felt like. Barely enough to cover his rent in a Back Bay apartment he shared with two other guys. He made only three sales during his first six months. Even worse, the tension in the office was palpable. The day-to-day operations were left up to Terry—the one out of the five partners who wasn't silent, although sometimes Steve prayed that Terry would lose his voice.

Terry's constant haranguing cast a pall over the office. He wanted to know everyone's move at every moment, and his lack of trust combined with unresolved anger issues effectively paved the floor of the SCS offices with metaphorical egg shells. Steve thought about quitting every day, but strangely enough, the more miserable he became, the more determined he was to succeed, just out of spite.

Steve opened up to Silvio, his stepfather, during a deep sea fishing trip off the coast of Aruba. Silvio was after a sailfish; Steve was after the daiquiris. He was hoping the distance between the Caribbean and Boston would give him some perspective.

Silvio launched into what appeared to be a golden memory: "When I was your age, Steve, just starting out in day trading, it was all about working harder than anyone else. Twenty-four hours at a time, as much as I could. When you're young, you can do that. That's your edge."

"Boston business hours are substantially less than twenty-four hours a day."

Silvio looked out over the cerulean sea, their boat gently rocking amidst calm waves. "In that case, you'll have to work smarter, not harder."

Steve didn't know what "smarter, not harder" looked like. He had made hundreds of cold calls, and no one was interested in SCS's services at any price—lower than the rate card, higher than the rate card, or the actual rate card rate. He'd tried all three.

The incentives turned out to be a farce. He took a potential client to a Celtics game, but the suite was full of random people. The client stayed glued to the game the whole time anyway, popping up between quarters to refill his plate with wings and slaw. What was he supposed to say to him to get a contract? "Say, Bill, who empties your trashcans every night? How about we match their price and throw in the recycling for free?" The milieu was all wrong. But he did make friends with the bartender. Turns out he was an inventor, too; they exchanged business cards.

Then there was the trip to the Turks and Caicos. It didn't make sense to compete in that fight because Steve had no intention of being at SCS for more than a few months. He'd mentioned the trip to some of the sales team. Turns out the "prize" didn't include airfare, and the week in question was always during hurricane season. Moreover, the trip wasn't awarded at all if the company as a whole didn't make its goals. The guys on the sales team shook their heads when Steve mentioned the customer service rating. "Total scam," seemed to be the consensus. When he pressed for more details, they mumbled about "the-customer-is-always-right malarkey and how it's impossible to satisfy some people."

One Friday, Steve was the only one in the office; everyone else had come up with an excuse to get out early. Out of curiosity, Steve rifled through Jake's files to see how he managed to close more deals than anyone else. Glancing at his paperwork it became clear—Jake was undercutting the competition by 25 percent or more, a wide margin. Even Steve knew he could make sales if he priced their services that low. And probably get a really high customer service score.

Armed with this secret knowledge, Steve had more than a dozen contracts in the works within three months. His commissions started piling up; it wasn't enough to lease a Beemer, but it was a start. Within six months he had overtaken Jake as the company's top sales person. He even got a congratulatory email from Terry that was cc'd to the whole staff. In response, Jake had taken to being ultra-secretive, guarding his computer and desk with high-security measures. Visitors to the office could smell the blood in the air. The sales staff communicated with each other through suspicious glances and clenched teeth.

But what goes up must come down, and when the fiscal year ended and the partners reviewed the numbers, Steve found himself back at his father's country club, across the table from Clarence.

"Explain to me," Clarence began, in a manner that indicated he already knew the answer, "how sales in your territory can be up 50 percent and yet we actually lost money."

Steve offered the truth, as he saw it. "You said I had leeway with price. No one would buy our services at the rate card price, so I lowered them until I reached what the market would support. I thought that was what business is all about."

Clarence looked ready to strangle him. "We have expenses. We have to pay people. There's overhead. It's not all about you."

"Terry sent me a congratulatory email just a month ago. In fact, my customer service scores are putting me in the running for Turks and Caicos."

"I should fire you." A vein bulged in Clarence's neck. "Somebody should have caught this sooner."

Steve was livid. He had gone above and beyond the call of duty for this stinking job. He proved he had what it took to be a successful salesperson, and now he was being punished. "I couldn't make any sales at your inflated prices. I tried."

Clarence pursed his lips. Steve stared him down. At last, Clarence broke the silence. "I promised your dad a fair shot. But you need to make up for the damage you've done."

"Those contracts are good for a year. We can't renege on them."

"You're going to double your sales over the coming year and you're going to find me another salesperson—a good one. We have a referral bonus; it will be worth your while."

"Another one of your great incentives?"

"It's like a thousand dollars. Have Helen look into it."

Steve left the club fuming. He was being punished for his success. Still, his pride was on the line, and he didn't want to fail. It took two months to hunt down the details of the referral bonus program, and it was still only a measly $100.

By March it was too much for Steve to stomach. He lost his top sales-person status and wasn't able to meet his quota. Jake resumed the top spot without being held accountable for using the same tactics that were forbidden for Steve.

So finally, Steve quit, bought a one-way ticket to Aruba, and found himself booking half-day and full-day fishing charter excursions from a floating dock on a white sand beach. His father was furious, but it was great to be away from the grind of Boston. It cost a lot less to survive in Aruba, and it turned out to be a much better place to network with venture capitalists than San Francisco.

## UNQUITTABLE

- Incentives work best with self-motivated individuals, but they won't nec-essarily create motivation in lazier individuals. Remember, all incentives are not monetary in nature. Additional time off, event tickets, special public recognition, perks, and other rewards can be used in addition to financial incentives.

- When structured properly, referral bonuses turn your entire workforce into efficient recruiters. Effective referral systems pay well (usually $500 or more), have very simple rules, are communicated regularly, and payouts are celebrated publicly.

- Use balanced scorecards. If only one metric is measured, you'll get what you measure, but there may be unintended consequences. Think through how people will behave with incentive systems, then measure a set of metrics to ensure balance is not lost.
- Good incentive systems drive performance and behaviors that support the company's financial, strategic, and organizational goals.

### QUITTABLE

- A lack of a formal incentive program may be a symptom of a larger problem. Failure to recognize high performance and desired behaviors is likely to alienate employees and lead to high turnover.
- Individuals may resort to devious means to get ahead if an organization fails to give individuals a legitimate way to compete with coworkers.

# CHAPTER 6

# Career Paths

The career path of previous generations has been expanded to include lattices as well as ladders. Once upon a time, the only direction was up, and climbing each rung may have entailed stepping on a few heads. Now, lateral career moves have become more common as people's careers splinter, diverge, and curve as wildly as a river. Individuals may move from operations to sales, then communications or research and development, picking up new skills and experience along the way. The keyword is *move*. Most people (but certainly not all!) envision a significant amount of growth in their careers, with desires of earning more money, gaining more autonomy and prestige, working up to their potential, and maybe most importantly, achieving higher levels of personal happiness.

Today, organizations with progressive talent management strategies provide defined career paths for people to accommodate these needs. Ladders, career paths that move vertically within a function, allow people to advance when they are satisfied within a specific department. Lattices, career paths that move among various functions, allow people to grow and often explore different jobs within an organization without having to leave that group. Employees benefit as they are not pigeonholed in a function they may not enjoy. Additionally, the company benefits as the employee becomes well-rounded and better able to understand the company's big picture. Companies with lattices also benefit from lower employee turnover and better attraction performance.

## JAMAL'S CAREER PATH BLOCKADE

Jamal ladled out a heap of spaghetti and handed the plate to his mom.

"This looks delicious." She grabbed the Parmesan cheese.

"Good news, Ma. I got a job."

A smile spread across her face. "Fantastic. Where?"

"At Traverse Inn. I'm in Shipping and Receiving to start and they said I can move up to the Front Desk if all goes well."

"Front desk—like, wearing a suit and everything?"

"Those clerks make $12 an hour, that's way above minimum wage. There's a lot of opportunity to move up if I play my cards right. The place is owned by a big corporation called McElroy. They own hotels all over the country."

She was pleased, but cautious. "Please do your best to keep your grades up. You're too good at school to throw it all away."

"I won't go out for football next year. I'll work instead."

"Let's cross that bridge when we get to it. I like to see you play."

"If I'm working, maybe you won't have to work so many double shifts. I can help out a bit."

"You should save your money for college, Jamal."

"I'm going to treat you to a lobster dinner with my first paycheck, Ma. You deserve it."

She laughed. "I'm fine with spaghetti. Especially when you make it."

Boxes hit the floor and the boom echoed throughout the delivery area. Travel-sized toiletries tumbled out and rolled across the floor under shelving units. The floor was slick with hair conditioner. The hand truck had crashed into a tall shelving unit, and falling forward it wrapped its shelves around the runaway truck's scuffed metal gears. Jamal, an innocent bystander, was beaned in the head by a falling box of toilet paper, splattering the cherry slushy he was holding across his t-shirt. He stood frozen in place, the five other guys around him in various states of despair and fear but thankfully uninjured.

Approaching angry footsteps grew louder. "What's going on back there?"

Brian and Will laughed nervously.

Doug rounded the corner. He saw the disaster and his eyes grew wide. "Anybody hurt?"

"No, sir," Jamal answered.

"Then what the hell happened?"

It was Jamal's first week on the job. He wasn't about to volunteer information.

"We had a runaway hand truck," Brian said, barely containing his laughter.

"You're fired, Watson."

Brian's smirk disappeared. "Wait—that's not—"

"Out."

Will stopped snickering too.

"You too, Dulmage. I've had enough of the both of you. And I'm taking the cost of this lost inventory out of your last paychecks."

Brian and Will had been the main perpetrators, playing games with the equipment, and Doug knew it. Will and Brian looked momentarily like they would protest and thought better of it. Brian muttered something as they turned to leave, only part of which was audible.

"I'll pretend I didn't hear that," Doug yelled after them as they headed toward the door. He turned to the rest of the group. "If I ever see something like this again, you're all fired and you'll be sued for damages. McElroy has the money it needs to obliterate idiots like you." He pointed to the mess on the floor. "You've got fifteen minutes to clean this up and put everything back like it never happened."

It was an inauspicious start to his career, but Jamal knew he'd dodged a bullet. A couple feet to the right, and that metal shelf would have gashed his skull. On the bright side, he had just moved up two spots in seniority in Shipping and Receiving.

"Hey. What's your name again?"

Jamal stopped stacking boxes and looked around. Doug appeared to be talking to him.

"Me? Jamal."

"Come with me, Jamal." Doug turned on his heels and started walking briskly toward the Operations office.

Was he in trouble? He searched his mind for what he might have done.

They reached the office, and Doug wheeled around to face him.

"I've been watching you. You're a good worker."

"Thank you, sir."

"Call me Doug. You remind me of myself when I was your age, lots of initiative. I started with McElroy thirty years ago. I had your job, and now I'm head of Logistics for a three-county area. The company rewards people like you. Tell me, Jamal. What kind of plans do you have for the future?"

"College, I hope."

"That's what I like to hear. You want to move up to a different position, make more money?"

"I kind of had my eye on desk clerk, or something with the books. I'm really good with numbers."

Doug slapped Jamal on the back. "Just stay away from the idiots and it's a no brainer."

"I appreciate it, sir. I won't let you down."

Jamal had a spring in his step the rest of the day. He'd watched his brothers hop from one job to the next, never gaining any traction. The good jobs they swore were right around the corner never materialized; they'd get laid off or fired before they could climb their way to a decent salary. It was always someone else's fault: the boss didn't like them; a guy in the shop had it out for him; he couldn't get to work on time because of traffic, a flat tire, the alarm didn't go off. Meanwhile, his mom worked double shifts and still paid their cell phone bills, while she herself went without one. Jamal fantasized about surprising his mom with a brand new phone of her own. He also fantasized further down the line about having his own business. He had no idea how to get there from here, but he was going to try.

In December of his senior year, Jamal told Doug he had applied for an opening as a front desk clerk, thinking Doug would be happy for him, maybe give him a good recommendation.

"You don't want to do that, son," Doug said.

"What? Why?"

"It's a dead end. There's more opportunity where you are."

"But it's a big raise, and it works better with my school schedule."

Doug shook his head. "I'd hate to see you lose your seniority."

Jamal was perplexed at Doug's attitude. He thought his boss would be supportive. "I was thinking that within a couple years I could be a reservation manager. It would be good to have both front-of-house and back-of-house experience."

"Front-desk is overrated. You get one guest who complains about you and you're fired. If it's money you're after, I guarantee that if you stick it out you'll be an operations supervisor in four years."

"I've been here over a year and I'm only making fifty cents more an hour."

"I wish I could do more, but that's McElroy policy."

Jamal applied for the job anyway, and the interview was weird. The HR manager kept asking him questions about why he wanted to transfer from Operations. She didn't seem impressed by his obvious answers: higher pay, broader experience. Instead, she focused on his lack of customer service experience, even though he had been interacting with vendors as customers for over a year. She also asked him why he wasn't satisfied in Operations, and wasn't convinced when he told her that he was satisfied.

"They hired someone from the outside," he told his mom two weeks later, over a dinner of her famous rice and beans.

"Did Doug give you a good recommendation?"

"I'm not sure. I get the feeling they want me where I am."

"Why don't you try another hotel chain?"

"Maybe I will. I just thought I'd have a better shot where I already was."

His mom shook her head. "People are crazy sometimes. No reason for what they do."

"I don't want to end up like Jerome and Jermaine, going from one place to the next."

"I know, but you have to find a place that respects your hard work."

"Doug says he does, and that I can make it to supervisor in a few years."

"Hmm is that so? I get the feeling Doug is looking out for Doug."

Jamal shoveled the rest of his rice and beans into his mouth and eyed the leftovers on the stove. His mom had always been a good judge of character.

Six months later, a housekeeping supervisor position opened up. Jamal had already started picking up some housekeeping duties in addition to shipping and receiving. The supervisor position would include a lot of scheduling and working with HR—a chance to branch out into other areas of hospitality. He asked Doug if he should apply for it.

"They're looking for someone with supervisory experience," he said.

"How can I get any experience if all these jobs require it?"

"You've only been here two years. You have to pay your dues."

"The job pays $14 an hour."

"For starters. You can move up real fast. It will be a good opportunity for you in a year or two."

Jamal's frustration made him want to scream. How could he acquire new skills and experience when the company wouldn't let him?

He applied for the job and managed to snag an interview. It was a different HR rep this time, but the story remained the same.

"Do you have any supervisory experience?"

"I often cover for the operations manager when he's gone."

"Have you worked in Housekeeping before?"

"I intersect with the Housekeeping staff on a regular basis as part of my current duties."

"But you have no formal supervisory or Housekeeping experience?"

"Well, no. But I'm excited by McElroy as a company and I'd like to continue being part of its team. I feel it offers a lot of opportunities for growth."

"Thank you for your interest. We'll be in touch."

The job went to an outsider, a 21-year-old manager of a Dairy Quick on the other side of town. She lasted three months then quit to become the manager of a new restaurant opening down the street. Jamal was near apoplectic. By now his whole family was urging him to quit and get a job somewhere else; he was beginning to think it might be the sensible thing. The heck with company loyalty.

He was processing the daily incoming linen order and joking around with Philippe as always.

"When will you let me drive your truck around the block and show you how I can drift a cube van?"

Philippe laughed. "Driving this box takes real skill, man. Hardly anyone can drive a stick nowadays. I can find those gears in my sleep."

"That thing is dirty, though. How do you have such clean sheets in there when the van looks like you rolled it through a swamp?"

"Don't criticize. This van sparkled this morning. You're the last stop today and it's seen some massive potholes."

"So have I, man, so have I."

They laughed and Philippe got serious for a moment. "Hey, are you looking for a job or anything?"

Jamal shrugged. "What do you have?"

"My boss is leaving. He practically runs the whole operation."

"Why don't you apply?"

"Not my thing—I like driving around all day. But you have people skills and that ability to multitask. They'd love you."

Jamal perked up. "What's the pay?"

"About average, I guess. But they have cookouts and give away free stuff all the time. Sometimes there's prizes—last year my buddy went to the Super Bowl."

"How long have you been there?"

"Five years. They pay my health insurance, which lots of places don't even do anymore. My son's got a preexisting condition, so it's a godsend."

Jamal shook his hand. "Thanks, man. I just might check them out."

Lund Linen Supply was a small, family-run company, the opposite of McElroy. But they had been around for forty years and many of the employees stayed for twenty years or more. While the business was hardly exciting, Jamal knew that it would always be an important player in the hospitality industry. A hotel lived and died by its reputation for clean sheets and towels. He interviewed for the operations manager position and was surprised when they offered it to him. He felt hopeful about his career prospects for the first time in years.

"You're making a mistake," Doug said. "There's no ladder to climb over there."

Jamal sighed. "McElroy won't let me climb this ladder."

"You're going to regret it. Small company, they could go out of business at any moment."

"Then I can come back here with my supervisory experience and finally get the job I deserve."

Doug shook his head. "There's just no helping some people."

In his frustration, Jamal remembered his first day, when those two idiots crashed the handcart into the shelving unit and caused so much damage. He got it now, their cavalier attitude and lack of respect. In Jamal's youthful naiveté, it had taken several years to see through the veneer of the McElroy Group.

## JASMINE AND LIAM ADD UP THE POSITIVES

Jasmine could not get the numbers to match up, no matter how many times she tried. She'd had the same problem in school and had survived her accounting class by a fraction of a point. Plain and simple, numbers made her sweat.

It was her first week in Finance at Positive Electric. Only five months and three weeks to go, and then she would head to Sales and Marketing. Her first six-month rotation in the three-year new employee Career Path program had been in Human Resources, an unexpectedly interesting department. She learned a lot about how the company ran and about senior positions that had gone unmentioned in business school. More importantly, she had made valuable connections with some great people. It was social, and social was fun. Unlike these spreadsheets.

College had been a blur for Jasmine. She was a cheerleader first and a student second. She logged long hours with her squad, and fall weekends were jam-packed with games and travel. She dated athletes, associated with a wide circle of friends, and loved every minute of it. Classes were sometimes an afterthought, although she managed to graduate with a degree in business and a respectable GPA. Her saving grace was her sparkling personality and effervescent smile. Her optimism had kept her afloat whenever she encountered an academic snag.

The spreadsheet on the screen did not care about her smile or the fact that she could do three back handsprings in a row. It stubbornly refused to work. It was hard for her to care about fringe benefit rates and leveraged costs. She had to ask Liam for help for the fourth time this morning. He was always gracious, but she didn't want to depend on him. It was important that she figure this out herself, even if her stay in Finance was temporary.

For Jasmine, Positive Electric's Career Rotation Program for new college graduates was a dream. She was armed with a business degree but clueless about her future. She had been sad to leave college, with its constant swirl of friends and activities, and she was headed into adulthood saddled with $25,000 in student loans.

At first, Positive Electric didn't excite her. They didn't manufacture a cool product and they didn't organize flashy events like destination weddings or music festivals. Her dream job—an NFL cheerleader—was tantamount to a volunteer position. Jasmine needed a salary to make a dent in her student debt. She reluctantly applied to Positive Electric after a few other options didn't pan out. Luckily, she interviewed well, but the spreadsheet before her now was not responding to her fabulous smile and witty remarks.

Sales and Marketing was the bright light at the end of the tunnel, but it was still a long way away. Thankfully there was Liam, for whom she had developed enormous respect. He had just finished the Career Path Program and landed permanently in Finance. Liam was comfortable with numbers; he already knew he wanted to be a CPA and the company's tuition-reimbursement program was going to help him out with some of the coursework. As an added bonus, he dressed with style and had played baseball in college. Jasmine would always be partial to football, but she definitely appreciated a strong pitching arm.

In the end, the spreadsheet won. It got tired of her feeble attempts to manipulate its formulas and froze. She rebooted her computer, but the data she had been working with all day that was due in fifteen minutes was gone. Poof!

She gasped for air. "No. No, no, no, no, no."

Liam wheeled over in his ergonomic chair. "Something wrong?"

Jasmine looked at him, wide eyed. "It's gone!"

Liam looked around, on the desk, the floor. "What?"

"My spreadsheet. Oh my God!"

"Just print it out again."

Jasmine faced him, terror in her eyes. "Not the hard copy. The actual file!"

"Did you save it?"

"Yes…No…I don't remember. I made a lot of changes." Jasmine sunk her face into her hands. "They're going to kill me."

"They might torture you for a while, but they won't kill you."

Jasmine raised her head to glare at him.

"Let me take a look." Liam commandeered her laptop and pounded the keyboard like a hacker in a movie. She held her breath.

Five minutes later, he turned to her with the verdict: "Yep. It's really gone."

Jasmine cried in despair. "What should I do? I've got an hour to input all of this," waving her hands in front of a jumbled pile of papers on her desk, "and make sure everything adds up."

"I'll help."

"Oh, Liam. I could kiss you!"

He laughed nervously. She had an inkling their friendship might be ready for the next level.

By the time Jasmine's stint in Finance was over, the spreadsheet debacle was a distant memory and she and Liam had become an item. She admired his technical and mathematical acumen, and he respected her innovative big-picture thinking.

When Jasmine landed in Sales and Marketing, the clouds parted and the sun shone down. Birds sang and the pot of gold at the end of the rainbow turned out to be her sense of belonging, not to mention some nice sales commissions. She had never studied sales or held a sales position before, but three days into her rotation she realized that her cheerleading background was coming in handy with promoting the company's products and services. Instead of flourishing pom-poms, she had brochures.

Outside sales calls were the most fun. She was out of the office, meeting new people, and each sale felt like winning a game. Clients adored her, and she discovered a passion for giving presentations—it was nothing more than performing in front of a crowd. The best part of sales was the training that came with it. New team members were paired with more experienced reps, and she was learning so much through her mentorship with Joe. Jasmine could see herself becoming an account executive within a couple of years, and maybe eventually a regional sales manager. The travel appealed to her. However, she could also envision a path where she might want to stay closer to home. There seemed to be a significant crossover between Sales and Marketing, and she was interested in learning more.

Jasmine and Liam discussed their divergent experiences in Sales and Marketing over sushi one evening:

"I can read numbers," Liam said, "but I can't read people. For me, it was six months of torture."

"I love people, not numbers. That's why Sales suits me."

"I like sitting at my desk all day and solving problems."

"How can you sit still that long? I need to move around, get out of the office."

"You've got physical energy. I've got mental energy."

She dabbed wasabi on her sashimi. "Good point."

The department neither of them liked was Production. As much as they valued Positive Electric as a great place to work, Jasmine and Liam didn't like the minutia of engineering or manufacturing. Making sure the widget machines were running at capacity just didn't excite either one of them.

"Nothing against manual labor," Liam said.

"Of course not," Jasmine responded.

"The shop floor is so loud."

"It's not the noise that bothers me, it's the possibility that one of those machines will tear me in half if I'm not careful.

"Another reason to like Finance. Dismemberment is rare."

They both laughed and agreed that their time in Human Resources and Customer Service was fruitful. Not only did it help them understand these areas of the company better, it also allowed them to get to know the people they would interact with later on, no matter where they ended up.

The Career Path Program was beneficial for the company because it served a cross-training and team-building function that improved communication and relationships over the long term.

"As much as I like Finance, I realize that many other areas of the company rely on numbers," Liam concluded. "There's always a place for the math guy. Even Operations needs performance analysts; it's not money, but it's numbers. Different units of measurement, both essential."

"The flip side of that is people," Jasmine said. "You can't build a successful business without forming good relationships along the way. That's what I like best."

"I remember they gave us this chart of career pathways my first day at the company, it was like a grid. I'd always thought of a career track as a pre-determined, ascending tightrope."

"I remember that! It was like a video game. You could move in any direction, across many functional areas. It's like once you get hired, they trust you to be good at whatever you choose to do."

"Yeah," Liam said. "Like they hired you as an individual, not because you fit in a box."

## UNQUITTABLE

- Well-documented career ladders and lattices allow talented individuals to be intentional about their careers. They demonstrate that an organization values growth as much as their talent.
- Career paths should be introduced during the recruiting process as an employer branding tactic. They promote organizational loyalty because they allow people to envision multiple possibilities for their future.
- Career paths indicate that an organization has given significant thought to the skills and behaviors needed for different positions.
- Rotational opportunities allow new talent to explore multiple areas, expand their skills, and create camaraderie with people in diverse areas. All of this increases professional development and counts as team building.

## QUITTABLE

- Organizations without documented career ladders and lattices aren't putting people first.
- Without clearly defined career pathways, people don't know their internal job options and may feel trapped in their current positions. They may begin to look for other opportunities at other companies.
- Organizations that want to retain people but do not offer them a chance to develop their skills are not being fair to themselves or the talent. Stringing individuals along with empty promises of promotions is disingenuous and will hurt your employer brand.

# CHAPTER 7

# Career Sculpting

Career sculpting isn't the same as mentoring or coaching, but all three have a lot in common. Whereas mentors may focus on big-picture career pathways and coaches on resolving specific issues, a career sculptor counsels an individual on crafting a job that takes advantage of their talents, strengths, and interests. Career sculpting allows talent to broaden their current position by incorporating new opportunities and abilities into their routine. This tool is especially effective in smaller organizations that have less defined career pathways or flat management structures that don't leave much room for maneuvering. Giving talented individuals agency over the breadth of their duties will pay off in increased job satisfaction and a healthier organization.

The key terms in career sculpting are *passion* and *energy:* What topics are they passionate about? What tasks do they find energizing? Academic writers are known to have very strong feelings about punctuation, while advertising copywriters just want to make an impact. Both love words and probably don't want to become tool and die makers. However, at some point, both would welcome the opportunity to expand their daily routines by adding new skills into the mix. Sometimes, a person doesn't want a whole new job—maybe she just wants a chance to expand her horizons. Wise employers are happy to accommodate this type of growth. Any time an employee offers to help with a task (assuming competence, even if it's a bit outside the parameters of the job description), it's time to consider sculpting the career to fit the individual, instead of making the individual conform to the job.

Below, Chris needs a new challenge to keep him in a growth mindset at his job. Luckily, his employer has a career sculpting program that matches him with someone to guide him through the process. The solution benefits the company as much as Chris. Meanwhile, Carl is bored to oblivion. He agrees to join his company's career sculpting program, but he encounters a cookie-cutter arrangement that seems more like a vanity project for HR than a tool used to reinvigorate the work force.

## HOW TO HAVE A MIDLIFE CRISIS

Freda always looked forward to Chris's annual review. It was a chance to connect and toss around a few ideas for the coming year. Chris was an undeniable asset to the company, and Freda had no problem giving him top scores and recommending him for the highest raise possible. After ten years, however, Chris was bumping up against the pay ceiling as an account manager. Lately, it seemed as if he had lost a bit of his enthusiasm, and she was eager to discuss it.

After they walked through the review criteria, she verged into more personal territory. Chris talked about how much he enjoyed coaching his second-grader's Little League Baseball team.

"It makes me a better person, learning to be patient with children," he said. "Even at his young age you can tell which kids have talent, but at this point it's all about instilling a sense of good sportsmanship."

Freda nodded. "I went through the same thing when my daughters were young. One was in dance, one was in Girl Scouts. It's not about the activity itself, but learning to interact with other people and develop social graces. I guarantee that these will be some of your favorite memories."

"For sure," Chris said.

"Do you have any other concerns?" Freda asked.

"To tell the truth, I do. You know I really enjoy what I do, and I admire the company a great deal."

"But?"

"Well, I'm feeling a bit…stale. Like I'm going through the motions."

Her hunch had been right. "That's understandable. Tell me more."

"It has nothing to do with you or the company. It's just me. I don't feel challenged anymore."

"Are you telling me you're coming after *my* job?" Freda teased.

Chris laughed. "Not at all. You know I'm not cut out to be a people manager. I really feel an affinity for the products and I know that's where my strength lies."

"I agree."

"I'm not sure what the solution is. Going back to school right now isn't feasible, and switching careers seems too drastic."

"And yet you feel like you're sleepwalking through your days."

"Am I that obvious?"

Freda laughed. "Midlife crisis if I've ever seen one. You in the market for a sports car?"

"Has this happened to you?"

She thought for a moment. "I had been at the same company for ten years before LongStar. I was forty and felt like I wasn't getting anywhere."

"I don't want to reinvent the wheel. I just want to add some air."

Freda tapped her pen against her notepad. "You're a perfect candidate for LongStar's Career Sculpting program."

Chris perked up. "I've heard of that, but never paid much attention."

"You team up with a career sculptor to discuss your interests and goals and work toward a solution that benefits you and the company. I haven't done it myself, but I could have someone in the program contact you."

"How long does it take?"

Freda shrugged. "As long as it needs to."

Chris gazed out the window. It was worth a try. Would it be a lot of psychology mumbo jumbo? At the very least it would get him away from his desk for a while. He'd have a chance to really think about his future, something that wasn't possible at home with two boys getting into the type of mischief that sometimes resulted in stitches. "Okay. Let's call it a plan."

Gerald was impressed with Chris. He had known him only in passing before becoming his career sculptor, but now he looked forward to their biweekly lunches. They were both adventurous eaters, laid-back but diligent about deadlines, and they both had an offbeat sense of humor that not everyone understood. Despite their similarities, the two men's paths were unlikely to cross significantly at LongStar because Gerald was a senior financial analyst in a different division than Chris. While Gerald loved his job, he had volunteered to be a career sculptor to spread his wings and help alleviate some of the isolation he felt at work. He was a sociable person by nature and it felt good to help the company in a different capacity. He also had a knack for listening to people and serving as a sounding board. Gerald and Chris discussed a range of topics over their lunch meetings, only a portion of which were work related. His job as a career sculptor was to listen and facilitate any reasonable changes that Chris suggested. The idea was to find out what energized Chris and what he found dull.

The men were at a new Ethiopian restaurant downtown, and Chris was telling Gerald all the random items on his bucket list as they devoured zizil wat: restoring a 1963 Buick Riviera, rowing through the Blue Grotto in Italy, learning to fly a hot-air balloon, and racing a motorcycle on the Bonneville Salt Flats.

"One of those things is liable to get you killed," Gerald joked.

"Did I mention that I make the world's best guacamole and I plan on selling it at farmer's markets when the boys are a bit older?"

"No such thing as too much guac," Gerald said. "But what I'm sensing is that you could use a little more adventure in your workday."

Chris paused between bites. "I never thought of work as an adventure."

"Have you ever considered going into New Business Development?"

Chris looked thoughtful. "Would I get out of the office more often? A change of scenery would be nice."

"Be careful what you wish for. They might send you to Timbuktu, Oklahoma."

"I'll go anywhere once," Chris laughed. "As long as I don't need a Sherpa."

"Knowing LongStar, you'll be good with a sturdy pair of boots and an umbrella."

At another lunch, they discussed *The Curious Leader,* a book given to everyone in the Career Sculpting program. It was a business management book, the type that Gerald liked to read for fun. The main idea was simple: The best business leaders are those who constantly ask *why?* Each chapter included exercises to increase one's capacity for curiosity and wonderment.

"I really connected with this book," Chris said. "As a father to two boys who are always asking 'why,' it struck me that at some point in our lives we stop asking. The trick is to maintain a child's level of curiosity as an adult. We have so many obligations that we forget how to look at the world as if it still has something to teach us."

Gerald nodded. "How can you relate that insight to your career at LongStar?"

"As an Account Manager, my job is to make sure the client is happy. If they're not happy, I need to find out why and fix it.

"Most of my questions are along the lines of, 'How can we give them a good deal on this?' or, 'What can I say to change their minds?' Maybe I need to back down a couple levels. Instead of being so focused, maybe the best questions are broader, like 'Are we attracting the right clients to LongStar?' or, 'Have we really explored every corner of this concept?'"

"I always ask myself why I didn't invest in Google when I was 23," Gerald responded.

Chris laughed. "What questions do you ask yourself about your job? I mean, finance is finance."

"You'd be surprised. Numbers can be quite creative—and I'm not talking about cooking the books. Budgets are created out of thin air—just like ad campaigns. How many people do we need on an account? Should we sacrifice this one major client for two smaller ones in order to get work in a growth sector? Should I pursue the path to the CFO's office, or should I be content working on real projects? Would I miss the hands-on stuff each day?"

"I also liked the author's suggestion to ask dumb questions. That was a new concept for me."

"That's a classic in business—ask a smart person a dumb question!" Gerald said.

"I'm not a cynic, but when companies come up with these complicated mission statements, I want to ask, 'Isn't the only real mission to make money?'"

"Same with core values," Gerald said. "Our core value is profit. We sell our product for money."

"But I would never say that in a room full of executives."

"Of course not."

"It's just a thought experiment."

"Absolutely."

Later that afternoon, a fortuitous email landed in Gerald's inbox, which he forwarded to Chris. It was a list of upcoming, special projects within the company. They ranged a new social media campaign targeted specifically toward rural millennials to a sales team at national conferences with the intent of building relationships with potential suppliers.

Gerald picked up the phone and called Chris's extension. "Are you seeing what I'm seeing?"

Chris clicked through to the email. "I do. Conferences. Schmoozing. Maybe I can go to Oklahoma."

"You should talk to Freda."

The Houston weather in February was a welcome respite from the Indiana snow. Chris was looking forward to meeting potential clients at the convention and then taking the rental car through the world's longest car wash. He also appreciated how the conference was only three days; he didn't like being away from the family for too long. This was the fourth conference he had attended since he had exited the Career Sculpting program with a fresh, clear direction assisting the New Business Development team. The process was formalized through a meeting with Freda, who signed and dated changes to his annual review regarding how much time he would devote to these alternative endeavors.

As he made his way through the convention hall, he perused the exhibits and collected interesting literature on both companies he felt would be good partners for LongStar and those who might be potential competitors. He eventually made his way back to the LongStar exhibit to grab his computer and prepare for his 1:00 p.m. seminar on integrating ISO procedures into project planning. He was proud of his presentation, and it was always well attended. It was definitely beyond the expertise of the LongStar Sales Managers, and having this bonus content was an asset to the company at these conventions. It really raised their profile.

Chris enjoyed sharing his expertise, and these conferences gave him something to look forward to during those long months of traditional account management. It was just enough of a change to energize him again, and it took nothing away from his work-life balance beyond missing a few Little League practices a year. His wife had adapted to his absence by inviting her mother up from Florida when he was gone. It was a special treat for the boys to be spoiled by Grandma.

During his absences from the office, his position was backfilled by one of the division's part-time project specialists. This allowed her to expand her skill set and effectively become cross-trained. Not only did this prevent him from walking into a dumpster fire when he returned from a conference, but also it ensured that LongStar had talent in the pipeline in case they suddenly found themselves short an account manager.

In all, Chris's career sculpting experience with Gerald lasted six months, and it might have lasted longer if the conference opportunity hadn't presented itself. It started with a couple of formal assessments designed to gauge his skills and interests, and then transitioned to their informal meetings talking about what kind of work is meaningful to Chris and how that could be merged into the company's workflow and goals.

Chris had always thought of himself as having insight into his motivations, but Gerald's perspective really opened up the conversation and got him thinking about things he'd never considered. It wasn't about where he wanted to be in five years, or what other jobs he wanted. It was about how to change his current position to make it more energizing.

At his next annual review, Freda noticed the difference. "How's that midlife crisis going?" she asked.

"I turned my crisis into opportunity," he said, jokingly.

"There's definitely more spring in your step these days."

"Going to conferences and presenting to people recharges my batteries. I get to keep an eye on where the industry is going and think about LongStar's role in it. I love to network."

"It's an important part of business development," Freda concurred.

"Best of all, I get to synthesize the conference info during strategy sessions with the business development team. Sometimes I pick up on stuff that isn't even on their radar yet, and sometimes I verify the hunches they already have. I like being their eyes and ears since they can't get to every conference."

"That's great."

"I made some valuable connections, too. I'm speaking with the Talent Team about a guy I met who gave an inspiring sales leadership talk. It might be worth it to bring him in."

"Do you still have time to do your old job?"

Chris laughed. "Funny you should mention that. I've actually been hard pressed to take care of all the things I used to. I've spoken with a couple of the newer members on my team, and I've transferred some of my old duties to them. It frees me up to do more of this new stuff, and it gives them their own chance to grow."

Freda nodded. "I love it when life works out that way."

## A PROGRAM IN NAME ONLY

The pencils in Carl's desk drawer had been securely speared into the ceiling tiles above his head. All twenty-four of them. It was his greatest accomplishment in months, and the only note of decoration in the Purchasing Department office. Carl had been at Big John's for fifteen years, and had many more to go before he crossed the golden finish line of retirement. Looking for a new job was out of the question; he'd be competing against younger whippersnappers who had more education and would work for less money. Carl had a mortgage, two teenagers, and no degree. His only exceptional skill was his facility with a crossbow, which didn't really help him on a daily basis.

He thought about taking some business classes at night school—as if that would help—but the company wouldn't pay for it, so he socked the money away for his kids' college. Their current plans were to become professional video game players—hopefully that would change.

Last year, Big John's went and spent a bundle on new purchasing software. People moaned and complained like it was the end of the world. On one hand, Carl got it—he hated change as much as the next person. On the other hand, the software was pretty easy to use and he adapted to it quickly. He became the department's go-to person for troubleshooting and he taught everyone how to customize their reports. It was a brief reprieve from the snail-paced passage of time at the plant.

Despite his expertise with the purchasing program, Carl didn't have nearly enough expertise to join the company's IT team, nor did he really want to. But he would prefer incorporating some IT duties into his purchasing job.

One Friday afternoon, the Wi-Fi network was down and Carl couldn't access any online wrestling videos. After making the maximum allowable trips to the break room and bathroom without arousing suspicion, he clicked open the company newsletter, which had been sitting unread in his inbox for a while. There was a blurb about something called a Job Sculpting program. It read:

> Do you want to expand your professional horizons here at Big John's without expensive or time-consuming training? Check out our Job Sculpting program for qualified employees. You can expand your skillset and increase your value to the company. Who knows how high you can soar if you don't spread your wings?

It piqued his interest enough that he emailed the HR department for more information. HR replied with an application to fill out, which had to be approved by his manager. Well, that was going to put a kink in things. His "manager," if you could call him that, was Big John's controller, Dirk Neymar. Their relationship was not so much strained as nonexistent. Dirk worked up front with the big boys and didn't venture down to purchasing very often, which was adjacent to the shop floor. He was a relative newcomer to the company with clear designs on running things once Mr. Griskow kicked the bucket. Carl couldn't do much to help him consolidate power, so Dirk left him to his own devices. What would his response be to Carl wanting to join the Job Sculpting program?

Against Carl's better judgment, he spent a significant amount of time filling out the application over the next couple of weeks. He was pleased with some of his responses:

- **What do you like about your current job?** I have a lot of experience in purchasing and I'm good at my job. I like the new purchasing software and trained the whole department how to use it.
- **What skills do you have that are underutilized in your current position?** I like technology. I don't know how to program, but I like creating custom reports and spreadsheets that show how we're doing.
- **What are some Big John's job titles that seem like they might be interesting?** I don't know about current job titles, but I would like to stay in Purchasing but have some IT duties. Not sure what you would call it.

He stuck the application in an inter-office envelope with a sticky note asking Dirk to sign it. To his slight astonishment, the envelope came back to him next day, Dirk's name scribbled on the bottom of the last page. So Carl sent it on to Human Resources and promptly forgot about it.

Three months later, Carl got an email from HR: His application for the job sculpting had been approved. To tell the truth, Carl wasn't sure he still wanted to go through with it—the moment had kind of passed. But he had extra time in his schedule and decided to head down to HR for a discussion. It couldn't hurt.

He met with Ashley, the latest addition to an ever-changing HR roster. He didn't know what to expect, but given Big John's history of innovation, it wasn't much.

"What skills do you have that are underutilized in your current position?" she asked, referring to a blank application on the desk in front of her.

"Do you have my original application? I answered that question already."

Ashley glanced around the office. "Did you bring a copy with you?"

"I submitted it months ago."

"The HR manager probably has it. He's not here today."

Carl sighed. Was it too late to leave? "I like computers. I'm not an expert or anything, but I'm pretty good at figuring out how to troubleshoot them."

Ashley took notes, looking up only briefly. She followed up with a series of questions about seemingly random things:

"Do you find it easy to stay relaxed under pressure?"

"Do you ever do things out of sheer curiosity?

"Are you usually highly motivated and energetic?

"Are you often envious of others?

"Would you rather improvise than spend time coming up with a detailed plan?"

He kept waiting for Ashley to put her clipboard down, look him in the eye, and talk frankly about the Job Sculpting program at Big John's. Instead, she finished the quiz, thanked him for his time, and said they'd meet again next week at the same time to talk about the opportunities that match his interests. He returned to his office, equal parts annoyed and perplexed.

A week later, Carl reluctantly dragged himself down to HR for his second meeting. He didn't have any other pressing obligation and the half-baked program wasn't really firing him up. He and Ashley sat down in the same HR conference room, and she slid a paper toward him, her expression quite pleased.

"I scored the test we went through last week and here's the result: You're a Rational Philosopher. That means you value thinking over feeling and having a plan over improvising. It also means you prefer having a stable career because you crave dependability, consistency, and clearly defined roles."

"I can't argue with that." Although he didn't see it as especially relevant at the moment.

"You have a respect for authority and hierarchy, and you like having clearly defined responsibilities," she continued. "You're dedicated and good at following orders but sometimes have problems with authority. You're dedicated, loyal, and like to finish what you start. You don't like to spend much time in meetings and prefer to problem-solve by trial and error rather than by consulting others."

"Thanks…I think."

Ashley missed his sarcasm. "The good news is that your profile syncs nicely with your current position."

"You don't say."

"Can you tell me why you're looking to do something different at this point?"

"I'm not," Carl said for what felt like the tenth time. "I just want to expand my current position to give me some new opportunities. I've been here fifteen years."

Ashley shifted in her seat. Perhaps she was finally sensing his anger. "Your profile also matches that of an operations manager."

"That job requires a college degree."

"You don't have one?"

"Well, no. Doesn't your computer tell you that?"

"I don't have access to personnel files."

He wanted to bang his head against the table.

"Do you want to hear about the other job opportunities available at Big John's right now?"

Carl felt his irritation rise. "I thought job sculpting was about adapting my current job, not getting a new one."

"We're hoping to do that in the future. But the company isn't ready to support that yet. Mr. Griskow believes that if we start letting people do anything they want, we'll need to rewrite all the job descriptions, and that will cause a ripple effect with regard to the pay structure and other things. So, mostly, what we're doing is examining your skills profile and matching you to the opportunities at the company that are a good fit."

"I was hoping I could learn a few things from the IT department, maybe help out people on my end of the building."

"Oh, right. The HR manager ran that suggestion by the IT manager, Raoul, and they agreed that maybe it wasn't a good time to do that."

Carl felt like he was undergoing a bait and switch at a used car lot. He also felt like it wasn't worth the effort to explain this feeling to Ashley. So he humored her. It was his only recourse at the moment. "What kind of jobs do you have?"

She tapped on her laptop and brought up the corporate website, which listed all current openings: assistant shop supervisor, line worker, IT intern, accounts payable clerk.

"Any of those sound interesting?"

"I see why Raoul didn't want to cross-train me. He doesn't want to jeopardize his IT intern opening." He pushed back his chair. "This isn't going anywhere. Thanks for your time."

As he made his way back to the dingy Purchasing Office, he was surprised at the strength of his vitriol. He was angrier at having a false prospect dangled in front of him than if the company had never mentioned anything about job sculpting at all. The bitter taste in his mouth would transform into a nagging blob that swirled inside him, one that would periodically bubble up and make him wonder why he had taken this job all those years ago and why he stayed when he should have gotten out. Now he was trapped, for the sake of all those he was responsible for. He swiveled around in his chair and leaned back, staring at the ceiling. He'd have to order more pencils.

## UNQUITTABLE

- Good managers help people find suitable opportunities for professional development.
- Good career sculpting programs take care to connect individuals to jobs, responsibilities and activities that best match capabilities and areas of interest.
- One-on-one career coaching is a basic element of the career sculpting process.
- A good career sculpting program allows ample time for exploring and setting goals.
- Job descriptions are used as guidelines; however, they should be flexible and allow for the pursuit of learning, interests, and proficiency.
- Businesses that cultivate a growth mindset take individuals up on their offer to branch out. In a business where a fixed mindset prevails, people are territorial about their jobs and view others as a threat if they encroach on their duties.

## QUITTABLE

- Employers that offer no individual coaching probably aren't great places to grow and learn.
- Organizations that are not flexible enough to incorporate a person's skills, capabilities, or interests into his or her position, when the person volunteers them, may not be ideal environments for growth.

# CHAPTER 8

# Exit Interviews

As long as there are places to work, people will come and go and exit interviews will be a part of the circle of life. This final conversation is a chance for the employee to say what worked well, what didn't, and end things on a positive note. If conducted with the right attitude, setting, and structure, exit interviews are a great way for organizations to gain valuable feedback. A good exit interview is scheduled during the final day or two of employment and uses both open-ended and closed-ended standardized questions. Ideally, a human resources representative or an impartial third party conducts the interview. It should never be conducted by the departing employee's immediate supervisor.

It's important to conduct exit interviews with all voluntary separations, not just managers or high-ranking employees. Asking the right questions—and listening to the answers—may yield important information to guide continuous improvement efforts. This is a company's last chance to exercise professionalism on their own terms, and even practice a bit of employer branding while they're at it.

## IT'S NOT ABOUT TALKING, IT'S ABOUT LISTENING

"Tell me about your new employer," Taryn asked Joseph. The pair were seated in overstuffed chairs to lessen the formality of the exit interview. Taryn was the regional HR manager for Westwood Markets, a role she enjoyed because of the variety in her days. Today she was at the Harbortown location, simultaneously working on annual reviews and exit interviews. As casual as she tried to keep the conversation, she stuck to the script, allowed it to flow appropriately, and took good notes. Consistency was the key. As much as everyone leaving Westwood Markets was an individual, it was important to try to find trends in the data in order to strengthen the company.

Joseph was the produce manager at Harbortown, the highest performing location in the chain. He'd been with the company for four years. "I got an offer from Family Price Foods to be an assistant store manager," he told Taryn. "The money is better, but the decision was hard. I was afraid it would take years to ascend the ranks at Westwood. People don't leave."

Taryn nodded sympathetically and typed on her laptop. Family Price was Westwood's biggest competitor in the region, and this wasn't the first time they'd poached a Westwood manager. Probably wasn't the last, either, but they needed to understand the trend. Taryn used the exit interview to not only gather data for the company, but also to promote the company's employer brand. She wanted to make sure people left the company on a good note. Westwood's policy was to strengthen bridges at this juncture as much as some employees sought to burn them.

"What did you like about your job at Westwood?"

"Lots of things." Joseph said. "The people are great. I worked at a drug store before this, and they hired some real weirdos. The people at Westwood are normal by comparison."

She laughed. "No weirdos. That's good."

"I moved up from associate to manager quickly, with a great bump in pay. That was awesome."

"What didn't you like about your job at Westwood?"

"Some of the customers?" Joseph laughed. "Seriously. Every now and then you'll get someone on a rampage and there's nothing you can do to make them happy."

Taryn nodded. "Hazard of customer service jobs everywhere."

"My goal is to be a general manager. I figure this is the best way to make it happen."

She didn't blame him. It's not that the company lacked career pathways, per se, it was more that there wasn't a lot of movement in those pathways. The true definition of a blessing and a curse. "Tell me, Joseph, would you recommend Westwood to a friend? As a place to work, I mean."

"Yeah, of course. At least to some friends, others would never be able to keep up. But, for instance, my friend Eric has a degree in filmmaking and makes minimum wage working in public access television. This would definitely be a step up for him."

It was an insightful answer, revealing that Joseph saw Westwood as a place for a career rather than just a job. It meant the company was doing a lot right. He also thought highly enough of the place to know that not everyone would make a suitable employee. Taryn had no doubt that Joseph would make a good general manager someday.

"Last question, Joseph. If you could change anything about working at Westwood, what would it be?"

"Oh, wow," he said, looking off into the distance. "That's tough. I guess, well—I know this isn't my department, but I don't like how the cashiers are rated on how fast they scan items. This puts some really great people at the bottom of the list. They may be slower than others, but they're super nice and chatty with the customers. I'd much rather deal with them than with some super-fast person that never says anything." He shrugged. "Just my opinion, though."

"Thanks for being honest. It's nice that you care," Taryn said. "Anything else specific to your department?" She sensed a hesitation and waited; the silence became slightly awkward before he broke it.

"Well, to tell the truth, Produce is a tricky department. There's so much waste, margins are nonexistent."

"True."

"I really feel there's a better way to sell a higher percentage of inventory. I don't pretend I have all the answers, but the company could come up with a better strategy."

He hit another nail on the head. There's no way he could know it, but there was a lot of talk at headquarters about this very topic. As far as exit interviews go, this was an easy one for Taryn. Joseph was leaving Westwood on good terms, and she encouraged him to apply for any manager openings in the future.

"If things don't work out in your new job, we'd love to have you come back. Clearly, you know what you're doing, and we're sorry there's not another position for you to move into right now."

As much as the exit interview was a valuable means of obtaining feedback, it also served as part of the company's employer branding strategy. The idea was to leave on friendly terms and make sure that employees would say good things about Westwood when they left for other pastures. After Joseph left, Taryn sent an email to the general manager at Joseph's location, authorizing him to send a gift basket of Westwood items to Joseph's house the next day. Whatever they thought he'd like—wine, sausage, pistachios, fruit, coffee. It was the least they could do for a manager leaving on good terms.

That afternoon, Taryn had another exit interview at the opposite end of the spectrum. Rosie had been a bagger at the Harbortown location for several years. Westwood was the only grocery store chain Taryn knew of that would actually give a bagger an exit interview. The Westwood mission statement was, "Our family providing your family with quality products and services." As far as Taryn and the rest of the management were concerned, a bagger was part of the Westwood family. Rosie had mild cognitive impairments associated with Down syndrome, but the general manager acknowledged that Rosie had always approached her job enthusiastically. She seldom called in sick or took time off. Then, somewhat unexpectedly, Rosie submitted her two weeks' notice.

"Hi, Rosie, it's nice to meet you," Taryn said. "I want you to know that our conversation is confidential."

"Okay."

"I'm sorry to hear you're leaving your job at Westwood. Can you tell me why you made that decision?"

Rosie stared at the table, avoiding eye contact with Taryn. "Am I in trouble?"

Taryn was taken aback. "No, of course not! I talk with everyone who leaves the company. We want to know if anything's wrong so we can fix it."

"Oh." She still looked uncomfortable.

Taryn gave her a minute to respond, but she remained silent. "Are you leaving this job because you got a new one?" she asked, finally.

"I want to work at All Foods Warehouse, but they haven't called me yet."

"Did you apply there?"

"Yes." Rosie looked up, tentatively. "Are you mad?"

"Of course not. You're allowed to work wherever you want."

More silence.

"Can you tell me what you like about your job at Westwood?"

She nodded. "I made a lot of friends. Me and the cashiers joke around all the time and they help me when someone has a lot of groceries. Like two carts full."

"What don't you like about your job?"

Rosie fidgeted in her seat and looked away. She was clearly distressed. Finally, in a small voice, she said, "My boss called me stupid."

Taryn's head snapped up from her notepad. "What? To your face?"

Rosie looked to be on the verge of tears. "She said it when I could hear, a lot of times. I know I'm not smart, but I'm good at my job."

"I'm so sorry that happened, Rosie. Did you tell anyone else at the store, a manager or someone?"

"My mom said I didn't have to work there anymore if they treated me bad, so I said I quit."

"What else can you tell me about your boss, Rosie? I want to make sure this doesn't happen again. I will personally talk to her. Do you want to file a complaint instead of quitting?"

"My mom tells me not to complain, that people won't change."

"We don't let our employees say things like that to others. It's wrong."

"She's always laughing at me."

Taryn was so angry she felt like storming out of the room and confronting Rosie's supervisor on the spot; however, she knew that would be counterproductive. What she had on her hands was a serious personnel issue, and she would open an investigation herself. She would suggest that Rosie transfer to a different location in the short term. More importantly, she would stay here and listen to everything Rosie had to say.

Still reeling from the accusation of harassment, Taryn conducted a third exit interview that afternoon. Serena had been a cashier for five years at one of their busiest locations.

"Tell me about your new employer," Taryn asked, hands poised above her keyboard, ready to take notes.

"I'm going to McManus. Retail. The hours are kind of lousy but I get bonuses for meeting certain goals, so I'm hoping the money is better."

"What do you like about your job at Westwood?"

"Lots of things. The pay was pretty good, and I liked that I could work around my kids' school schedules. Some of the people were cool."

"What didn't you like about your job?"

Serena leaned back in her chair. "So you want me to spill the beans, is that it?"

"We're looking for constructive feedback. If there are issues we need to address, we want to fix them so we're a great place for all employees."

Serena considered this for a minute. "I'd say me and my boss didn't see eye to eye."

"The assistant store manager?"

"Yeah. She really had it out for me."

This was a delicate area, and Taryn would have to tread lightly. When it came to personality clashes, more often than not, both parties were at fault. "Is there anything we could do differently to make Westwood a better place to work?"

"You could get more people from headquarters to visit and see for themselves what's going on. Sometimes I get the feeling they don't really care."

This wasn't the first time Taryn had heard this. "What would they see going on?"

"I don't like the way some of the customers get treated. It's not right."

"Get treated by whom?"

"Some of the cashiers aren't sociable, but that's because of the managers. They keep making us come in when we're supposed to be off. Everything trickles down, but if the customer is treated poorly, the company looks bad."

"I agree, Serena. That's an important point." Taryn carefully noted what Serena had told her. It wasn't unusual to find out about these issues only after people had decided to leave. "Would you recommend Westwood to a friend?"

"You mean to work here?"

"Yeah."

"I got two of my friends hired here. Benny works in meat and seafood, and Errol is a beverage manager. They both liked it a lot. Benny transferred to another store and Errol's still here. But things have changed since we got a new store manager. I still like Westwood, but not this location."

Taryn nodded. "I appreciate your honesty. Is there anything we can do to help with your transition?"

"I considered moving to a different location myself, but the other stores are too far away from where I live. I chose McManus because it's close. So I don't think there's much that can be done at this point."

"Serena, I want you know that we appreciate your hard work for Westwood. If anything changes with your future job, you are welcome back here."

"Thanks."

They stood and shook hands. The meeting ended on good terms, but Taryn knew she had work ahead of her.

A year's worth of data from exit interviews, and the data was irrefutable. Westwood's overall turnover rate was an enviable 6 percent for full-time employees and 42 percent for part-time employees, but the numbers were significantly higher in four locations as well as in the Accounting Department at headquarters. Taryn suspected that those stores had underperforming managers. The Accounting Department would be a whole different ball of wax.

Sure enough, when she sat down for a deep dive into the data, she found the patterns she expected. Multiple interviewees mentioned issues with store managers at the four locations. Three managers in particular appeared to hassle workers who showed up five to ten minutes late to work when the busses were running late. Three other managers showed a pattern of not granting time off to workers who were sick or taking care of others who were sick. These managers would be enrolled in sensitivity training and expected to get their numbers in-line with the other locations.

The Accounting Department was a surprise. Given that the department was practically under Taryn's nose, she should have been more attuned to it. It seemed like she was always interviewing for accountants, even though the department was small—only ten people working under the CFO.

The Accounting exit interviews revealed a previously unknown truth to Taryn: Accountants were ambitious creatures! In the five exit interviews in the past eighteen months, four revealed they were leaving because the opportunities for career growth were limited. The CFO, herself only 40, seemed to be much more interested in achieving ambitious growth rates and massaging the numbers to bring everything in line with the CEO's vision than managing people.

As part of her fiscal, year-end activities, Taryn presented her findings to the executive team. One of the things she liked about her job was how she could use numbers and statistics to tell a story about the company's progress.

"So as you can see from this last chart, by asking detailed questions at exit interviews and tracking the data diligently, we identified issues that required action at five locations. Four stores and the Accounting Department. The goal is to save the company money by reducing employee turnover. By retraining managers at these locations, our goal is to reduce turnover from an average of 12 percent to 6 percent. This would mean thirty-six more people would stay, representing $448,000 over the previous fiscal year that wouldn't need to be spent on recruitment, hiring, training, overtime pay, and learning curve costs."

The top brass perked up at the dollar amount. Nothing to sneeze at, especially in an industry built on razor-thin margins. She concluded: "When our goal of being a work family breaks down, we do our best to fix it. That's how the exit interview process supports the Westwood mission statement: 'Our family providing your family with quality products and services.'"

## COOKIE BITES THE DUST

Cookie is a real go-getter. She leans in to everything she does, whether it's making baked goods (that's how she earned her nickname) or leading the HR Department at Delicious Foods. The only thing she likes more than surprising coworkers with a tray of homemade brownies is talking. Cookie talks to everyone, about everything, and just about all the time. For extroverted optimists like herself, this results in some world-class conversations ranging from the FIFA World Cup playoffs to stock tips from her ex-brother-in-law who once ran a hedge fund but now works as a landscape artist in Arizona. For the more subdued employees at Delicious Foods, Cookie's personality could be a bit intense, especially at 7:30 a.m. Doug, the founder and CEO, belonged to the latter group.

Last year, they had a conversation that went like this:

Cookie: "Doug, do you have a few minutes? I've got a great idea and I want to run it past you."

Doug (looks at watch): "I've got a meeting in five minutes."

Cookie: "Perfect! So you know that conference I went to last week—"

Doug: "Human Resources for Human Beings?"

Cookie: "That's the one. It was so awesome. The weather was great that day and afterward we went to this Mexican restaurant that had this band, and the singer looked just like Colin Farrell if Colin Farrell wore a sombrero and played a giant guitar. And the guaca—"

Doug: "The conference—"

Cookie: "I went to this workshop about exit interviews and it turns out they're something that we should totally be doing. In fact, I'm hearing about them everywhere these days. If you do it right, they take hardly any time and can provide valuable feedback that can save the company money over the long term."

Doug: "Save the company money, you say?"

Cookie: "Yeah, and that's not all. I can tell you more. We can lower turnover rates by finding out why people are leaving. You may think you know why someone is leaving but if you never ask them, then you don't know for sure. It's science."

Doug: "I thought people left the company because they got a better offer somewhere else."

Cookie: "See, that's the crazy thing! Turns out that's not always the case. People leave for a variety of reasons. Sometimes it's money, but sometimes they have issues with a manager, they want more responsibility, or they need to spend more time with their family. Or maybe their life is spiraling out of control and they need to see a mental health professional but they don't realize it."

Doug: "Oh, dear."

Cookie: "Exit interviews are the way to go. It's really a no-brainer. Think of all the data, we could do so much with it! And without it we can't do anything. We've got to start somewhere."

Doug's head hurt, but Cookie had a point. He just wished she'd said it in an email. He appreciated her willingness to try new things; all he had to do was give the word and she'd be off inventing some new process. Doug could use a few more Cookies at Delicious Foods, just as long as they kept the hallway ambushes to a minimum. "Sounds like a good idea."

"Thanks, Doug. You won't regret it. Hey—you know what would be great? A mariachi band for the company picnic. I'll suggest it to Diane, see if we can work something out. I just learned how to make churros. It's never too early to start planning. I should also check and see how the avocado crop is doing this year because there's been a run on them lately, which is really driving up the price of guacamole, and if they're too expensive we may want to have a barbecue instead."

And on that note, she was gone just as mysteriously as she had appeared. Doug made it to his meeting in the nick of time, feeling like he had just braved a strong weather system.

She worked fast. Within twenty-four hours, Doug and many others received the following email:

To: All Delicious Foods, Inc. Supervisors
From: Betsy Delaney, Human Resources Manager
Subject: Exit Interviews

We are pleased to announce that effective immediately, all supervisors will begin conducting exit interviews with employees on their last day in the office. This new company policy is designed to provide valuable insight into why individuals are terminating their employment with Delicious Foods. The goal is to reduce our 26 percent annual turnover rate and get in-line with industry standards. Given the high cost of interviewing, hiring, and training, each percentage drop in turnover represents sizable savings for the company. Moreover, we hope to make Delicious Foods a better place to work. Feedback from these exit interviews may inform all aspects of company policy, helping us to grow and get better together!

Supervisors are required to fill out the attached form for each departing staff member. Supervisors are to conduct one-on-one interviews lasting approximately thirty minutes to determine the following:

1. Why is the person leaving?
2. What did they like about Delicious Foods?

3. What didn't they like about Delicious Foods?
4. Anything else you feel is relevant.

Supervisors are to forward the results to Human Resources. HR will tabulate the results and suggest new policies based on this valuable feedback. Please don't hesitate to contact me if you have any questions or concerns.

Sincerely,
Betsy (Cookie) Delaney

One thing Cookie really liked about her job was that Doug gave her a lot of leeway to do what she wanted. While the administrative red tape at Delicious Foods was minimal, it could still be difficult to rally the troops. Nevertheless, Cookie was excited to read the exit interviews. The first one landed in her inbox a week later:

Name of employee: Chad Brown
Position: Warehouse Assistant
Length of employment: 9 months
Supervisor/Interviewer: Bill Hicks
Reason for leaving: Got a better position.
What individual likes about Delicious Foods: Got to take home expired packages of Devil Dogs.
What individual doesn't like about Delicious Foods: Too many rules.
Notes and comments: None.

The data wasn't as illuminating as she had hoped. Maybe they would get better with practice. But six months later, the exit interviews remained brief and predictable:

Name of Employee: Barb Dewey
Position: Administrative Assistant
Length of employment: 17 years
Supervisor/Interviewer: Anna Wokolsky

Reason for leaving: Retirement

What individual likes about Delicious Foods: The office girls are so nice!

What individual doesn't like about Delicious Foods: Starting work at 7:30 a.m.!

Notes and comments: Barb had a great time working at Delicious and she will definitely pop in every now and then to say hi.

Cookie was having a hard time quantifying the data for anything useful, but she wasn't sure what to do differently. Finally, she got a chance to conduct an exit interview herself. She was determined to capture some relevant information.

Name of Employee: Sean Robinson

Position: HR Associate

Length of employment: 2 years

Supervisor/Interviewer: Betsy (Cookie) Delaney

Reason for leaving: Graduated college, got full-time job.

What individual likes about Delicious Foods: Great opportunity to learn the HR trade

What individual doesn't like about Delicious Foods: Not a whole lot of room for growth opportunities.

Notes/Comments: Sean was a great worker and learned a lot in his two years of part-time work. He would have liked to have been promoted into a full-time position, but none were available at the time.

She was satisfied with this report. It gave the valuable insight that at least one person leaving the company would have stayed if there was a suitable opening. Unfortunately, Delicious Foods was a small company and it wasn't feasible to turn the HR assistant position into a full-time role.

A year later, Cookie was distressed. She cornered Doug in his office while he was enjoying a bagel with schmear. "Doug, I just don't understand it."

He looked up mid-bite to see Cookie charging toward him, waving a spreadsheet. He was trapped.

"The turnover rate hasn't budged. I've got all this data about why people are leaving, but it hasn't changed anything. They got a new job or their spouse is moving or they're retiring. How does that information help us become a better company? I should present this at the next Human Resources for Human Beings conference as a case study—or no, I shouldn't, because it would make us look bad. Maybe I could disguise our name. Do you think it's time to hire a consultant?"

"What's the turnover rate?" Doug asked.

"Ugh!" Cookie spun around, hand to her forehead, and plopped herself into a chair, legs sprawled. "Twenty-six percent."

Doug put down the bagel. "That's too high."

"It's absolutely too high! Three times too high! I just don't understand it. Some supervisors aren't even doing the interviews like they're supposed to. But even if they did, the person would just say they got another job."

Cookie paused, gathering strength for another torrent of words. Doug ventured a guess: "Has it ever occurred to you that people don't tell their supervisors the truth?"

She tilted her head in confusion. "Why in the world would someone not tell the truth?"

"Because maybe the supervisor was the problem."

A constellation of expressions crossed Cookie's face: disbelief, doubt, suspicion, and finally possibility. "Wait—what?"

"You expect people to be honest with their direct supervisor? Maybe you should be handling all the exit interviews yourself," Doug said.

Cookie leaned back and twirled around in the chair. "That might be a good idea."

"You're welcome."

"I could ask the questions I want. It would be like an interrogation. In a good way. A good interrogation. I can get people to open up to me, and find out what's really going on. You're right. They won't tell their supervisors the truth. This needs to be a skip-level meeting. We'll get some real data. This will be great."

"We've got to get this turnover rate down. I'm counting on you."

Cookie rose and strode from his office with a mission, and Doug got to finish his bagel in peace.

Cookie had no idea what she had gotten herself into. With Delicious Food's astronomical turnover rate, she had to find time in her schedule for as many as three exit interviews a week, in addition to all the recruiting, interviewing, and hiring that was her usual job. The first thing she discovered was that the questionnaire was only a starting point. On a Tuesday afternoon, she completed an exit interview with Mac, a warehouse assistant.

Length of employment: 7 months

Supervisor: Bill Hicks

Reason for leaving: Looking for new job, might go back to school

What individual likes about Delicious Foods: "The work was easy. Sometimes boring."

What individual doesn't like about Delicious Foods: "Pay sucks. Didn't get along with supervisor."

Notes and comments: Mac had been asked to leave; he'd been written up for insubordination twice and frequently arrived late to work.

Soon Cookie had performed more than a dozen exit interviews, and sure enough, patterns emerged. Bill Hicks was a problem—nobody had anything nice to say about him. And lots of people complained about the low pay. Cookie wrote up her findings in a memo to Doug, suggesting that Bill receive management training and that the company revisit their pay structure. She reinforced the latter with data from the Department of Labor regarding the industry as a whole. She eagerly awaited an answer.

Crickets. But that wasn't unusual. After forty-eight hours of silence from Doug, it was time to track him down. Cookie found him in the parking lot, of all places.

"Did you get my email? The one about the exit interviews? I've got some suggestions on how we can move forward and get this turnover rate down. Hey, your truck looks nice. Did you get new rims?"

Doug, who had been loading some boxes into the back of the cab, stopped and considered the whirlwind moving toward him at an alarming speed. "Can I get back to you? I haven't had time to think about it."

"What's to think about? It's clear what needs to be done. The proof is right in the statistics."

"Listen, Cookie, you know I admire your enthusiasm. But your suggestions involve significant expenditures. I need more time."

He was right because he was the CEO; there was nothing she could do at the moment. "I understand." She paused, trying to find the right words. "Let me know if you want me to walk you through the data. It's pretty interesting."

"Thanks, Cookie. I'll let you know."

But he never did. He kept brushing her off when she mentioned it, so she finally stopped asking. It probably had something to do with Bill Hicks, who was Doug's cousin and had worked there since the company began. As for the salaries—she knew that was a pipe dream. Her only goal had been starting a conversation, but he didn't even seem up for that.

At the next fiscal year-end meeting, Cookie reported on the stubborn turnover rate, which had dipped only to 24 percent.

Doug blew a gasket. "You've had over a year to work on this. How could you have missed your goal by such as wide margin?"

Cookie was stunned. "I sent you my thoughts months ago. The exit interview data—"

"We're not raising base pay or spending money on workshops for supervisors. What else you got?"

Everyone stared at her. Nothing. She had nothing.

"So now you have nothing to say?" Doug was goading her, his voice loud and stinging.

"I'm working with the community college. I'm planning on—"

"You've got six more months." And that was that. They went on to the next item on the agenda.

Cookie continued conducting exit interviews for another couple months, but the gesture was futile. All the data in the world couldn't fix bad business decisions. Perhaps it was time to get her own resume in order.

## UNQUITTABLE

- Exit interviews are conducted for all employees who voluntarily leave the organization.
- Interview data is regularly reviewed and used to improve the organization's culture, processes, policies, benefits, physical facilities, and management behaviors.
- Good interviews enlist an interviewer who is impartial, a good listener, and not the employee's supervisor.
- Good exit interviews leave departing employees with a positive impression of the company. Well-performing employees may receive a parting gift.
- Interviewers make it clear that good employees who leave the organization are welcome to return in the future.
- Successful exit interviews capture information that can be quantified and analyzed.
- Exit interviews should be championed by an owner or CEO committed to making the organization a great place to work.
- Make the receipt of an employee's paycheck a face-to-face event. Receiving the check should be tied to participating in an exit interview.

## QUITTABLE

- Interviews are conducted sporadically, or not conducted at all.
- Under no circumstances should the interviewer be the employee's manager.
- Interviews that capture information that is then never conveyed to decision makers are failed opportunities.
- Unsuccessful interviews are those that collect data (but don't use it to drive improvement) and are disconnected from a larger HR strategy.

# CHAPTER 9

# Corporate Universities

Corporate universities standardize training and career pathways in a company. These programs are a tangible investment in talent where lessons align with company and employee goals. Participants receive a consistent, quality message, which is useful in small- and medium-sized companies and essential in huge multinational companies. Corporate universities also reduce turnover by allowing people to explore career paths and learn the essentials for success in multiple positions throughout the organization. They help reinforce the company's aspirational culture and employer brand, thus improving candidate attraction and employee retention. Additionally, they reduce promotion-related failures by ensuring an employee is properly trained for a new position. Lastly, and highly important in today's environment, they play into the well-documented millennial desire for professional development.

Corporate universities are usually associated with large companies: McDonalds, GE, Apple, Pixar, Deloitte. That doesn't mean they can't be successful in small and mid-size operations with careful planning and consideration. Even a rudimentary training program can be built upon over time to create a corporate university with a standardized approach for addressing talent needs. In the following scenarios, two companies approach the issue in their own way; one recognizes the value of allowing people to learn and flourish, and the other practically pushes people out the door.

## FAN GIRL RISES TO THE TOP

Jana was fangirling over Sharon McGillroy, the CEO of FarmBerry, Inc. Here she was, in the flesh, impeccably dressed and addressing the FarmBerry Academy students with a natural vivaciousness that made the audience smile.

Jana had been at the company for five years, working her way up from HR administrator to HR associate to HR manager. She was the first in her family to go to college, and her ambition was a good fit for FarmBerry Academy, the company's corporate university. Sharon was a role model for what Jana wanted for herself.

Sharon was talking about eNPS—the employee Net Promoter Score. Jana, much to her surprise, found the topic fascinating. FarmBerry enjoyed a really high eNPS score, which meant that employees were highly engaged and likely to recommend the company to friends and family as a good place to work. That much was already obvious to Jana from her time in HR. It was rare for the company to hire outside individuals for high-level jobs. Many positions were filled by promoting up-and-coming achievers. She herself was living proof, and so was Sharon, who pushed herself through the glass ceiling and landed in the C-suite in under twenty years at the company.

"FarmBerry's high eNPS score is nice, but I relate to people more than numbers," Sharon said, addressing the group of twenty-five students. "When we hire someone, we're making an investment. Quality people make quality products."

Jana nodded. FarmBerry Academy was what initially attracted her to the company. After struggling through six years of college to get her bachelor's degree and working a string of jobs best forgotten, she had accumulated enough student loan debt to destabilize a small country. An MBA was out of the question at the moment, but the Academy was the right program at the right time. Jana's sister, Sasha, said that the company was trying to brainwash her, turn her into a robot.

"Liking your job and wanting your company to be successful doesn't make you a robot," Jana said, explaining the program over dinner at home that night.

"They'll lay you off as soon as things go bad," Sasha said.

"You're such a pessimist."

"I'm a realist. Companies don't care about people."

"The company is made of people. They have to care about us," Jana said.

"Everyone is replaceable."

"Maybe where you work."

"Girls!" Their mother chimed in.

Jana and Sasha achieved détente with an exchange of facial expressions, but the conversation got Jana thinking: Was FarmBerry Academy a ploy to turn her into a sycophant, or was it helping her achieve her dream of a rewarding career?

"We don't cut corners on our products, and we don't cut corners on our people," Sharon continued.

Jana wasn't stupid. She understood the precarious nature of work in the twenty-first century, and she knew that blind loyalty to an employer could lead down a dark path. Her own father had suffered that fate, having been laid off after seventeen years as a municipal employee. At 50, his prospects of starting over were dispiriting, to say the least. He found himself going from the top of a pay grade to $10 an hour.

Thus, while Jana's enthusiasm for FarmBerry was real, it was informed by her knowledge that the world was often unfair. Jana had heard enough horror stories from friends and family about other companies—big ones—that skimped on employee development. Reputation mattered more to them than people. Here at FarmBerry, Sharon was saying that people were the company's reputation, and Jana desperately wanted to believe it.

FarmBerry Academy—still in its pilot phase—consisted of six core courses, each with forty hours of class time spread over eight weeks. It would take a year to complete. Sharon was giving the introductory lecture in the first class, FarmBerry History and Product Basics. The rest of the class would be taught by a roster of managers armed with a heavily vetted curriculum of PowerPoint slides and group activities. The other core classes were Communication, Marketing, and Customer Relations; Business Strategies; Vendor and Supply Chain Management; Technology Horizons; and FarmBerry Culture and Values. Jana was familiar with all these concepts due to her business degree, but she was eager to learn how the company adapted them for their own needs.

What she liked best about the Communications class were the case studies, which were both hilarious and enlightening. One involved a viral YouTube video by a couple of pranksters. Two girls are demonstrating how to make a Thanksgiving cranberry sauce using FarmBerry's Raspberry-Cranberry Chutney. They scoop some out of the jar and the camera zooms-in on what looks like mouse droppings nestled in with the cranberries. The girls scream and drop the jar on the floor. A sheepdog enters the frame and licks up the spilled sauce as the girls shriek and run. This fake video caused FarmBerry's sales to nosedive, especially after lazy news networks picked up the story and ran it at face value. The young women involved, when contacted by FarmBerry, eventually admitted they had doctored the chutney with chocolate shavings. The case study really opened Jana's eyes to how easy it is to damage a brand's reputation and sales, and the herculean effort it can take to overcome that damage. None of Jana's college classes instilled in her such a visceral reaction; she never felt the connection between what she was learning and their real-world implications.

The Vendor and Supply Chain Management course exposed her to many new concepts, all of which related somehow to her work in Human Resources. Almost everything was hands-on, and the students even took a field trip to a nearby orchard to see first-hand what went into growing organic apples and pumpkins. The equipment that harvested the apples was impressive and helped Jana understand farming as a high-tech, modern industry and the farmers as agricultural experts crucial to FarmBerry's business. One of the great things about FarmBerry's continued growth was that it enabled more of its suppliers to fully convert their crops to organic, something that wasn't economically viable for farmers without the security of a major buyer.

Two houses, two children, and an MBA later, Jana achieved her career goal: vice president of Human Resources for FarmBerry, Inc. Her student loans were history and she had moved into the office right next to Sharon's. She was still a Sharon fangirl, but their relationship had deepened over the years and now encompassed talk about Sharon's grandchildren and Jana's camping excursions in her vintage Airstream trailer.

Jana's relationship with Sasha had mellowed as well. In fact, Sasha now worked at FarmBerry as a customer service manager and an instructor at the very corporate university she once chided her sister for attending.

The corporate university had changed over the years, thanks to Jana's involvement. It was now the primary vehicle for all staff training rather than a set curriculum for a chosen few. Instructors had incorporated virtual reality to teach manufacturing processes, and test-kitchen baking sessions were a popular offering. An important lesson Jana had learned over the years was that the corporate university served functions beyond staff development. It was an environment ripe for networking and teambuilding—the type of experiences that create a cohesive corporate culture.

It was hard to connect the dots between Jana's VP position and her time in FarmBerry Academy, but, without a doubt, the experience gave her solid insight into the challenges specific to the company. For example, rumors started to spread on social media several years ago that some of FarmBerry's products included GMOs, violating their claim that all their products were natural and organic. Jana, who had recently become a public relations manager in hopes of working her way across and up her career lattice, knew that the company's preferred way of dealing with such a crisis was quickly and honestly. Within twelve hours of the allegations, she had drilled down to the heart of the controversy and crafted a response on social media that was candid and complete. It turned out that one of their suppliers grew both genetically modified and organic crops. FarmBerry bought only the organic crops, but somewhere along the way the farm's name and association with GMOs led activists to believe that FarmBerry had purchased the GM crops. Once the issue was identified, both the farm and FarmBerry released statements affirming that no GM raw materials had been sold to or used by FarmBerry.

Experiences like this allowed Jana to see the corporate university as a two-way street. The corporate university is an acknowledgement that the company believes in and wants to invest in its people. It is also a tool ensuring people have the knowledge, skills, and abilities to keep the company financially vibrant.

## DISCORD AT ACCORD

Fifty-seven open positions! It was far from Accord Insurance's all-time record but definitely enough to make Marcus cry. Even worse, most of the positions were above entry level, so he couldn't scoop up a bunch of students from the local community college and pay them $9.75 an hour. These were manager and supervisor positions—jobs that required experience in the insurance industry.

Of course, Marcus wasn't exactly dumbfounded about why he was constantly playing whack-a-mole with job openings. When the lowest person on the totem pole makes minimum wage, it takes a long time to attain even a mild approximation of the American Dream. Then there was Accord's toxic corporate culture that rewarded power grabs and punished consensus-building. It was as if those at the top were willfully ignorant of the company's name.

During the holidays, for example, a memo went around stating that there were to be no holiday gatherings on company time because it was "inconsiderate to the customer." And everyone knew better than to hope for a holiday bonus of any sort. Instead, everyone got a bonus that was equal to 0.5 percent of his or her salary on the off chance the company met its sales goal for the year. Problem was, by the time this bonus was green-lit and distributed, it was March and the snow had already melted and everyone's presents had already been paid for or accumulated interest.

Marcus accepted a position in Operations at Accord because he was desperate. His dad had left home suddenly and he had to find a full-time job in a hurry. He couldn't stand on his feet for long periods of time due to a health condition, which ruled out most restaurant and retail jobs. Of the few options remaining, the one that came through first was Accord. The pay was terrible, but at least the position came with benefits, which, at the time, was almost more important than the money. He figured he wouldn't stay there long, but life has a funny way of upending one's plans. After two years, his supervisor recommended him for a position as an HR assistant, getting him a bump in pay. Because of his pre-existing health condition, he was hesitant to take his chance at another company and risk a gap in medical coverage. So he settled in at Accord.

The fifty-seven openings weighed on Marcus. The company preferred to promote from within as a way of preserving and developing "talent." But the opposite often happened, like with Gino.

Gino started out in Customer Service. He was a pretty good worker—he had to be with a baby girl at home to support. He was dependable enough that when a position opened up for a claims clerk, he applied and got the job. From what Marcus knew, Gino was excited. Yet before the year was up, Gino had quit. He'd spent a total of thirty-two months with the company— twenty-four in Customer Service and eight as a claims clerk. Marcus was somewhat surprised—Gino was clearly an ambitious guy and surely needed the pay raise. In passing, Gino said something about "not wanting to spend his work hours wondering if he was going murder someone by the end of the day."

At first Marcus took this as a joke, but statistics told a different tale. In one of his more jaded moments, Marcus took a deep dive into the data. It revealed that employees who were promoted at Accord quit at a higher rate than those who quit from the positions they were hired into. Gino was far from an aberration: In the first year following a promotion, turnover was 26 percent, versus 19 percent for the rest of the company. Once again, this didn't make sense on the surface given that promotions generally came with a raise. But Gino's comment was telling, and it reminded Marcus of how he had felt when he transferred from Operations to Human Resources. Part of the corporate culture was that you should be able to figure things out for yourself. Training was for newbies and typically amounted to "Here, watch me. Got it?" The higher-ups believed that in-depth training was expensive and didn't pay off because turnover was too high. Scratch that surface and you see a Catch-22 staring back at you.

One of Marcus' pet projects was instituting an exit interview policy that would capture information about why people chose to leave. He was pretty sure that lack of training would be at the top of the list. Not far behind would be the lack of work-life balance (reflected in the company's draconian, inflexible policies regarding time off) and the underwhelming pay scale.

Brent Hall was the CEO of Accord Insurance. Marcus had never met the man personally, but his reputation was that of a walking scowl who hated excuses. People's entire careers hinged on his moods, which were as changing as the weather. No one knew where he came from or what he did to become the CEO, but conspiracy theories proliferated. Some swore he was a member of Hell's Angels. A senior manager claimed he saw him working out in a local gym, and he had what looked like scars from multiple gunshot wounds on his upper arm. Needless to say, when Brent's email popped into Marcus's inbox, a psychic scream issued forth from his soul. The subject line was simply "Rebecca Showalter" and inside was a meeting time: Friday at 3:00 p.m. The message was cc'd to the head of HR.

Marcus divined a wealth of information from the attached document. Rebecca Showalter was the latest promotion in the company to be fired for some perceived shortcoming. She had been promoted from risk consultant to risk manager, and within two months a series of one-hundred-year storms ripped through the Southeast and sent Accord's claims through the roof. The Claims division was in chaos, as were the Claims divisions of all insurance companies. Brent Hall wanted to know why Showalter had been promoted to risk manager and by whom, because she was obviously incompetent. He wanted some heads to roll and ordered a complete review of the criteria for the position. That Marcus got the email meant that his head was in danger of rolling right out the door. He spent his lunch hour updating his resume, too nervous to eat his leftover tuna casserole.

He made his way down the hall to the CEO's office at the appointed time, the flickering light overhead spelling out a Morse code of doom.

"Close the door," Hall said.

The HR director, Harvey, was there, too. Marcus's boss's boss. He was standing next to Hall's desk, arms crossed, like a henchman.

Marcus closed the door and took a seat.

"You know why you're here?"

"I have a pretty good idea."

"Tell me why Rebecca Showalter was promoted to risk manager when she clearly wasn't qualified."

Marcus paused. He was already toast, so he owed it to his dignity to be honest at this point. "She was the most qualified candidate who applied."

"She was a risk consultant beforehand, right?"

"For six years."

"What made you think she was up to the crucial task of minimizing risk for our company?"

Marcus worked hard to keep his nerves in check. "I believe the intention was to have the outgoing manager provide several weeks of shadowing and training."

"What happened?"

"The scheduling didn't work out. The position wasn't filled until after the departing manager left."

"That's it? That's your excuse? I don't believe this." Brent Hall threw his hands up, incredulous. "Harvey, help me out here. How can we give one of the most sensitive positions in the company to someone who isn't trained to handle it?"

Marcus couldn't wait to hear his response. Harvey cleared his throat. "I agree that we could boost our training efforts. Last year I proposed instituting a corporate university program to create a more robust talent pipeline. We could promote cross-training and more formally assess the skills of our current workforce."

Brent Hall stretched back in his chair, hands behind his head. "I remember that plan. The price tag was six figures."

"It's not uncommon for companies to spend that much to ensure a long-term advantage."

"I'm not putting up that kind of money to train people so they can quit and take their skills somewhere else."

Marcus wondered how Brent Hall could be for real.

"Your training experiment is not even open for discussion until you get the turnover rate down to something reasonable."

"There's a positive correlation between training and employee tenure," Harvey said in a measured tone that was more professional than what Marcus himself could have mustered. "A comprehensive training program could prevent another Rebecca Showalter situation."

"Showalter is gone. We need to replace her with someone qualified. I've got claims adjusters bringing the most asinine numbers to me from these storms. We have to get a handle on this."

"I'm afraid we don't have anyone in the pipeline. We'll have to recruit from outside the company, which will take longer."

"And?"

"And we may have to increase the salary."

"There it is." Brent cracked a smile. "You HR people are so predictable."

Marcus felt a peculiar need to back up Harvey. "I think a training program would really benefit the company," he said. "Especially for those who are promoted to positions that are significantly different from their prior positions."

Brent ignored him. "This is HR's fault and we have to show the board we're serious about it not happening again."

Brent zeroed in on Marcus. "I think you know where I'm headed. We're going to have to let you go."

Marcus felt sick.

"I wish it didn't have to end this way," Brent said, "but I'm sure you understand."

Marcus didn't understand anything except for what Gino said about wanting to kill someone. He waited for Harvey to back him up, but the HR director knew to keep his mouth shut.

"It's just business," Brent said. "Thank you for your service, Marcus. I wish you success in your future endeavors." Hall rose from behind his desk and offered his hand. Marcus shook it, and then Harvey's. He mumbled something about it being an honor and left.

Now there were fifty-nine open positions at Accord Insurance, but none of them were his responsibility. By the time he gathered his few belongings and tucked them in the trunk of his car, his nausea had been replaced by a tentative hopefulness, as if a burden had been lifted from his shoulders. The next few months would be rough, but for the first time in several years, he would leave the office free from the dark cloud that had followed him for so long.

## UNQUITTABLE

- Corporate training programs must be backed by a responsive, visible, and committed management team.
- Well-rounded programs and corporate universities Include modules on job skills, knowledge, and abilities, as well as corporate culture, industry

information, communications, customer service, and a host of other topics intended to develop employee skills for themselves and the company.

- Good training programs are accessible to a wide range of employees at various times throughout their tenure with an organization.
- Include classes and seminars aligned with specific career paths. They optimize employees' chances of succeeding when they transition to a new position.
- Include tools to track an employee's skills, knowledge, and abilities.
- Your corporate university needs a champion—an individual who is responsible for ensuring it is supported, funded, updated, and operated effectively.
- Your program should change over time in response to the needs of the organization and talent environment.
- Build in a dedicated annual budget to cover development and delivery costs.
- Market your corporate university as a key element of your company's value and identity.

## QUITTABLE

- Corporate training programs are not viewed strategically by senior leadership.
- Training programs are stymied by insufficient or nonexistent training budgets.
- Training consists mostly of on-the-job training that is neither standardized nor consistently implemented.
- Training programs without an owner or champion will wither and die.
- Training that doesn't focus on career pathways ignores what is most important to employees.

# CHAPTER 10

# Flexibility

Is there such a thing as too flexible? There's the usual work-life balance—being able to work at home while waiting for the cable guy, or offices with summer hours that allow people to leave at noon on Friday. But what about companies that offer "unlimited vacation," a notion that drives baby boomers (and anyone who's ever had to work on an assembly line) insane? How about absconding to Europe and literally phoning in every day from a time zone that puts the individual on a completely different schedule? A soft-hearted manager may allow one person to arrive half an hour late every day due to child care arrangements, but suddenly people without children feel they deserve the same option. What's fair?

Flexibility is both a mine field and a gold mine. At a time where the lines between work and leisure are constantly blurred, many of us are constantly tuned into work on some level regardless of our physical location. A majority of companies have flexible work arrangements, but most of these arrangements are informal.[1] They often take the form of managers allowing people to work at home or come and go ad-hoc to accommodate the needs of their family. However, less than half of managers believe that those who telecommute regularly are as productive as in-office staff.[2] And many companies don't promote their flexibility program because it is hard to quantify into an official policy—especially if you can't offer it to everyone.[3] Let's face it, some jobs are just more flexible than others. You can't work at home if you're a nurse, mail carrier, or a teacher (but shout-out to all the teachers who put in hours of work at home after the school day is over).

If you're looking for the silver-bullet flexibility system, keep looking. Every business has its own unique culture, customer needs, and job requirements. Given this, you have to design a flexibility program that works for you, your employees, and your customers.

Ultimately, an organization's willingness to be flexible boils down to trust. A culture of trust emanates from the top down and colors the whole workplace. Westwood Markets operates from a place of trust, unlike Super Cleaning Services. Which place would you rather work? Which do you think has a higher turnover?

## VIGNETTES OF TRUST

Charles cracked open a cold one. It was another perfect summer Friday afternoon on Spring Lake. Gentle breeze, wisps of clouds, and the mesmerizing slosh of water against the boat's hull. He had approximately six hours before Jim and Jennifer could get away from the office, round up the kids, and make it to the cottage for the weekend. He couldn't understand why more employers didn't value the three-day weekend, especially in the summer. Is anyone productive on a Friday afternoon when the weather is this nice? Cooping people up in a chilly office with tinted windows that don't open is a form of torture. However, Charles knew that this summer schedule was practical only for certain staff members at Westwood Markets. A manager always had to be on site at the store locations, but those who worked at headquarters, like him, were allowed to work four ten-hour days during the week and take Fridays off. Some people divided their hours to get every other Friday off, and some took only a half day on Friday. Still, others took Monday off. The point is, people got to tailor their schedules to maximize the time they wanted to spend doing something else. And Charles wanted to spend his time on his boat, with his Irish Setter, Dexter, by his side. It was as good for the local economy in Spring Harbor as it was for Westwood Markets.

Terrell needed to see a dermatologist for the weird mole on his neck. He had booked an appointment three months out—the soonest he could get in. Then he got a phone call saying they had a cancellation and could he come in this afternoon? Heck yeah, he could! There was no way of knowing if the growth on his neck was harmless or something more sinister; if it was bad news, he wanted it yesterday.

As soon as he got off the phone, he made a beeline for Randy in Receiving. "I need a favor."

Randy turned to Terrell in mock rage, responding way too loudly: "No more mani-pedis on company time, Williams. I'm not covering for you again."

The guys on the loading dock erupted in laughter.

"Fine. If that's the way you want it, Myers, you can take someone else to see Taylor Swift."

Their bromance was fodder for all sorts of workplace shenanigans.

"I got a last minute doctor's appointment to check out this thing on my neck."

Randy caught a glimpse of the offending mole. "Dude!"

"Can you cover for me at 2:00 p.m.?"

"Get out of here before I catch the plague."

"Thanks. I owe you one."

"You owe me two, but who's counting?"

It was neither the first time nor the last time that Westwood Market's flexible policies saved Terrell's work-life balance from tipping over. Randy, the meat department manager, and Terrell, the warehouse manager, had been crossed-trained and could fill in for each other in a pinch. Company policy allowed each of them to cover for the other for a total of ten hours per week, without either having to use their time off. Best of all, the paperwork was a breeze. It was a simple line item on their timesheet. Companywide, it was a boon. The percentage of parents with young children who relied on it at least once a year topped 95 percent. There was no real downside. Good employees always figure out how to get their work done. Cross-training was also a great tool for expanding people's skill sets and helping them identify with other departments, like a secret weapon of empathy that covertly built team spirit without the painful group activities.

Westwood's annual holiday party was at the state university's indoor botanical gardens. The pathways were lined in fairy lights, and the humid air formed a cozy virtual blanket that protected the guests from the arctic elements outside. A string quartet played mildly familiar classical music while strolling servers offered shrimp pot stickers. The Westwood crew enjoyed the opportunity to dress up and introduce their spouses to the coworkers they talked so much about at home.

Bill looked forward to the event all year. He enjoyed seeing the Westwood workforce in an unfamiliar environment, under flattering lighting, without having to corner a single person about deadlines or meetings. As the Westwood CEO, people could be guarded around him; the holiday party eased some of that tension and allowed him to get to know people a little better. He wasn't the most outgoing person in the world, but he genuinely enjoyed chatting with everyone. He strived to put a human face on the impersonal world of business.

He approached a group from Accounting.

"You've outdone yourself this year, Bill," Sal said.

"My cousin got married here last year. I fell in love with the place."

"These pot stickers are amazing," Sharon said.

"Hey Tabitha," Bill said. "How old are your kids now?"

"Beatrice is six and Alex is four."

"How's Beatrice's speech therapy going?"

"It's really helping. It's a godsend being able to work from home on Thursdays."

"Glad to hear it."

"Her therapist is all the way out in Elmdale. It takes forty-five minutes to get here. Brendan works nights, so he needs to get his sleep and can't take her."

"Is that why you're solo tonight?"

"Bingo."

"Tell him I said hi."

Bill excused himself and went in search of more spinach dip. He knew via her manager that Tabitha's schedule was working out well for the department. Overall, Westwood's Work Flex program had dramatically decreased unscheduled absences and even lowered the turnover rate. Providing options for people to manage their lives is just good business.

The Work Flex program thrived on trust. Bill had thought about the issue so much he considered writing a book. He even had a title: *Trust*

*Discussed.* His system boiled down to a combination of modeling good communication techniques and making all corporate decisions transparent. This was simultaneously obvious and counterintuitive. All Westwood managers received communications training, whether they worked in a store or at headquarters, and this complemented the Work Flex program. Managers are trusted to make the best decisions for their teams, and employees are trusted to make the best decisions for themselves. Work Flex was bolstered by two-way communication, working more often than not. When it didn't work, the six-month written agreements between employee and manager were not renewed.

Jamie was hired at Westwood after the department store he worked at went extinct. He was the son of a shop rat and a hair stylist and had grown up with an us-vs.-them mindset when it came to work and bosses. Yet, after less than a year as a stock clerk, he began taking business classes at the community college with the goal of eventually moving into management. His father accused him of being a traitor to his blue-collar roots, but Jamie tried to explain that it wasn't like that. Westwood actually seemed interested in helping him develop his skills. The department store hours were 9:00–5:00 p.m. or 2:00–10:00 p.m., with two fifteen-minute breaks and a thirty-minute lunch break—all of which required punching in and out. The only exceptions were when the supervisor called and made him work extra hours because someone didn't show up. Which was just about always.

Westwood was downright civilized by comparison. To start, the store was fully staffed and people tended to show up on time, cutting down on early morning phone calls from frantic supervisors. Regular shifts were 7:00 a.m.– 3:00 p.m. and 3:00–11:00 p.m. But people had leeway with their schedules as long as at least one stock clerk was available first thing in the morning and night. Jamie usually showed up around 6:45 a.m. He liked being the first one there, turning on the lights and easing into the day before the place sprang to life. Thermos of coffee, a bagel, and a little bit of paperwork. Sometimes he snuck a day-old doughnut from the bakery department.

This routine was sometimes disrupted by transportation woes, whereby either Jamie or his brother needed a ride, resulting in getting to work late or having to leave early. Unlike his supervisors at the defunct department store, Westwood managers were pretty relaxed as long as they knew where you were and when you were coming back. Their trust won Jamie over and he began to appreciate the company. Even more, it made him want to rise through the ranks. His supervisor at the department store had been a sour stereotype with bad breath and a chip on her shoulder. Terrell, Jamie's manager at Westwood, did hilarious impressions of the store's weirder customers and had great attention to detail. Jamie admired him and could see the benefits of climbing the corporate ladder. In fact, Jamie and the rest of the clerks had so much fun in the warehouse that sometimes it didn't seem like work at all. But they hit their goals, moved their inventory, and got stuff done. In fact, Terrell only occasionally scolded people, and it was always because they deserved it. Jamie respected him enormously.

The dermatologist lopped off the mole on Terrell's neck and sent it out for a biopsy. Turns out it was precancerous, requiring a couple follow-up visits which further impacted his work schedule in the following weeks. Randy was happy to help him out—he'd gone through a similar health scare in his own family recently and understood the urgency. Terrell appreciated that he wasn't forced to burn through his vacation time for something that was not fun at all. As a thank-you, Terrell offered to detail Randy's truck for free on his day off. He didn't have to do it, but he was a firm believer in good karma.

## SUSPICIOUS MINDS

It was 9:05 a.m. and Greg hoped that when the elevator doors slid open Terry would be somewhere else—getting coffee, pounding his fists on the copy machine, berating a night supervisor at the warehouse—anywhere other than sitting at his desk in this fishbowl of an office. But the doors whirred open to reveal Terry in all his glory presiding over the comings and goings of every staff member of Super Cleaning Services. Greg could feel Terry's 1,000-watt stare burn a hole in the back of his skull as he made his way down the hall to his desk. Five minutes! At any other company it would be within an acceptable margin of error.

"It's Monday, Greg," Terry called after him.

Greg took a deep breath and turned around. "Traffic. Won't happen again."

As soon as Greg got to his office, he slammed his backpack down. *That power-hungry idiot needs to back off.*

Swirling beneath Greg's anger was a basic question: Why was Terry even in the office? The guy owned a 5,000-square-foot, French Tudor mansion on Lake Atwood Boulevard with a forty-foot cabin cruiser docked in a backyard boathouse. He didn't need a day job. The four other silent partners rarely showed their faces in the office; what did Terry have to prove? From what Greg could tell, Terry just liked being a boss, or rather, being bossy.

Jared passed by Greg's open door, coughing due to bronchitis, again. Janet, making her way back to reception with a plate of apple slices, turned away from him in a valiant effort to protect herself. Super Cleaning Services gave people only one sick day per year.

Janet deposited the possibly contaminated plate of apple slices at her desk and walked over to Terry's open door, knocking lightly enough to arouse his attention but not hard enough to trigger an outburst.

"What?" He didn't look up.

"My mother has a doctor's appointment tomorrow at 1:00 p.m. I'll need to take a couple hours off."

"Who's going to answer the phones?"

"The junior salespeople can take turns."

"They don't know how to transfer to voicemail and stuff."

"I could set the phone to the general voicemail message until I get back."

"You're supposed to be here during business hours."

"It's her gallbladder. She's 85."

"Use your sick time. Or call her an Uber."

She wanted to punch him. She had used her single sick day to take her daughter to the doctor when she had strep throat two weeks ago. And it was only February. "I can come in early or stay late later this week to make up the time."

"Business hours are 9:00 a.m. until 5:00 p.m. That's when you need to be here."

Janet was taking care of her children and her mother single-handedly. "Yes, Terry. I know. I'll do my best."

She slinked back to her desk, contemplating shoving an apple slice up his nose. She was resigned to doing what she had to do, which was take her mother to the doctor; she would just be sneaky about it. She was the one who processed the time sheets each week, so Terry would never know how she accounted for her time. He talked a big game, but in the end he wasn't a detail guy.

She ate her apple and tried to get through her emails, but she couldn't concentrate. She went to the kitchen for another cup of coffee. The sink was full of dirty mugs. She turned to Craig, who was standing nearby scrolling through his texts while waiting for the toaster to pop.

"Why can't you guys clean up your own mess? I'm not your mother," she snapped. Craig's head jerked up.

She tossed her plate in the sink and stomped off, forgetting the coffee.

*That's so Janet,* Craig thought. *Spreading her bad mood around the office like a virus.* He'd been at Super Cleaning Services for five months, which was about four months too long. If he stayed longer than that, he risked becoming a hollow-eyed, soulless zombie like Greg. Disheveled and on his way to a serious drinking problem.

Terry sauntered in to the kitchenette, which was Craig's cue to get back to his desk and look busy. But he was too slow.

"What's up, Craig?" Terry asked. Even when he was trying to be friendly he sounded accusatory.

Craig was watching a video of a kitten attacking a birdcage occupied by an insult-hurling cockatiel. "Reading about office vacancy rates in the city, getting some new ideas for strategy."

Terry tipped his coffee cup to him. "Keep it up."

Craig rolled his eyes. Terry stuck his nose in everybody's business because he didn't have anything else to do. Every outside sales meeting was met with a barrage of questions: where, who, how long, how much? The lack of trust coupled with the lack of vacation time made Super Cleaning Services a perfect storm of dysfunction.

Back in his office, Terry put his feet up on his desk and grabbed the phone. "Janet, get me Craig's spreadsheet. I want to see what he's been up to."

"It's on the network, but I'll email it if you can't find it." She hung up.

He would need to have a talk with her. She was not the friendly face of customer service they needed at Super Cleaning Services. Next, he put in an order for lunch delivery, checked his online stock portfolio, and booked a tee time for his trip to Hilton Head.

Craig's spreadsheet popped up in his inbox, and his mouth puckered into a pout. These abysmal numbers couldn't be right. He picked up the phone again. "Janet—is Craig's spreadsheet updated?"

"How would I know?"

That attitude again. "This should be accurate through last Friday."

"You'll have to ask Craig."

He slammed the phone down. It was so hard to get people to do their jobs! He turned back to his computer, opened his calendar, and booked two meetings—one to put Craig on notice, and one to talk to Janet about her attitude.

Terry and Gil met up at the club for their monthly meeting. The other three silent partners were in Florida. Single malt Scotch arrived on command, and they placed twin orders for prime rib. Terry loved the club. A lot of the people he'd grown up with had abandoned its mahogany and leather grandeur in favor of what—he wasn't exactly sure. But he adored its genteel warmth and commitment to tradition. Gil, who spent half the year in Scottsdale, was just as dedicated to the club, enjoying a swim in the ancient basement pool three times a week.

"I don't like the numbers," Terry said. "We're not seeing the growth we expected, and turnover is way too high."

Gil perused the report and nodded. He took off his glasses and tapped them against the table. "What do you think the issue is?"

Terry sighed. "I hate to say it, but we've got a real attitude issue."

Gil looked thoughtful.

"It's these young guys in sales," Terry said. "They run around like secret agents, failing to report basic information or let me know where they are. I don't get it. Then there's the receptionist. She's got the worst attitude of all."

"How so?"

"She always needs to take time off. Sick mom, sick kids. I don't know what her deal is."

"Maybe she's got a sick mom and sick kids."

"She needs to show up when she's supposed to. We're a small operation."

Gil put his glasses on again and paged through the report. "I notice that our numbers started trending downward two years ago. Around the time you replaced Nick as the General Manager."

Terry sipped his Scotch. "What are you saying?"

"Just making an observation."

"Look. We get these guys straight out of college and they don't understand they need to pay their dues. They all want to take long weekends to go to music festivals and weddings. We need them in the field five days a week or we're never going to get anywhere."

"My niece just got married in Cancun," Gil said. "I sent a nice present from the registry like a normal person. I don't think they expected us to actually go to Mexico."

"We're under no legal obligation to offer any paid time off at all. And I resent people who ask for time off after they've just been hired. I much prefer granting vacation days as a reward for meeting sales goals. That's just how the world works."

Gil motioned for another round. "So how are we going to change these numbers?"

"Let's raise quotas. We might have higher turnover short-term as the riffraff decide to go back to Burger Box, or wherever they came from. The ones who stay on board will need to buckle down. They won't have time to cop an attitude."

"What about the receptionist?"

Terry drummed his fingers on the tablecloth. "First chance I have, she's out. But I have to do it right so it doesn't come back and slap us in the face. We don't need any EEOC trouble."

The server appeared with prime rib and the conversation turned to the NFL draft.

"You'll have to make it quick, Jared," Janet said, sliding in to the diner's back booth. "Soccer practice ends in forty-five minutes."

"This won't take long," Jared said. "I've got a business proposition."

Janet looked puzzled. "Is this some kind of mob thing?"

"I'm serious."

"Then why ask me?"

"You're the smartest person at Super Cleaning Services."

Janet laughed. "That's not saying much."

Jared stirred creamer into his coffee. "The place is a disaster. I want to form my own company."

"Your own company? Doing what?"

"Cleaning."

"To compete with Super Cleaning Services?"

"Yeah."

"Isn't that a conflict of interest?"

"See, I knew you were smart. Super Cleaning Services was cobbled together from chewed gum and Q-tips; there's no noncompete clause anywhere in the company documentation."

"What kind of start-up money do you have?"

"An inheritance that should be enough."

"If you're looking to make money, real estate is safer."

"Look, you want in or not?"

"I need to think about it." She looked out the window at her car in the parking lot. A brown sedan with 150,000 miles and a cracked windshield.

"I've already drafted a business plan."

Janet sipped her iced tea. "Freedom from Terry. That's a pleasant thought."

She thought about Jared's offer on her drive to the park to pick up her son. By the time she arrived, she'd made up her mind. Sandwiched between taking care of her mother and her kids made this no time for taking risks. And yet, just knowing that Jared was going to make a move awakened something inside that continued to gnaw at her for the next couple of days. It was as if before her meeting with Jared, she wouldn't give herself permission to entertain the thought of leaving. Now, the floodgates had opened. It made dealing with Terry easier, imagining giving her two weeks' notice. The look on his face would be priceless. If Jared was smart, he's poach Craig, too. He was doing just enough to get by at Super Cleaning Services, but she knew that if he put even minimal effort into his job, he'd be dynamite.

## UNQUITTABLE

- Flexibility is an attraction and retention tool. It has become an essential strategy in the war for talent.
- Counterintuitively, good flexibility programs are highly structured. This helps employees comfortably use their flexibility program as intended.
- The key to flexibility—especially when it involves people working outside the office—is communication. This means documenting processes and programs and offering them to everyone.
- Flexibility is an important tool in helping people maintain their mental and physical well-being by providing them with control over their own circumstances.
- Research shows time and again that well-crafted flexibility programs lead to:
  - Improved engagement
  - Improved productivity
  - Lower turnover
  - Better attraction
- Studies also show people with well-crafted flexibility programs work more hours and take fewer sick days.
- There is no silver-bullet flexibility program. Every organization needs to create a system that works for their own business.

## QUITTABLE

- Inflexibility causes resentment, which itself can spread through an organization like a disease.
- Lack of flexibility often causes individuals to resort to deceitfulness.
- Making flexibility "exceptions" for a single individual or department often leads to resentment among other employees and departments.

# CHAPTER 11

# Performance Management

Performance management refers to the package of techniques that help individuals succeed and thrive in the workplace. The last thing a performance management system should do is determine who gets a raise and how much. What it should do is act as a framework that captures current performance and creates a pathway to improved performance in the future. It promotes collaboration instead of competition. The result may be a pay increase, but that's not its purpose. It probably won't surprise you that effective performance management is somewhat time intensive and takes place year-round.

A good performance management system is standardized, consistent, detailed, and multifaceted. It has various avenues of input, is results-oriented, and serves as a vehicle for an employee's career advancement. On the flip side, it provides a roadmap to assist underperforming staff members in a manner that is understanding, fair, and motivating. The process identifies expectations, goals, and objectives, and provides customized, helpful feedback.

Because the process is standardized, managers in all areas and at all levels of an organization can be trained to use it consistently. A good system quantifies multiple factors that benefit the individual and the organization: teamwork, talent development, and employee loyalty. Employee performance is just as important as career development. It's a good time to talk about accountability and align performance with the organization's overall strategy. A good performance management system facilitates coaching, not judging.

## "IF I TAKE CARE OF THEM, THEY'LL TAKE CARE OF THE REST"

Anjanette loved her company's performance management system! She met with her twelve direct reports for brief stand-ups every week; had thirty-minute, one-on-one check-ins twice a year; and conducted written reviews twice a year. It was intense, but that's what it takes to manage performance. She felt like an orchestra conductor, getting a great performance out of her team. It doesn't work to let things operate on cruise control and then slide in once a year for an almighty performance review. Elevate's PMS (as it was affectionately known) kept managers and staff in constant communication about individual needs, making sure that those needs were aligned with corporate goals.

Despite studying engineering in college, Anjanette had real affection for the social aspects of her job. Her friends thought she was slightly daffy each time she widened her eyes and launched into a spiel on Elevate's awesome system. They stared in disbelief when she dropped the punch line: The system was completely divorced from compensation decisions. It focused solely on employee development, not employee evaluation.

"You mean you don't need to rank people from best to worst and then divvy up a miniscule pot of money between them, ultimately giving the proverbial finger to underperformers and thereby weaponizing their disdain for the company?" asked her friend Melanie.

"Exactly," Anjanette responded.

Anjanette's enthusiasm was bolstered by her roster of high performers, and saying nice things about nice people was the easiest way to garner good karma. In fact, it was a cornerstone of the system—learning how to provide positive, constructive feedback on a regular basis, in both formal and informal situations. Some people had no problem writing nice things on an annual review but found it difficult to give compliments to a person's face.

Elevate's PMS operated under the theory that short, frequent check-ins are more conducive to a company's and an employee's long-term growth than Ye Olde Annual Review, an office relic as antiquated as an IBM Selectric typewriter. A few Elevate managers grumbled about how time consuming the system was, but Anjanette's motto was, "If I take care of them, they'll take care of the rest." This had proven to be true so far, as Anjanette's employees exhibited enviable loyalty toward her.

Today, Anjanette was meeting with six of her direct reports. Of the half dozen, she had five good eggs and one hard-boiled number with a green ring around his yolk. She was saving him for last. First up was Ron. He started out at Elevate as an intern and was hired as a junior loan officer in the consumer division before quickly switching to commercial lending, a track with significantly more growth potential. He was a rising star on Anjanette's team—indeed within the company—and was on track to get his MBA within the year. It would take a lot to derail him. During their weekly coaching meetings—the short stand-ups—he kept her abreast of his MBA progress, which he was hoping would lead to a bump in pay or a promotion. His five-year goal was to have Anjanette's current position as loan manager. Rather than feeling threatened, she encouraged his ambition, because by that time she herself hoped to be a director.

"Hey, Ron, how's it going?"

"I passed my stats final." He shut the conference room door and took a seat. It was his semi-annual written review, scheduled to last thirty minutes. He'd already read an electronic copy that Anjanette had finished the day before, so there weren't any surprises.

"Last time we talked about techniques to improve your strategic thinking. Can you give me an example of how you put those concepts into play recently?"

Ron considered the question for a moment. "This ties into something we discussed in one of my classes—the difference between strategic thinking and strategic planning. Basically, the former subsumes the latter. Currently, I'm comfortable with strategic planning—when I sit down and focus on how to address an issue given a particular set of circumstances, I can brainstorm ideas that are likely to put the company on the right path."

"Interesting," Anjanette said.

"But strategic thinking is the next step. That's more of a consistent outlook on life in which I frame all issues to optimize outcomes. So, the flow chart I created to document enhancements to the consumer mortgage loan process is an example of strategic planning. However, strategic thinking would entail keeping a roster of continuous improvement ideas in my head at all times to facilitate the planning for the commercial mortgage loan process."

Anjanette had a soft spot for Ron's way of thinking. She could practically see the gears turning in his head sometimes, almost to the detriment of where he was walking. His commitment to education signified that he was still actively engaged in the learning process. Many people his age assumed they already knew everything. They chatted for a few more minutes, and then they both moved on to the next task on their respective daily schedules. Before lunch, she made a few notes in her records about their conversations, noting how Ron was becoming more management oriented.

Xavier, the bad egg, showed up five minutes late to his check-in with Anjanette. He might have thought that was acceptable, but Anjanette didn't, not with his track record. Xavier was an underperforming loan officer, and Anjanette's notes on him accounted carefully for his infractions since his hire date. Six months ago he was entered into the company's more rigid performance improvement track, designed to give extra aid to those needing help in meeting performance expectations. Some individuals were more coachable than others, and Xavier had proved to be a challenge.

Xavier was really into motorcycles. He liked to ride them, work on them, talk about them, and dream of them. He was in a motorcycle club that took itself—in Anjanette's opinion—just a little too seriously. Xavier took long lunches in faraway spots so he could ride midday, and took ten days off each August to participate in some massive rally in the desert. He always came back with a new tattoo. This year, it was "Ride or Die," inked around his neck, visible with everything except a turtleneck. He was in clear violation of the company dress policy, which forbade any tattoo visible while the employee was in business attire.

Neither Anjanette nor the other managers were about to trample over an individual's right to self-expression, within reason. But when it came to Xavier, what started out as a few quirks had morphed into something more transgressive. His accumulated violations had become impossible to ignore: unexcused absences, long lunches, irascible behavior. And that didn't even count the safety violations! The Performance Improvement Track was presented to him as an opportunity to improve within a reasonable time frame. If improvement goals were not met, however, he would face consequences, up to and including being "released to the market."

On the Performance Improvement Track, Xavier's workday was more structured than his coworkers'. In addition to the weekly stand-up with Anjanette, he had a sit-down meeting with an HR rep and Anjanette that was documented closely. For six months, he had to:

1. Verify his start and finish times each day through software on his computer.
2. Document hours spent on each project or loan and have it signed by Anjanette.
3. Schedule all time off at least a week in advance.
4. Pass random drug tests.

The tattoo was the last straw. Anjanette wrote him up for violating the dress code and escalated his case up the chain. Today, the paperwork had been drawn up, and Xavier would be released. Anjanette knew it was the right decision. He had been given a second chance, yet he failed to exhibit any interest in adhering to Elevate's mission or showing respect for his coworkers. Xavier wasn't a good fit for the company. She caught a glimpse of him as he was being escorted out of the building, and he didn't seem too upset. It was Anjanette's experience that most employees know when their termination is justified. She let go of the frustration he had caused her. The Elevate PMS had done its job, establishing a pattern of behavior at odds with the contract he had signed when he accepted the position with the company. She looked forward to a revived morale on her team and finding the next Ron.

Part of the Elevate PMS was the 360-degree review for managers, a process coordinated by a consulting firm. These reviews were conducted every two years and were designed to reinforce Elevate's culture of transparency and trust. The review was never a hit job because all participants were coached on making reviews useful through positive comments and concrete suggestions. It included input from Anjanette's direct reports, those above her, select people in other areas of the company she frequently dealt with, and even some external customers. Unlike a traditional performance review, the 360 was more about how she impacted others' work, rather than her actual accomplishments. Thus, the report never came back stating that "this person is the reason why this company is so successful and her salary should be doubled immediately." Even though she secretly hoped it was true.

The report always snuck up on her because she wasn't involved in the process at all. She had heard vague rumblings through the hallways that the results would be released any day now. Sure enough, on a Wednesday afternoon after lunch, it popped up in her inbox. She opened the document, fresh from HR. The results were categorized under the headings of leadership, interpersonal skills, problem solving, motivation, and efficiency. The answers, of course, were anonymous. A high-level summary was accompanied by specific responses:

- **Does this employee exhibit leadership qualities in the roles he/ she plays in the company?**
  "Anjanette serves as an unofficial mentor to me. She willingly shared advice as I moved into a supervisory role which made for a smooth transition. To me, Anjanette personifies the definition of leadership."

- **How would you recommend that the employee improve his/her interpersonal and relationship building skills?**
  "Anjanette can be abrupt when she's overwhelmed. Sometimes emails are not responded to in a timely manner. However, she goes out of her way to address serious or pressing issues with a one-on-one approach until a solution is reached."

  "I find Anjanette overbearing. The best managers allow people to work independently on their own and trust them to get their work done. I felt it was unnecessary to meet with her every week."

- **Does the employee effectively solve problems?**
  "Yes. Some of our more sophisticated mortgage products can be difficult to explain to clients. I had a client who wanted to terminate a resold loan after he received new information contradicting what we told him during

the closing process. Anjanette intervened and worked hard to get to the source of the misunderstanding, which turned out to be faulty information from another bank unfamiliar with our products."

- **How does the employee demonstrate that he/she is motivated and committed to success in the company?**

  "Anjanette considers managing people and business equally important. She is also a member of the Continuous Improvement Team, which adds valuable insight into processes and products throughout the company. Even though her work with this team uses valuable time each week, Anjanette remains constantly available to her staff and coworkers for everyday issues."

- **Are the employee's work methods and approach to accomplishing his/her job effective, efficient, and continuously improving?**

  "Part of what makes Anjanette effective is her hands on management style and daily communication with each member of her team. However, rather than micromanaging her staff, she empowers them to take control of issues and carry out the proper course of action."

Who doesn't like to read good things about oneself? It wasn't hard to guess who made the comment about being "overbearing" and she wasn't too concerned about how it would impact her results. Only ineffective managers are friends with everyone. She was just glad they didn't send a questionnaire to her husband, otherwise a bunch of people in HR would have learned about her poor laundry skills and the time she killed all the houseplants by accidentally spraying them with vinegar.

## MOPPING THE FLOOR WITH GREG

There was a lot of yin and yang in Greg's life, and he balanced them as delicately as a freshly poured Martini making its way from the bar to his mouth. As the years passed, however, he felt this balance swing out of control, yin sloshing over the rim of the glass and dribbling down the yang of his shirt.

At first, his job at Super Cleaning Services (SCS) seemed like a dream. He wasn't chained to a desk, he got a generous bonus for meeting his quota each month, and the hours weren't bad. He spent his days meandering through Boston's high-rent district, wooing new clients and keeping the old ones happy. It wasn't as exciting as selling Italian sports cars, but if he wanted to catch a midafternoon ball game at Fenway only the kiss cam would tell.

The problems started when Terry took over as general manager. SCS was owned by five guys—four silent partners and Terry, who more than made up for the others' silence with his opinionated micromanagement. Jared, the sales manager who had hired Greg, clashed with Terry immediately. Jared hired people who worked well independently and he trusted them to do their jobs. He was reserved and honorable, exactly what you'd expect from an Englishman and former sales director of a country club. But Terry was hotheaded with a Napoleon complex. He not only wanted to know where everyone was at all times, but also for everyone to report their sales daily. He even kept a running tally on a whiteboard in the kitchen like some 1980s Wall Street brokerage firm. Salespeople were pitted against each other rather than encouraged to work together. The only people who escaped Terry's wrath were SCS's actual cleaning crews, because Terry promptly left the office at 4:15 p.m. and never saw them.

Jared objected to Terry's new vision for SCS, so it wasn't surprising when Jared quit one afternoon after a heated discussion with Terry about revising the rate card. With his overcoat folded neatly over his arm and his umbrella in the crook of his arm, he sauntered out without a final "Cheerio." The air became thick with impending doom.

Terry scanned the room like a cyborg checking for stowaways on a spaceship, and his gaze landed on Greg. "You—you're the sales manager now."

Startled, Greg turned around, but there was no one there. Terry meant him.

And that was that. There was no training, no talk of a promotion or raise, although he did have a comfortable surprise in his bank account the next payday. He moved his stuff into Jared's old office and read a few management books left behind on the shelf. It was going to be a very seat-of-the-pants transition.

Three salespeople quit within a month as Greg tried to figure out his role, leaving him to pick up the slack and look for replacements at the same time. Greg knew Terry would blame him for the deepening crisis, so he wanted to start a paper trail to cover his you-know-what. According to one of the management books left by Jared, the best way to do this was to conduct exit interviews. Unsurprisingly, all three exit interviews with the departing salespeople revealed the same nugget of information: None of them liked Terry and all were looking for a company that would take them and their professional success more seriously.

"Is there anything we could do differently?" Greg prompted Jen.

"A performance review would be nice," she replied, "just to document that I met my goals for the year. It's a small company, I know, but there needs to be a record for new people to review when there's a turnover in management."

Greg couldn't agree more and duly documented their conversation. "Is there anything else you'd like to share?"

Jen paused, then spoke carefully. "We're being real, right?"

"Of course."

"Then I'd say that I'm not a fan of this silent partner business. I feel like we're supposed to be some sort of cash cow for them, but this is my livelihood and they're not treating it with the respect it deserves."

He knew exactly what she meant. "I wish you success in your new position."

"Is there anything we could do differently?" Greg asked Warner.

"This whole exit interview is a sham. My clients love me and I love them. I worked on these relationships, you know? I created them."

"I hate to see you go."

"Not your fault, but I think you know what this is about."

Greg knew, but he wanted Warner to give him specifics, something he could document. "If you could change something about your position that would make you want to stay, what would it be?"

"I want that loser Terry to slither back to his yacht club and let people do their jobs."

Greg laughed. This was one of Warner's milder propositions.

"I'm serious." Warner said.

"Barring that, how could SCS improve its sales team?"

"Like I said, trust us. We don't need handholding. If the service is needed and priced right, we can sell it."

Greg took notes on his laptop. "I appreciate the feedback and good luck at your new job. What is it you're doing, exactly?"

"I'm the new business development manager for Belle Agua, a new bottled water marketed for the Latino market."

"Good luck with that."

"It's already a fifty million dollar business."

Last up was Aliyah, who had sent Greg a resignation email just two days earlier. She was leaving SCS to help her uncle open a second location of his Vietnamese-inspired pizzeria, Bahn Mizza. Of the three departing employees, she was the most vocal.

"In addition to regular performance feedback, SCS needs to overhaul their accounting system and draft a coherent business strategy. We need a better way to track business expenses and pay reimbursements."

"That's a lot. What about things specifically related to sales?"

She opened a folder and began to read her printed list. "Develop a list of credible leads. Market to a niche population. Institute a sales training and mentoring program. Conduct an operations audit. Create an incentive program for the cleaning associates—"

"Can I have a copy of your list?"

"I already sent it to Terry."

Greg winced. "These are all great ideas, Aliyah, and I really appreciate your enthusiasm. I'm sorry you won't be around to help implement these changes. Please know you're welcome back anytime."

"Vietnamese pizza is the future, trust me."

"I have no reason to doubt you."

Greg scheduled a meeting to talk with Terry about the accumulated exit interview results. But as was Terry's modus operandi, he cancelled the first meeting and pushed back the next. In between, Greg got a stray email lambasting him for letting Aliyah email him directly with her list. Big surprise.

Eventually, Greg, armed with data and bracing for a storm, cornered Terry in his office. "The sales team thinks a more focused business plan and a structured system for tracking expenses and performance would go a long way in establishing a professional protocol for the company," Greg nervously blurted out, perhaps more forcefully than he anticipated.

Terry looked at him blankly, as if trying to remember who, in fact, the sandy-haired young man in front of him was. When Greg's name flickered into his consciousness, his mouth engaged: "They're salespeople. Their job is to sell. My job is to manage the business."

"Three salespeople mentioned these issues in their exit interviews."

"Exit interviews? You're going to believe the rantings of a disgruntled employee? As far as I'm concerned we're weeding out the riffraff. We're running a tighter, leaner operation now."

Greg, as inexperienced as he was, knew that calling employees "riffraff" wasn't the best way to develop and maintain talent.

"I'd like to establish regular performance reviews for the sales team," Greg said. "It will go a long way in helping them focus on their goals."

"Their performance begins and ends with whether or not they're hitting their numbers."

"There's more to it than that—"

"Such as?"

Greg wanted to punch him. "Whether or not they're trending in the right direction. Give them a little encouragement and advice."

Terry shrugged. "Suit yourself. You're the manager."

Greg cleared his throat. "I was also curious about the procedure for my performance management."

Terry looked puzzled. "What do you mean? Your team hits their numbers or they don't."

"Well, there's other things, too. Like the strategy for how I can help grow the company, or the opportunities available down the road if I hit all our goals."

"You don't want to be the sales manager at SCS for the rest of your life?" Terry grinned crookedly.

Was he joking? Greg truly didn't know. Still, he'd come this far. He had to see this conversation to the end despite his rising ire. "What about career development? Or a performance review? At lots of places, performance management is tied to the company's core values or mission statement."

"We clean buildings. That doesn't require a mission statement."

His exasperation mounted. "As a manager, I'm trying to do right by the team. As an employee, I'm asking for the same in return."

Terry shrugged. "Okay. We'll talk about it at your next performance review."

"I was hoping to meet quarterly."

"Seems like overkill, but okay. Send me a meeting invite."

Meanwhile, Greg put in a purchase order for an off-the-shelf performance management software. After playing around with it for an afternoon, he realized that it was more complicated than he had anticipated. It would require a level of commitment from HR that was impossible given their meager staff and Sisyphean task of hiring enough people to cover their current cleaning contracts. Instead, he instituted a simpler system, an annual performance review based on a person's hire date. It was a one-page list of questions that the manager and the employee both answered. Then, the manager would schedule a short meeting to discuss the results and devise a plan for the coming year, including three major goals.

It was basic, but it was something. Greg was proud of his continuous improvement initiative; people like to know where they've been and where they're going. He sensed a morale improvement with the remaining sales staff that he hoped would pay off big down the road. More than that, he started to feel like a real manager. The operations manager even caught wind of Greg's plan and stole the questionnaire to use with the cleaning crews.

One afternoon, Terry summoned Greg to his office. Their quarterly performance meeting was still two weeks out. Greg strolled down the hallway, expecting a very rare but well-deserved pat on the back.

"What the hell's wrong with you?" Terry barked.

"Sorry?"

"Sales are down and gross margins are eroding."

"Sales are down because we're short-staffed. Per person, the numbers look pretty good."

"Have you seen the bizarre contracts your guys are coming up with? We're practically paying our clients for the pleasure of scrubbing their restrooms."

"I'm planning to address—"

"You've got two months to get margins and sales up."

Greg was dumbstruck, but he knew he had to hold his ground. "Or what?"

"You're out of here."

"I've been working as hard as I can to keep the sales department together."

"It's not about working hard, it's about working smart." Terry looked smug, like he'd just uttered something brilliant.

Greg fumed and considered his next words carefully. "I don't know what the expectations are for my performance. Am I managing people or am I responsible for sales? Maybe if we sit down and establish some objectives we can look at the big picture." It pained Greg to use so many buzzwords.

"This business is as simple as it gets," Terry countered. "You're a sales manager, you manage sales and the people who make them."

That didn't help anything.

"How much do you want sales to improve in two months?"

"I want them to be better than what they are now." He was in full Napoleonic mode.

"Can we come up with some goals at our performance management meeting on the fifteenth?"

"Our what?"

"Performance management meeting. Two weeks from now. We agreed to meet quarterly."

Terry shook his head. "I'll be out of town. Can you meet with Doug?"

"But I report to you."

"I can't hold your hand, Greg. I've got a lot of important things to do. You're going to have to take the initiative here."

Greg left Terry's office feeling equal parts angry and queasy. The easiest thing would be to quit, but he wasn't 22 anymore. He had bills to pay and a resume that needed continuity and an upward trajectory. Plus, he had developed an uncharacteristic sense of responsibility toward the sales team. He wanted to protect them from Terry's bluster—it was the only way to keep morale up. He harbored a slight hope that the other silent investors would recognize Terry's idiocy, but he didn't dare reach out to them behind Terry's back.

Greg maintained the performance reviews to the best of his ability. The problem was that he couldn't provide solid input on career development because he didn't know SCS's future goals. The company didn't have a mission statement, only a motto: "Our superlative service is crystal clear." It wasn't much of a strategy. Greg started doing the reviews quarterly; it was a lot of work, but also the right thing to do. The one-page format worked well, but efforts to create individual action plans were stymied by the lack of a larger business trajectory. For example, his conversation with Micah went like this:

"Your performance is quite good for being so new to the company."

"Thanks. I appreciate it."

"Do you have anything to add to my comments?"

Micah paused. "Under performance challenges, you wrote that 'Micah could complete more closings with a forceful follow-up sales pitch. He lets too many potential clients slip through his fingers.'"

"You disagree with that?" Greg inquired.

"It's a conflicting message. I thought we were supposed to stay away from the hard sell. My strategy was to establish a relationship with my leads and check in on a regular basis."

"We have a directive to increase our sales significantly this quarter. I appreciate your strategy, but it may not help us meet our numbers."

"If you allow me to expand my territory, I can probably meet those goals."

"I can't allow that at the moment; we have a hard time getting crews out beyond our current boundaries."

"Then I don't understand how we're supposed to grow."

Greg sighed. How *was* the company supposed to grow? He tried changing the subject. "I want to highlight some of your successes. The Trilovent deal was big, and you managed it single-handedly. That's a feather in your cap."

"Thanks. I feel like Jared laid the groundwork for that one and the lead just fell into my lap."

Greg was happy to acknowledge and celebrate the sales team's successes, but it wasn't enough. He could hold all the performance management meetings in the world, but they wouldn't change the fact that he couldn't lead if he didn't know where he was going. His bump in pay from becoming a manager wasn't worth being deprived the tools and vision necessary to be effective at his job. He'd also gained a lot of respect for Jared and how he had endured an untenable situation. It had been so long since Greg had enjoyed an afternoon at the ballpark he could hardly believe those days had ever really happened.

## UNQUITTABLE

- Many people think performance management systems are limited to employee reviews. The best systems rely on trained managers and supervisors who continually coach employees. Simply reviewing an employee quarterly, semi-annually, or annually is not enough.
- Effective performance management systems usually separate performance management from performance as it relates to salary increases.
- When it comes to underperformance, a performance management system documents an employee's infractions and efforts to correct the behavior. This information may become invaluable if "release to the market" is a possibility.
- The system should apply to everyone in the organization, though some elements—such as the 360 review—may be reserved for managers and higher-level individuals.
- Even the smallest organizations can benefit from a well-run performance management system.
- Criteria for good performance should be determined for each department across the company to ensure individuals are being evaluated fairly. The criteria should adhere to the company's strategic, operational, and cultural objectives and strategies.

## QUITTABLE

- When employee reviews are conducted sporadically or not at all, you're telling individuals they are not a priority. Why, then, would they make their job a priority?
- A performance management system that assesses individuals only on performance metrics and ignores how they embody the organization's culture and core values is missing the point.

- Also missing the point are employee reviews that don't include discussions on career development.
- Organizations with managers and supervisors who are not trained or committed to coaching their employees are doomed to lose talented individuals to organizations that do.

# CHAPTER 12

# Mentoring

There's a national generational turnover currently happening in the workplace, so the time to capture as much institutional knowledge as possible before it retires to Arizona was yesterday. Even if your organization isn't populated with retirement-bound baby boomers, a solid mentorship program creates a web of knowledge, goodwill, and relationships that can strengthen your organization. Stop thinking of a mentor as an aging, good-natured employee willing to take a younger coworker under his or her wing, but as anyone willing to empower new employees to live up to their potential. Take age out of the equation; it's experience that matters.

A good mentoring program is crucial when creating an unquittable workplace because strong relationships are the foundation of a thriving organization. Mentorships are an ideal way to not only pass down institutional knowledge and expertise, but also deepen relationships with good communication. While it can take place informally, a formal mentorship system allows managers to intentionally direct resources and the program's parameters, such as who will be invited to join, how long the program will last, how often partners will meet, etc. Such programs also need a budget and a champion.

Like everything else, mentorships can be done well or poorly. In the positive scenario below, a formal mentorship program results in a years-long friendship that benefits the company as much as the individuals. Recruited from diverse areas of the company, the women learn from each other, form connections that strengthen the company, and contribute to a positive, well-functioning environment. At Accord Insurance, however, the CEO thinks a mentoring program is a great idea but delegates its implementation to others. Without careful planning, the rollout is haphazard and no one understands their role. Wishful thinking is not a sound talent strategy.

## FERTILE ABUNDANCE

"Did you know that a company's most valuable asset is its people?" Evie threw her head back and laughed.

"Did you know there's no *I* in *teamwork*?" Claire slapped the table and snorted.

"Wait, wait—" Evie burst out giggling again. She eventually collected herself and adopted a serious tone. "We need to create a paradigm shift to incentivize synergistic collaboration to transform our data-driven processes into a win-win situation."

"Brilliant!" Claire gave Evie a high five.

The two women were decorating for Larissa's baby shower, but transforming the conference room into a Disney princess wonderland was proving difficult. Store-bought decorations could only do so much to disguise the generic office décor, and the fluorescent lighting wasn't helping.

"What are we going to do while Larissa is on maternity leave? She puts everything in perspective," Claire asked.

"I will text her relentlessly. I refuse to let her abandon us," Evie said.

"Who's abandoning who?" Larissa entered the room wielding a tantalizing assortment of cupcakes on a tiered serving dish. She was as stylish as ever in a bright red dress that few could pull off so effortlessly, pregnant or not.

"Hey! Get out of here," Evie said. "We're not ready yet."

"You can't ban me from my own party. Pretty soon I'm going to be stuck at home with an infant and a two-year-old. I need all the adult time I can get."

"Then sit down at least," Claire pulled over an oversized, ergonomic chair. "We don't need you going into premature labor."

Claire, Evie, and Larissa met when they were grouped together through LongStar's mentoring program. Larissa had been with the company for fifteen years as an accountant (one of the "Original Eleven" employees, present since day one) while Claire and Evie had worked there for two and three years, respectively, in different departments—Claire in media relations, Evie as a copywriter. The mentoring program paired mentors and mentees through an interview process. Evie remarked that it was like a job interview crossed with a dating app.

The process worked. The three of them had become friends as well as coworkers, despite the fact that Larissa was 40 with nearly two kids and a vacation home while Claire and Evie were still struggling with student loan debt and elusive landlords. Prior to Larissa's most recent pregnancy, the three of them enjoyed semi-regular spin classes. Claire and Evie would have made the baby shower a much bigger deal, except this was Larissa's second girl and she pretty much had all the princess paraphernalia she needed.

The LongStar mentoring program was Kevin Trainor's vision. He rolled it out five years after he founded the company as part of his talent development strategy. It was based on his belief in paying it forward and back. He had his own mentor early in life, a family friend who helped Kevin through his father's death from cancer. Earl had been a guiding light for Kevin and made sure he got through college and graduate school, and then backed him when he launched LongStar. The company's first mentors included local professionals from all walks of commerce, because it wasn't all about improving the company's bottom line—it was about developing talent at LongStar so the company could grow roots and strong branches at the same time.

Larissa had jumped at the chance to become one of the company's first mentees long before she owned her vacation home. She was paired with Scott Crandall, a dapper gentleman who served as the corporate counsel for the local hospital. He was everything she was not—quiet, well-spoken, dignified—but somehow it worked. What they had in common was far more important: a love for their jobs and a desire to live up to their potential. Larissa learned important life lessons from him, such as how to remain impartial and not take things personally, how to balance work and family, when to ask for help, and how to change entrenched viewpoints to solve problems.

Kevin asked Larissa to become a mentor herself two years ago. She jumped at the chance, even though she was about to go on maternity leave. It would be a great way to form new relationships in the company, and it was always nice to get out of the accounting bubble.

She was surprised how much the program had changed from its original incarnation. For starters, it was more formal. She first attended a training program to learn how to be an effective mentor. It was a combination of a webinar, take-home reading assignments, an in-person guest speaker, and a workshop with group and role-play activities. "I'm learning how to be a guru," she told her fellow finance team members. "All I need now is a white robe and a pair of Birkenstocks." She learned the difference between coaching and mentoring and how to share her expertise in a way that would foster leadership skills rather than turn mentees into Larissa clones. Still, when the moment came to face her mentees, she was nervous.

Evie was excited to meet Larissa. The kickoff for the new mentoring cohort was held at the company's rooftop lounge on what turned out to be a sunny June day. People grabbed their morning muffin of choice and gave Kevin a warm round of applause for his opening remarks.

Evie loved her job as a copywriter, but she was ambitious. She hoped the mentor program would not only give her insight into different paths she might enjoy, but also pair her with a successful woman to emulate. Confidence was not her strong suit, especially when it came to making her case to authority figures. She had seen her mentor, Larissa Rabinowitz, before and admired her composure, crafted from equal parts high heels and confidence. She wanted some of that.

Claire Chen sat down next to Evie. "Who's your mentor?"

"Larissa Rabinowitz," she said.

"Me, too. I'm Claire."

"Evie. I've seen you around. PR, right?"

"Yeah. You?"

"Copywriting."

"Cute shoes."

She clicked the heels of her espadrilles and smiled. "Thanks."

After Kevin's opening remarks, Larissa, Claire, and Evie spent an hour on the rooftop deck getting to know each other. Larissa was friendly but professional, listening intently and never asking overly personal questions, just pertinent follow-ups. She discovered that Evie's dream was to become a best-selling novelist and Claire's was to open her own restaurant. However, both were excited about the career opportunities at LongStar and hoped to join the managerial track. As part of the matching process, they had taken a personality test that indicated their similar working styles. They all liked to verbalize their thoughts during the decision-making process, were adept at simultaneously juggling multiple projects, and tended to be "big picture" rather than detail-oriented thinkers.

For the first few months, the trio joined other mentoring teams for a working lunch once a week. They learned about SMART objectives: specific, measurable, attainable, relevant, and time-bound. They talked about goals and action plans. During these sessions, the mood was casual and friendly, and the food was free. Claire and Evie did most of the talking, and Larissa, verbal as she was, concentrated on listening. She had learned in her mentor training to ask open-ended questions that brought the mentees' visions into focus. They were a chatty bunch; Larissa worked hard to keep them on track. She was thankful for her mentor training in this regard, as she had to fight against her impulse to join their conversation about risotto recipes. When it came to creating individual action plans, Claire and Evie focused on how their work styles could be a benefit or hindrance. Larissa helped them think strategically about what they learned from "failures" in their early professional lives. How would they do things differently if offered a second chance? They talked a lot about the differences between managing people and managing projects. Larissa helped them relate their goals to the LongStar mission statement and core values. She felt like she was learning as much as her mentees.

Ultimately, Claire's and Evie's action plans dovetailed. Despite being in separate departments, both were interested in business-to-business advertising and representing LongStar on the trade show circuit. While Larissa had no experience in that aspect of the business, she knew a lot of people in the company and could advocate on her mentees' behalf. She also knew how to create a methodical plan to get from point A to point B (and points C and D when they were ready). She could use her connections to introduce Claire and Evie to other individuals who would assist them.

But most of all, the mentoring program was about pairing people up to learn about the company, not to become better at their jobs. The idea, as Kevin told them, was to invest in employee development so people would stay for a significant portion of their career and not jump ship when the grass seemed greener elsewhere.

It was unusual for Larissa to be teamed with two mentees, but everyone agreed to give it a try and it turned out great. Larissa told Claire and Evie that they could ask her anything—from the details behind Kevin's hot dog phobia to the real reason why LongStar parted ways with its long-time client, the Caturday Clothing Company.

After the first few guided sessions, each group was responsible for arranging meetings for the rest of the year. That's when the women took to walking laps on the high school track Thursdays after work. The fresh air and exercise stimulated good discussion. They retreated to a smoothie bar on days with poor weather. All three were willing to meet outside of work hours, even though it wasn't necessary with the program. At first, most of Larissa's mentoring was simply listening and giving positive reinforcement as her mentees got their sea legs in the business. They were young and still working on asserting themselves in meetings with people twice their age.

By the end of the year, Claire and Evie's action plans had been established and their SMART objectives achieved. Both women had taken advantage of the company's tuition reimbursement program and enrolled in a business course. Neither of them were making a commitment, just testing the waters. Larissa had encouraged each of them to be bold during their semiannual review and to share their action plans with their managers. Larissa had coached each through the "how do I prevent my manager from thinking I'm trying to steal his job?" discussion. According to Larissa, the key was to tap into the company's philosophy of abundance—that life at LongStar wasn't a zero-sum game, but full of unlimited opportunities that people can create for themselves and each other. This was in contrast to a philosophy of scarcity, in which people hoard resources and fear for their jobs as they gain seniority. Claire had heard Kevin speak of this abundance philosophy prior to the mentoring program, but Larissa's explanation really hit home.

The mentoring program had the added benefit of forging strong cross-departmental relationships that transcended fiefdoms. It was good for career growth and for LongStar. Over protein shakes one afternoon, Claire asked Larissa for her perspective on a social media campaign that had set off a crisis of confidence for her. Claire was tasked with reaching out to several Instagram influencers to get them to promote LongStar clients on their feeds. In theory, there was nothing wrong with this—it was a time-honored PR technique—but Claire had a problem with one of the influencers, one who had well over a million followers. This individual had been rather rude in their email exchanges and Claire didn't know what to do about the red flags this raised. She was under a lot of pressure from her superiors to make the deal, but it went against her better judgement.

Larissa thought about it for a while. She didn't have any similar professional experiences; after all, auditors were auditors and the emails she exchanged with contractors were completely different. She had, however, been in the business long enough to know that client relationships were a tricky thing. If Claire's Spidey sense was tingling, there was probably a good reason for it. She decided that her best course of action as a mentor was to ask a lot of questions.

"Have the emails been abusive?"

"It's more subtle than that."

"Has this individual been properly vetted?"

"Actually, I was the one who suggested her to the group."

"Based on what?"

"A story in *PR News* and because I personally follow her account."

"When is the deal supposed to be in place?"

"By the end of the month."

"Can you push the deadline and find a comparable alternative?"

"I'm afraid it would make me look bad to the team."

Thus the conversation continued, Larissa knowing precious little about PR but using her talent for clearheaded observation and impartiality. The gist of the situation was that Claire was afraid the relationship could go south and damage LongStar's reputation in a crucial segment of the market. This was always a possibility in the business, so Claire's fear was partly justified and partly due to anxiety over her first major social media campaign. They went over "worst case scenario" thought exercises. They discussed Option A and Option B, and then found an Option C—a middle path. It involved a limited contract with the influencer and Evie disseminating the questionable emails more widely upfront as a way of alerting others of possible pitfalls in the future. A CYA move, useful in any industry.

Thanks to the mentoring program, Claire and Evie eventually outlined career pathways that transcended media relations and copywriting and veered toward new business development. Claire realized she didn't have the stomach to deal with some of the personalities that inhabited the media relations and PR world, and Evie wanted to see more action on the front lines. Neither of them would have known how to make that transition without Larissa's help. In addition to introducing them to key individuals, Larissa got to share her hard-won experiences. All three gained a solid friendship based on shared interests that would last for years to come.

## A DEMENTORING PROGRAM

Brent Hall had a fantastic idea. Like all his good ideas, it had come to him in a dream. He immediately called a meeting with his HR director and a few others to flesh out his thoughts. His executive assistant, Molly, took notes, as usual.

"Accord Insurance needs a mentoring program. It needs to be world-class, like everything we do. We're going to recruit the best mentors and pair them with our most promising young managers. This will give us an edge over our competitors."

Molly wrote *mentoring program.*

"Our mentors will develop our managers' potential and make them want to stay at Accord. They'll never want to go anywhere else because they're going to love it here so much." Brent was really leaning into his idea, pacing the floor and gazing out into the distance.

Molly wrote *people will never leave.*

"We'll blend cutting-edge managerial techniques with employee branding components to let them know how good they have it here."

The director of human resources, Scott, cleared his throat. "Great idea, Brent. I take it you would like HR to spearhead this initiative?"

Brent snapped his fingers and turned on a dime to face the director. "You read my mind, Scotty. I know you're up to the task. It's a matter of drafting a plan and identifying qualified mentors, then it's full speed ahead."

Molly wrote *full speed ahead*.

Brent placed his hands on his hips. "Any questions?"

Silence.

"Alrighty then, let's get cracking."

On her way out the door, Molly overheard Brent as he strode down the hall to his next meeting. "Killing it, and it's only 8:30."

Back at her desk, Molly discarded her notes and forwarded an article on mentoring programs to Scott. The same one she had sent Brent two days ago, prior to his epiphany.

Scott read the article and got busy. He knew all about mentoring programs, of course, but like any major endeavor, a solid effort would require time and money. Brent Hall, however, was a seat-of-the-pants, results-oriented guy. Scott's directive was to pull something together quickly to prove the department's agility. It could be refined and scaled later. So, Scott identified one manager from each department with at least ten years of experience. It seemed like a good cut-off. He sent the chosen managers the following email:

> You have been identified as a potential mentor for Accord's inaugural Mentoring Managers program, an opportunity to share your deep knowledge of Accord Insurance with newly appointed managers. Each participating Mentor will be paired with a compatible Mentee. The two of you will meet on a regular basis to get to know each other and share institutional and departmental knowledge. This will help the Mentee secure his/her footing in a new environment and strengthen Accord's core values, ultimately creating a corporate culture that allows for industry dominance. Mentoring topics and curriculum outlines will be available prior to your first meeting. Let

me know if you're interested in pioneering this important continuous improvement program. The kickoff will take place on October 1.
We hope you are as excited about this opportunity as we are.

Scott received five responses from the thirteen emails he sent. Two managers
declined, citing scheduling difficulties, and the others expressed mild interest.
That was enough for Scott: He had his first three mentors. He compiled a
list of recently appointed managers and matched them with mentors based
on the reasonable similarities of their departments. Next, he developed a
curriculum—a hodgepodge of articles and studies culled from the Internet
and packaged in a bright, new format by an ambitious HR assistant. Four
weeks after Brent's brainstorm, Scott was ready to go.

Luke had been hired as a programmer at Accord, but had risen through the
ranks to IT manager in a scant three years. He arrived at the Mentoring
Managers kickoff without a good idea of why he was there—he hadn't
applied to a mentoring program—but it felt like a bad career move to blow
off the invite. He would rather be spending his time on the flurry of reports
the new month had brought than sit in a conference room for two hours,
but maybe there would be doughnuts.

It was a small group, only six people: three mentors, three mentees. His
mood brightened—this was obviously a very exclusive opportunity.

Luke's mentor was Ali, a systems engineering manager. He had a professo-
rial, graying beard and wore a rumpled button-down. Belinda, a woman from
HR, was running the kickoff session and passing out workbooks with sec-
tions devoted to "Getting to Know You," "Goal Setting," and "Management
Style." Luke felt like he was teaming up for a class project in middle school.
Ali was dealing with a seemingly urgent situation via text message.

After about twenty minutes, Belinda instructed each mentoring pair to
turn to each other for a game of Two Truths and a Lie. Luke had his stock
responses ready to go. He turned to a disinterested Ali and said, "I pro-
grammed my first video game at thirteen, I bake a mean lemon meringue
pie, and I have three Dalmatians."

Ali looked at him quizzically. "What is meringue?"

Luke and Ali met once a month after the kickoff, for about an hour each time. They stuck to the workbook. Luke talked about what he wanted out of his career, and they spent the rest of the time on management tips. Luke confided in Ali his concerns about performance reviews and how he didn't feel qualified to evaluate his department accurately yet. Ali told him that review scores are simply a function of past performance and first impressions, both of which he could access. That didn't help Luke's anxiety over how to split the meager pie of merit-increase money.

Luke had hoped the Mentoring Managers program would allow him to develop a partnership with Ali that would lead to less territoriality between the various tech departments at Accord. Many employees had skill sets that could transfer from one area to another, and Luke had a dream of forming a company-wide database with languages and certification of all IT staff. He ran the idea past Ali, who didn't seem too excited. In fact, Ali wasn't excited about much at all. That certainly wasn't unusual in their field, but then why was he a mentor?

They had lunch for their third scheduled meeting. The topic du jour was "Management Style." The workbook outlined three major styles—directing, discussing, and delegating—along with the pros and cons of each. Luke and Ali were each supposed to discuss their personal style and learn from the other.

"I feel these options are too limited, so I did a little research on my own," Luke said.

Ali seemed more absorbed in his chicken wrap than his mentee's viewpoint.

"Turns out there's something called the strategic management style, and it seems like what I'm trying to emulate with my team."

"Hmmm," Ali said.

"What would you say your style is?" Luke asked.

"Combination of all three. Nobody is strictly one thing or another."

"Yeah, but which one do you think takes precedence?"

Ali shrugged. "Not sure it matters. The key is hiring people who do their jobs without a lot of oversight."

"But what about career development and making sure employees live up to their potential?"

"People have a natural threshold in my experience. Some people are perfectly happy being code monkeys for the rest of their lives. Their focus is on getting back to their video games at five o'clock. The ones who want to climb the ladder will find their way."

"The strategic management article I read discusses having a big picture and selling team members the company's vision."

Ali chuckled. "Ever try to get a roomful of IT people excited about insurance?"

"But what about pride in their work? Creating the best system to facilitate growth? Things like that."

"That's a good point."

Luke had finally elicited a half-hearted compliment from his mentor, but the moment felt less than celebratory.


After the management style meeting, Luke revised his expectations for the Mentoring Managers program. It would look good on his resume and during his annual performance review, and that was enough. Having been a manager for less than six months and receiving no formal manager training beyond a quick online seminar, he was learning on the job. He supposed that was the way most businesses operated, but he felt like an imposter. A real mentor would have been invaluable, especially as a sounding board for certain situations. Just last week, two programmers, Ben and Skyy, got into a deadlock over who was responsible for creating a work-around for the customer service phone system while they installed new software. Each wanted to do it a different way and neither would budge. Luke preferred Ben's solution and gave him the go-ahead. Skyy was livid, and the bad blood between the programmers was casting a pall over the whole team. What should Luke do?

Belinda had pitched the Mentoring Managers program as ideal for these situations. Luke wanted to be a team player with regard to the mentoring program, so he emailed Ali for his advice, even though it was out of both their comfort zones:

> Hi Ali—
>
> I could use your mentoring advice for a situation with my team. A couple programmers aren't getting along and I don't know how to defuse the situation. Do you have a few minutes?
> —Luke

He received an immediate response: an out-of-office message. Ali would be back Monday and respond then. Except he didn't respond Monday or any other day the following week. Luke didn't want to pester the guy, so he waited until their next official meeting two weeks later. But it turned out Ali was at a conference and he missed the meeting.

Eventually, a détente of sorts emerged between Ben and Skyy and business proceeded as usual. Luke was relieved, but he also knew he hadn't solved anything. The programmers' undercurrent of animosity could flare up any time and he might have to step in. What would he do then?

Only four people attended the concluding session for the Mentoring Managers program in March: Luke, Ali, and another mentoring pair from Underwriting. It was a short session with neither pair providing much in the way of feedback. Luke said he appreciated the company's commitment to employee development and that he found the experience useful. It would be dangerous to say anything negative. Nevertheless, he did feel it was a misguided venture, half-baked in concept and shoddy in execution. In fact, rather than making him feel like the company was truly committed to his professional development, he had the odd suspicion that the program had been created to soothe someone's ego. It wasn't hard to guess whose.

## UNQUITTABLE

- Mentors must receive training to be effective mentors.
- Mentors must enjoy their role and truly want to help newer or younger employees, not see it as a burden.

- Mentors and mentees should be paired based on criteria that makes sense for the company and the people involved. Put some thought into it.
- Strong mentoring programs recognize the immense value of the relationships they foster.
- The best mentoring programs are based on reciprocity, mutual respect, defined expectations, and shared values. All these elements create trust.
- Mentors must have knowledge, but they should also want to share it with the best interests of the organization in mind.
- A great mentor is a facilitator who wants the mentee to develop according to his or her strengths. The goal is not to create a clone of the mentor.
- Mentors and mentees do not need to be officially managed, but they should regularly meet with a goal in mind for a predetermined length of time.
- Identify a champion, someone who will coordinate the mentoring program and defend it when times get tough.
- Track mentoring program outcomes in both the short- and long-term, including satisfaction with the matching process and subsequent promotions for mentees.

## QUITTABLE

- Organizations that fail to provide either formal or informal mentors are squandering rich opportunities and underutilizing readily available talent.
- Poor matches between mentors and mentees will minimize the program's value.
- Poorly conceived programs can backfire and foster ill will.
- Misguided mentoring programs suffer from poor communication, lack of commitment, mismatched individuals, and misaligned goals.

# CHAPTER 13

# Strategic Workforce Planning

Strategic workforce planning (SWP) may sound like a luxury reserved for multinational corporations beholden to the interests of stockholders. If you've read this far, however, you realize that it is yet another tool in your belt for developing and retaining talent. Ideally, SWP is baked into an organization's DNA and budget. It ensures that you'll have the resources you need to not only meet your goals and maintain growth, but also weather economic downturns or unforeseen disruptions in production. It requires hard, up-front work to clearly determine the organization's long-term goals and resource requirements. It requires knowing where you're coming from and where you want to be, and how to analyze the distance between those two points. Of course, talent is a huge part of SWP, like identifying, hiring, training, and retaining talented individuals. In fact, SWP joins all the pieces of the talent puzzle and gets everyone working together toward a common goal. The result, among other things, is having the talent you need, when you need it, to meet your strategic and financial goals.

In summary, SWP is a process to attract, develop, and retain the talent you need to achieve both short- and long-term goals. Here are some specifics:

## STRATEGIC WORKFORCE PLANNING IS

- A process comparing where your organization is today with where you need it in the future.
- A critical tool for making sure your talent management plans are aligned with your corporate strategy and goals.

- A series of time-based actions designed to attract, train, and retain critical talent.
- A continual process, not an event.

## STRATEGIC WORKFORCE PLANNING ISN'T

- A short-term strategy or a quick fix.
- One person's idea of how the organization should function.
- The sole domain of HR.
- Only succession planning; however, succession planning is a subset of SWP.

Ultimately, workforce planning means handling your current and future talent needs. Wishful thinking won't close the gap between now and the future—good planning will. HR needs to be intentional in recruiting and developing talent. Are job descriptions correct? Are they periodically updated to reflect the position's evolution? What skills would you like people to develop to obtain the kind of growth you desire? Do you need more marketing talent, more programming talent, more MBAs, fewer MBAs, a staff attorney, or a director of operations who can upright a listing ship? All these questions require data, which means HR will be involved.

In the scenarios below, Scooter is a big picture guy. He knows what Positive Electric Industries (PEI) should look like and has the foresight to plan for the future. It doesn't take a fortune-teller to have general idea of when your top performers are going to retire. You need to have people standing in the wings ready for a smooth transition, which means identifying key people and investing in their development. That's half the talent war right there. In a culture that provides no reason for individuals to swear allegiance to an employer, investing in your talent's future and providing clear, upward career mobility just might give them one.

At Big John's, the CEO wants to blame someone else for the company's poor performance. Having inherited the company, John has never had quite the same vision for it as his father and takes a lot for granted. Julio presents a solid plan, but it falls on deaf ears—or at least ears that don't like what they hear. It's hard to invest in people for the long term when you've got to make a quick turnaround.

## THE CHIEF PEOPLE OFFICER

The first thing people notice about Scooter P. Johnson is his energy. He's small, wiry, and powerful, with a gregariousness suggesting a background in cheerleading, or at least theater. His history in Accounting was a mystery to many who know him, and maybe even himself, because he eventually landed in Human Resources. It seemed like a much more natural habitat for him.

It would have been silly to call Scooter Positive Electric's chief human resources officer when he personified the title of chief people officer so well. He embraced his impish charm and accessorized with colorful bowties and socks, which in combination with his red hair and diminutive size lent him the air of a leprechaun. People who met him for the first time often stared wide-eyed, thinking, "Is he for real?" And those who had known him a while would smile and nod: "That's our Scoot."

Scooter's big push was to make Positive Electric a "destination culture," like a Silicon Valley start-up. College students would vie for internships, splashy business magazines would write fawning write-ups, and Positive Electric would win awards for being such an awesome place to work. It had never been a bad place to work, but Scooter had instituted an aggressive employer branding strategy through sheer force of will, propelling the company into the regional spotlight as a cutting-edge organization that understood the technology of the future. It was a pretty nifty campaign considering how tough it is to sell younger talent a company that manufactures electrical and electronic components for cars, trucks, trains, and aircraft. In fact, 67 percent of the company's engineers were over 55. Scooter needed to get some fresh blood in the talent pipeline, and fast!

In addition to bowties, Scooter collected HR certifications. Each course and conference allowed him to network with other professionals and expand his skill set. It was one of his favorite aspects of the job! One of Scooter's certifications was in strategic workforce planning, obtained before anyone had really heard of it. The historically staid industry of electric systems was changing drastically with the shifts to hybrid, electric, and autonomous vehicles. Scooter's passion was making sure Positive Electric's workforce remained at the forefront of this innovation. The company's officers forecast tremendous growth in the company's future, from global revenues of $11 billion today to $22 billion in ten years. But it wouldn't happen unless they mastered the talent game. They needed to find and train talent to replace the aging engineers, technical staff, and salespeople when they retired. Then, they needed to double their workforce in order to hit their expansion goals. This was going to require a herculean feat of strategic workforce planning. Quite frankly, Scooter, his bow ties, and his impeccably prepared team were excited for the challenge.

Scooter created not only a massive, color-coded spreadsheet, but also a "SWP for PEI" logo which he then emblazoned on t-shirts for the HR department. It was a team effort, and it required team spirit.

Within a few months, Scooter's team had accomplished the first three of the six major steps of his SWP for PEI plan:

1.  Get buy-in from leadership team on the process, resources, and goals. Luckily, the PEI CEO, Cressida Shelby, was cut from the same cloth as Scooter. She was similarly affable and forward-thinking, but she struck a more traditional pose in inspiring the company's workforce. This allowed her to maintain a weighty professional bearing, even if she did sometimes whisper ideas in Scooter's ear (like the company-wide best-dressed pet contest) and let people believe it was all his doing. Cressida knew PEI wouldn't reach its growth targets without a clearly defined path, so she had no problem investing in the time, research, and people necessary to getting there. If Henry Ford could invest in his assembly line to increase production and lower costs, she could manage the 21st-century equivalent.
2.  Identify the organization's current structure, size, skills, and skill gaps. This was a huge endeavor, so Scooter hired an outside consulting group for an unbiased assessment. This became an ongoing task in HR given that departmental reorganizations were as common as blue birds in spring. You always need to know where you were before you can get to where you're going.
3.  Determine the knowledge and skills of key figures that need to be transferred before their estimated retirement date. This step contained a fair amount of prognostication. Scooter's goal was to enact a constant knowledge-transfer program reinforced by many other PEI HR efforts,

including the mentorship program, career paths program, career sculpting program, corporate university, and talent dashboard.

Scooter is now facing the final three steps of the initiative:

4. Define PEI's future structure and organization to meet growth and diversification goals. This includes positions, the number of staff needed for each role, skills and knowledge required for each position, and a fair share of prognostication. There are still bumps and detours on the road, even if you know where you're going. They had to be ready for the paradigm to shift at any moment and to incorporate unforeseen changes into their plans.
5. Identify the gap between the organization if it implements Strategic Workforce Planning to achieve its long-term goals, versus the organization if it does not implement Strategic Workforce Planning.
6. Create a plan for attracting, hiring, and developing the talent needed to close the gaps. Connect all changes with the company's succession plan.

The last step sounded simple, but it was actually the hardest of all due to so much prognostication. Admittedly, SWP was an inexact science, but its effectiveness would increase with continued diligence. So, Scooter refreshed the SWP annually, sharpened the big picture, and let the company learn and grow from experience. An annual report also ensured continued project support from the leadership team.

Five years later, the company had made significant progress. HR, in consultation with senior managers, honed their vision each year. The plan had actionable deliverables and clearly defined owners. In fact, the action items were incorporated into managers' "Big Rocks" on their performance review for added accountability. The growth was on track and PEI had expanded their solar integration product line enormously, even as their hydromagnetics products dipped below projections as coal-fired power plants went off-line. One tactic was shifting the internship program focus to students studying electrical engineering for sustainable and renewable energy.

Now Scooter found himself applauding Cressida's heartfelt speech honoring PEI's "Gang of Eight," as they had been affectionately dubbed. The occasion was a mass retirement party at Gino's for eight seemingly irreplaceable PEI stalwarts. The company rented out the entire restaurant and a few hundred attendees offered toasts, gifts, and remembrances to the guests of honor: the director of new product development, director of European sales, chief compliance officer, senior R&D engineer, senior director of software engineering, senior director of communications, engineering operations manager, and director of procurement.

The nearly simultaneous retirement of so many high-level managers would give the average chief people officer a heart attack, but Scooter wasn't average. The Scoot Man and his team had seen the mass exodus coming and prepared. Successors for all the positions had been previously identified and groomed to take over, preventing a sinkhole of institutional knowledge. With successors to the Gang of Eight named, a ripple was felt downstream as individuals lower on the totem pole moved up a place or two. Succession planning for these key positions was a large aspect of the strategic workforce planning at PEI.

To build on the succession planning, Scooter made sure the mentoring program addressed needs at all levels, that the new cohort of mentors received training each year, and that they were paired with promising mentees. He liked to keep things fresh rather than recycle a handful of mentors year after year. It was also a strategic move; the more individuals who participated in the program, the stronger the buy-in at all levels. This kept the initiative safe each time Finance decided they needed to trim a little fat from the budget. "Keep on moving, nothing to see here," Scoot muttered under his breath whenever the bean counters darkened his doorway.

Three engineers who had undergone the career sculpting process took advantage of the company's tuition reimbursement program and received MBAs. An engineer with business skills was a double threat, and now PEI had more than their fair share of them. Additionally, PEI had one of the highest percentages of women engineers in the industry due to the corporate university's diversity in engineering courses. It was a boon for their corporate brand, and PEI was almost always mentioned in industry articles on the topic.

The business landscape had changed significantly in the five years since leadership had instituted the SWP program. New technology was arriving and the company had to respond quickly to shifting marketplace needs. HR had to stay nimble. They constantly communicated with managers regarding skill gaps and immediately designed training to address the needs. Their talent dashboard functioned like a contest and HR reps rewarded themselves with a lap around the office on the Scooter-Scooter whenever they hit a new low. The Scooter-Scooter was exactly what it sounds like—a scooter with a cutout of Scooter's face affixed to the front. It had a bell, but was often adorned with helium balloons as well.

Job descriptions were updated each year to reflect changes in PEI's business and the industry as a whole. It was incredibly time-consuming, but it was essential to attracting the right candidates and truly made department managers think carefully about the skills they needed.

Scooter was proud of his team's strategy and thankful for the C-suite buy-in on all the SWP endeavors. He didn't spearhead all the initiatives, but his position offered him a good view of the efforts. He was considering writing about the experience for the *Journal of Human Resources*, but he just didn't know if he could find the time! Right now Scooter had to locate the event director, set up the karaoke machine, and get the crowd on its feet with a spirited rendition of "Love Shack."

## THE DEATH OF BIG JOHN'S

Julio shut off the lights and left the HR department for the final time. His was the last car in the parking lot. Nobody had stayed behind to celebrate, and no one was even gathering at O'Malley's to pour one out in honor of Big John himself. After thirty-seven years, the company was kaput. Julio unlocked his car, threw his stuff on the passenger seat, and prepared to drive away. He took one last look at the forlorn building, its proud past now only a footnote in the history of another declining rust belt town. The Realtor would come by tomorrow morning to stake a for sale sign on the property, where it would probably stay for years.

Julio knew better than to blame himself for the company's death, but it was hard not to take it personally. Big John's had been in bad shape when he arrived five years ago, and he had consistently tried to head off the slow demise that had begun more than a decade ago. He preached to the leadership over and over again, but he could not convert them.

Julio pulled out of the parking lot and onto the main road, taking in the landscape of still cornfields framed by a glowing winter sunset. "*Que lastima,*" he said aloud. "The sun setting on the empire of Big John Griskow, God rest his soul." If only he knew how his son and his glad-handing pack of sycophants had driven the company straight into the ground. He'd have let John Jr. become a carpenter like he wanted, rather than force him to muddle his way through business school.

John Jr. hammered the final nail into the coffin a little over a year ago. Julio had prepared his first big, solo presentation for the company's annual business strategy meeting. It was on strategic workforce planning, and he was confident that tweaking the company's attitude toward talent development would really turn things around. Typically, he wouldn't have even been at the meeting—Haley reported the department's strategy for the coming year as head of HR. However, she had planned her family vacation for that week, in clear violation of unwritten rules, and Julio jumped at the opportunity to substitute for her and get time with the C-suite honchos. It was a move that could potentially catapult his career to new heights.

Julio had done a dry run of his presentation for Haley ahead of time. Haley, who had been the HR director for seven years and phoning it in since the day Julio had met her, sat with her arms crossed for the duration of his talk. When it was over, she stood up and said, "Good luck." It was a warning delivered as a note of encouragement. Julio's presentation at the business strategy meeting looked more like a high-noon standoff, and he was lucky to escape with his job intact. To say that John Jr. wasn't receptive to the dire charts visualizing the company's aging workforce and impending talent chasm was an understatement, despite the care Julio took in describing the situation as an "opportunity to embrace the new economy."

John Jr. cut Julio off halfway through his presentation. "What are you going to do to lower the $6,800 recruiting cost per employee? That's higher than anyone else in our industry."

"We have a turnover problem driving up costs," Julio explained. "It's hard to retain younger workers with the current pay structure."

"Our average pay is $14.75 an hour. Federal government says that's enough to raise a family of four. I've seen these kids come in here—they've got money to plaster their bodies with tattoos, so they must be doing okay. Let them pay their dues."

What John Jr. knew about paying dues was anyone's guess. His father had bought him a vintage Mustang for his sixteenth birthday.

Julio gestured to the PowerPoint slide on the screen, trying to keep his presentation on track. "Another important factor to consider is the average age of our engineering staff. Fourteen of our eighteen development engineers are over the age of 55. Nine are over 62."

"I don't see that as a problem, Javier."

"Julio."

"Think of all the money we'll save when they retire and we replace them with young guys at the bottom of the pay scale. Isn't that right, Sal?" He poked Salvador, the CTO, in the ribs with his elbow.

"The primary concern with so many impending retirements is brain drain. We need to hire some younger engineers soon so the knowledge transfer takes place before we're hit by mass retirements. Otherwise, we could lose critical institutional knowledge," Julio countered.

"Do you know how many kids are graduating with degrees in mechanical engineering each year? It's like 25,000. Every year." John reached for an everything bagel. "If we don't catch them this go around, there's a ton more coming right up."

"I appreciate that," Julio said. "But it currently takes us an average of 120 days to fill open positions. Some have been vacant for over two years."

John Jr. put the bagel down and looked Julio in the eye. "That tells me you're not very good at your job."

Julio was dumbstruck. Was he joking? The vibe in the room turned steely. Julio turned to face the screen, stopped on a slide showing how staffing company fees exceeded $3.7 million the previous year.

"Look," John Jr. continued. "I took a 50 percent cut in pay last year to help balance the budget. So don't tell me that I don't understand what's going on in my own company. I've made sacrifices to compensate for your department's incompetency."

No doubt about it—Julio was getting dressed down by the CEO. The heat in his cheeks threatened to burn him alive. His fight-or-flight instinct kicked in, but John wasn't done.

"Haley sent you in here because she was too scared to face me herself. Hiring and retaining good people has been a major problem around here for years and none of you have figured out a way to deal with it."

He stopped speaking, but kept his gaze focused on Julio. Others in the room squirmed in their seats. A muffled peel of laughter from beyond the confines of the conference room pierced the silence.

Julio swallowed hard. "We all want the company to grow. Strategic workforce planning is a way to prepare for the future—"

"What future? The future where we're all driving flying cars? I need people now. Post the positions, schedule the interviews, and hire the schmucks. It's really a simple process."

Julio's knees started to tremble. He willed himself to keep breathing, but nothing in his training had prepared him for blunt force trauma. "We're really looking for some buy-in on this new process—"

"I'm not going to buy-in to anything new. You're going to have to work smarter."

Julio clicked to the final slide, an optimistic graph showing an upswing in corporate revenue if the company was fully staffed. "Yes, sir. Thank you for your time."

He turned the screen off, quickly packed up his things, and left the room. He fought back the urge to punch the wall as he retreated to his office.

Of all the lessons Julio could have learned from the experience, he was savvy enough to learn the right one: Don't mistake another person's incompetence for your own.

Julio could have quit following that experience, and maybe he should have, but he stuck around for a couple of reasons. Primarily, he liked Haley and his other coworkers, but secondly, quitting wouldn't get him unemployment while he searched for another position in an uncertain labor market. Thus, for the next eighteen months, he had a front row seat to the company's slide into bankruptcy and oblivion. It was quite a sight.

Just a month after the ill-fated business strategy meeting, the head of engineering took a slightly early retirement due to a pancreatic cancer diagnosis. HR was still searching for his replacement when two more engineers retired. Soon, the exodus accelerated. By the end of the fiscal year, the company was down from 610 employees three years earlier to 480. Julio suspected that the departure of key individuals—those who motivated their employees and were well-liked by nearly everyone—hastened the departure of many more who found little reason to stay and absorb the leadership team's abuse on their own.

At some point (it was impossible to know exactly when) the company passed the point of no return, where a strategic workforce plan became a moot point. The talent gap became a sinkhole, and potential job candidates could smell the company's desperation and see the fear in Haley's eyes.

Key sales opportunities fell by the wayside and revenue took a nosedive. John Jr. spent more and more time out of the office, sparing those who remained from his tirades. It seemed as if the whole C-suite had checked out; Julio felt no sense of urgency from them about jump-starting a turnaround. He wondered if they had a secret plan to be bought out by an international conglomerate. He would have expected some unfamiliar visitors to the plant if that were the case, but no one mysterious materialized. Meanwhile, the revolving door of floor workers in the plant continued spinning, the insulting $11/hour starting pay not able to keep pace with competitive rates. Even the relatively happy HR team lost their administrative assistant to a better paying position, and then the opening was eliminated altogether.

Eventually, the loss of manufacturing talent and growing number of vacant positions led to quality and service issues. Once customers started leaving, sales tanked and profits turned to losses. It wasn't long before the company defaulted on its bank loans. The bank called for a meeting and demanded a turnaround plan within four weeks. The CFO's (who was also the son of an original Big John's crony) half-hearted attempt to pull something together necessitated steep layoffs. The HR department was cut to just Haley and Julio. The CTO left one Friday and never came back. Ultimately, the layoffs exacerbated the service and quality issues. Things went downhill fast and the bank called the loans. The game was up. Equipment was auctioned and Julio processed several hundred pink slips.

At the last moment, John Jr. pulled the rip cord on his golden parachute and landed softly into the nestled bosom of his gilded heritage. He switched out his business suits for a country club wardrobe and set sail on his sloop with his second wife. Julio never heard from him again.

The future was uncertain—it always was—but Julio had a couple of irons in the fire and was not above restaurant work if push came to shove. Haley, at the age of 45, was headed to graduate school. She harbored more resentment at the company than Julio, understandable given her longer tenure, but she was resilient enough to give herself a fresh start.

Turning onto the highway, Julio felt a new sense of possibility. More than ever, he truly believed that investing in people was the best insurance for any crisis a company could face.

## UNQUITTABLE

- Workforce planning is included in strategic and financial planning.
- Recognizing and developing leaders in all areas of an organization creates positive energy and goodwill.
- SWP includes knowledge capture and transfer initiatives.

## QUITTABLE

- Waiting until a crisis hits an organization to engage in SWP will be too little, too late. A complete program will take two to three years to become effective.
- When HR operates in a vacuum and is not included in strategic planning, the initiative is doomed.
- Succession planning is neither conducted nor built into the SWP.

# CHAPTER 14

# People Analytics and Talent Dashboards

Many individuals are attracted to Human Resources because they like working with people; if they wanted to work with numbers, they would have gone into engineering, computer science, or accounting. But wouldn't you know it—even people-oriented jobs intersect with numbers at some point. At least this time around you won't need to memorize a formula or solve an equation for "x." Instead, you'll use numbers to tease out relevant trends that help quantify your strategies. People analytics gives you a window to the patterns that impact your business; it turns hard data into actionable information. Chances are you already track a significant amount of people, program, and performance data. The goal is to use it wisely. Really great data allows you to make decisions that will improve engagement, morale, retention, attraction, and ultimately, financial results.

As a gumshoe on the case of suspicious activity at Westwood Markets, Chelsea finds clues by matching wits with the data. She uses her expertise to interpret the numbers and solve a big problem for the company. Meanwhile, Cookie tries to stanch the exodus at Delicious Foods any way she can following a haphazard merger and the installment of a new corporate overlord. She believes in people analytics, but her execution misfires. Good intentions are not enough.

## THE CASE OF THE CREEPING TURNOVER

The rain pounded against the windows. Chelsea settled into the worn leather chair she had carted with her everywhere since her first year at Purdue. She lit a scented candle to mask the aroma of Indian takeout, the remains of which littered her desk. It was going to be a long night.

Light from the parking lot slanted in through the blinds, casting deep shadows across the ficus in the corner. Otherwise, the room was dark. An oscillating fan rhythmically blasted stale air at Chelsea, creating the only noise in the room.

The building was empty. They were all gone—the accountants, the managers, the public relations team. Even the cleaning crew had departed. It was just Chelsea and her laptop. Time to get to the bottom of the mystery.

There was a dead body in the middle of the room. Figuratively, anyway. The corpse was in the shape of a steep rise in turnover throughout the company. Chelsea had to find out who the killer was and stop him before he struck again. There were a lot of theories, but theories weren't the same as clues. She needed to stick with the facts and not go off on wild speculation about love triangles, mobsters, and aliens.

Westwood Markets seemed to have it all. The high-end grocery chain had grown to 230 stores in the Midwest and Southeast over the past fifteen years. It had a reputation as the place for hard-to-find organic vegetables used in Southeast Asian cuisine. Customers were known to drive over fifty miles to get their hands on the infamous durian fruit—carefully packaged—at most Nectar Springs stores. The big chains and independent farmers markets wouldn't touch it. The staff even knew how to peel and cook the fruit; they were that good. *Engaged* is the term Chelsea and her HR colleagues used to describe Westwood employees.

That's what made the dead body so confounding. For years, Chelsea believed that employee engagement was tied to the company's unusually high retention rate. There had been high turnover blips before, issues pertaining to a single store or department, but that was usually an indication of an ineffective manager. Several years ago they isolated an issue with the Accounting department that was skewing company-wide statistics, and afterward the turnover rate dipped back down to historical levels—around 4 percent for full-time and 20 percent for part-time employees.

Low turnover was inversely proportional to job satisfaction. But the ratio went haywire this past year. As job satisfaction remained steady, turnover climbed to 7 percent for full-time and 29 percent for part-time employees. The question was, why?

A bolt of lightning and deafening crack of thunder reverberated through the still office. *Indeed,* Chelsea thought. She brought up the Westwood talent dashboard on her computer. If there were clues to be discovered, this is where they'd be.

The talent dashboard was a goldmine of information; she'd worked hard to get it to this point. It was hard to get people to care about tracking numbers in the Human Resources business. But Chelsea believed in quantifying behavior; it was the only way to measure trends and spot trouble points. The sports fans in HR got it: They knew that statistics were crucial to analyzing a team's or player's performance. The top brass loved it, too—they were suckers for reports, and hers had all the bells and whistles: bar graphs, pie charts, histograms, and scatter plots. They all moved in the right direction, until now.

She took a swig of kombucha tea from her bottle. It went down the wrong way and she erupted into a coughing fit. When it passed, she saw it—an unusually high rate of retirements. But what did it mean? She did more digging.

By the time a pattern emerged, the storm had cleared and a full moon was breaking through the clouds. Way back in the files—so old they weren't even on the Cloud—a pattern emerged. The first five Westwood locations opened fifteen years ago. They had hired experienced people in mid-career. People who had supermarket experience, who knew how to work with suppliers, who understood that the world of groceries was a margin business. These individuals stayed with the company through its growth and had done very well for themselves. Now, they were retiring. It was a few years earlier than top managers in other fields, but that was their reward for building a successful business: a long, healthy retirement full of meaningful endeavors. This even explained the rise in part-time turnover. A number of the original employees had reduced their hours to part-time in the past several years instead of retiring. This was especially true with those who worked at headquarters. Empty nesters not ready to pull the plug entirely on their careers, they were happy to dabble in their trade on a lighter schedule, contribute to the company's bottom line, and participate in knowledge transfer. This itself was the result of the company's flexibility.

"Ah ha!" Chelsea exclaimed, excited by the data. "If I remove the early retirees from the equation, our voluntary turnover level has actually decreased!" She leaned back in her chair, triumphant. A tendril of smoke curled toward the ceiling; the sandalwood candle had bit the dust.

The details could wait until morning. There would be a report to write, an action plan to create, and people to brief, but the hard part was done. There wouldn't be another dead body on her watch. At least not one killed by high retirement rates.

It was great to know the CEO was in her corner. "Let me know what you need," he said when she filled him in on the case. Truth was, she didn't need a lot. It was just a matter of implementing a strategic workforce planning program she had been working on for a while. As part of her SWP process, she and her team identified likely retirements in the coming years and beefed up their preretirement program, allowing pre-retirees to remain with the company on a part-time basis and become more involved in training and knowledge retention. Many of these employees also showed interest in joining the company's mentoring program and teaching at the company university.

Chelsea had always been a big fan of film noir movies from the 1940s. But working in Human Resources didn't have the same panache as, say, Sam Spade chasing bad guys all over San Francisco in his search for the Maltese Falcon. And yet, her job, when she used her imagination, called to mind the best detective plots from the Golden Age of Hollywood. Like a director with an eye for angles and shadows, it was all just a matter of how you looked at it.

## COOKIE'S MAGIC WINDOW

Two things happened at Delicious Foods on Monday, the company where Cookie had worked since she was 21. First, the vice president of warehousing threw a bottle of water at a floor manager. It missed his head but connected with a steel support beam, causing an $H_2O$ explosion that drenched several onlookers. Second, the leadership team announced a new "Customer Delight" campaign, which included t-shirts emblazoned with the corporate logo and the phrase "Customer delight, it's always right!" on the back.

Cookie knew the two events were related. Morale was low; tensions were high. Sales were falling and late shipments were skyrocketing. The trend began three years ago when Apple Private Equity acquired Delicious

Foods. APE, as the entity was known, had also acquired three other similar businesses. In total, they had revenues of $200 million and employed 410 people. Cookie was responsible for all the hiring and firing.

Cookie believed in "people analytics," or the idea that good statistics and data can drive HR decision-making. She also believed in maintaining a detailed talent dashboard as the major tool of people analytics. Cookie's talent dashboard was an Excel spreadsheet that tracked her recruiting and hiring efforts. She kept detailed data on the number of applicants for each job posting and the number of interviews for each opening. She knew there were more openings this year than last year, and that they were open for a longer time. The existing staff had to do more with fewer people, which inevitably led to communications snafus, longer hours, and conflict. The conflict impacted the bottom line, and the APE leadership team decided to solve the problem by launching the "Customer Delight" campaign.

Doug and Cookie chatted about this turn of events at his parents' fiftieth anniversary party that weekend. Cookie had created the centerpiece baskets for each table, a dozen heart-shaped cookies arranged in a gold vase tied with a red velvet bow.

"I feel like the company is slipping away," Doug said.

"How so?"

"These APE guys make me so nervous. They ask me questions I can't answer. And I have an MBA."

"Like what?"

"How come our turnover rate is skyrocketing? Why is morale so bad? How many days does it take to fill an opening?"

"I wish I had the people analytics to help you out."

"What about your talent dashboard?" Doug asked.

Cookie sighed and ran her hands through her hair. "I've had a hard time staying on top of it. We've got so many openings to fill that I don't have time to track down the data from the companies other than Delicious. I know how many interviews I do. I know how many people are quitting and that April is the top month for people to quit. But I haven't been able to determine any trends regarding why people are quitting. The reasons are all over the place."

"I wish I knew how to connect these statistics to the decline in morale," Doug said. "The APE team wants something concrete, but all the subsidiaries are so different. I need a better handle on the situation."

"I've reached out to the other HR teams, but I get the feeling they're just as overwhelmed. There doesn't seem to be the political will to invest in a company-wide system." Cookie said.

"I get the feeling the APE team is trying to find a reason to let me go."

"Oh Doug—they wouldn't! No one cares about this company more than you."

"They want answers I don't have."

"I wish we knew how to get them." Cookie wondered how she could improve her talent dashboard.

"You may be baking cookies full-time soon," Doug said, nodding to the vase on the table.

Cookie nudged him with her elbow. "I'll make you my business manager."

Later that night, Cookie couldn't sleep. She got out of bed, padded out to her office, and turned on the computer. She had to find a way to make the talent dashboard work. She brought up the spreadsheet. It was too basic. It had a sheet for every month, and on the sheet for each month were the job openings, where she recruited from, how many applicants she received, how many she forwarded to managers, how many people were scheduled for interviews, and if the position was filled.

It just wasn't enough. Right away she noticed two elements she wasn't tracking: whether or not the position was new or the result of attrition, and how many days between when the position became available and when it was filled.

She could go through the records and reconstruct much of this information, but it would take time. It would be a lot easier if she had a more robust HR program that logged some of this data automatically. She had a feeling it would reveal that the company's turnover had always been high. That's the nature of the industry—low paying, low-level jobs that serve as a stepping stone for most people. Did APE really expect Delicious to turn into a company where people were happy to spend their lives in a warehouse for $11/hour?

Even if she was able to address those issues, there were APE's other companies to worry about. She needed data from all of them. They were even smaller and less organized than Delicious—the types of places where the account managers still kept penciled-in numbers and names in spiral notebooks, or worse, in their heads. Talking to any of them about an eNPS score was going to get her some hostile stares; she was just learning about them herself.

Cookie's eyes glazed over in a darkened conference room three months later. In addition to the "Customer Delight" campaign (she didn't even know where her t-shirt was anymore), the APE management team had launched a standard materials management system in each warehouse. In theory, the concept made perfect sense. Holding people to it was another matter entirely.

Slide after slide showed numbers from who knows where—it wasn't her talent dashboard, that much she knew. Cookie couldn't see how the numbers could be accurate—no one had asked her to contribute to them. Was there a system somewhere she didn't know about? Her face began to burn when they got to the root of the HR problems, or "the people problems," as the CEO called them: poor morale, high turnover, long vacancies. The head suit looked directly at her. The subtext was that she was being blamed for not turning things around.

The iron bell was tolling for her.

If only human resources was as straightforward as baking! You mixed flour, eggs, sugar, and whatnot, and after fifteen minutes in the oven, you had a delicious treat. If something went wrong, you threw out the batch and started over. The way to people's hearts was through their stomachs. Cookie wasn't the first to say it, but she knew it was true.

Another way to people's hearts was by genuinely listening to them. Cookie was a great listener because she really cared that you had pneumonia, won a 5K, booked a cruise, babysat your niece, etc. She supposed it was a byproduct of having been raised in a big family—she could never get a word in edgewise as she and her six siblings competed for their parents' attention.

She learned to wield authority by conveying interest in people and keeping their secrets. You couldn't be in HR and be a blabbermouth. People confided in her, and she felt maternal toward them in return. Even at the tender age of 45, she gave off a grandmotherly vibe.

In the aftermath of the conference room debacle, when the upper management blamed her for APE's people problems, it was obvious that cupcakes and listening skills weren't enough. The APE team wanted to know why the turnover rate was 29 percent. How did the company lose 105 people in a single year? All Cookie could offer by way of explanation was anecdotal, culled from her exit interviews. Some people retired, some were taking time off to raise a family, some moved out of state, some got other jobs. There seemed to be an uptick lately in the number of people who were leaving for jobs at the newer manufacturing and distribution facilities in the area. The pay was a little better, the benefits about the same. She had a feeling people knew they would have more opportunities to grow their careers in another environment. If only her talent dashboard would reveal the truth! How was she to measure morale?

Cookie grabbed the "Customer Delight" t-shirt from her shoulder (it had somehow wound up in a pile of her winter boots) and wiped up the dripping cake batter from the counter. She had expanded into wedding cakes after taking a few basic decorating classes and spending an absurd number of hours watching YouTube tutorials. She worried that having to earn a living at baking would suck all the fun out of it. Only time would tell.

Over twenty years with a single company—the best years of her life. Her last few months there were painful. It was clear they were trying to make her quit, but she was holding out for unemployment insurance. She finally got it, along with an antianxiety medication prescription and a pain in her gut she was sure was an ulcer. She would always wonder what else she could have done. Doug had nothing but kind words for her when they met up with a few of the old-timers at a pub.

"I really liked my job, Doug. I did the best I could."

"I know." Doug dipped a jalapeno popper in ranch dressing.

"And you did, too," Cookie said. "I never received any formal HR training. I never figured out that fancy HR system APE came in with. It wasn't what I was used to."

"At least we both landed on our feet."

Cookie laughed. "You get to use your MBA and I get to use my Kitchen Aid mixer. But it still bothers me."

"What does?"

"The data. I feel that I if I could have accurately measured morale, I could have come up with a plan to turn things around. Right now it looks like they're headed for a fire sale."

"We did surveys. No one ever filled them out."

"That in and of itself is data."

"None of the other acquisitions were able to figure out a talent dashboard either," Doug said.

"I always wanted metrics that could show causality between low morale and a decline in sales, but it was never that straightforward."

Doug finished off his popper. "Well, you'll never have that problem now. You'll always know where you stand with cupcakes."

## UNQUITTABLE

- Talent dashboard data is updated weekly or monthly to ensure that it's useful and relevant.
- Talent goals are well-defined.
- Talent dashboards are used to monitor and improve the company's talent ecosystem.
- The organization tracks metrics that quantify elements associated with employer branding, including eNPS, morale, turnover rate, average time to fill open positions, and job inquiries received.
- Don't keep analytical information a secret. Stewards of the dashboard find opportunities to share the data widely and, preferably, up the chain. Use talent dashboard data to inform continuous improvement efforts.

## QUITTABLE

- Organizations have no talent dashboard or way to track critical data.
- HR tracks talent-related data, but doesn't use it to analyze or act.
- Even worse, the organization tracks data incorrectly or tracks irrelevant data.
- HR entrusts a dashboard to a single individual without working it in to their larger talent management strategy.

# CHAPTER 15

# Compensation Systems

There are lots of different ways to pay people. Some individuals thrive on commission, while others want to know ahead of time the exact amount on their paycheck. Some love bonuses when the organization meets its fiscal goals, and some believe a bonus shouldn't be tied to a goal they personally have no control over. Some love stock options; most of us aren't fortunate enough to be acquainted with them. Beyond the variation in compensation systems, there's an even larger question: How do you determine how much to pay an individual for the work he or she does?

Data about compensation is now more transparent than ever—it's as easy as cruising over to the Bureau of Labor Statistics website where everything is broken down by region, industry, education level, and a host of other demographic data. Employees and employers both know the score. But compensation is influenced by a variety of factors, adding a level of complication. What about lower pay but an awesome benefits package? Tuition reimbursement? Company car? Super flexible schedule? The option to work at home? Onsite childcare?

All these factors aside, studies show that compensation does not influence job performance.[1] People are internally motivated to perform well (or not) at their jobs.[2] In fact, attempts to improve performance by increasing pay often backfire by making someone who was intrinsically motivated more receptive to external criteria.[3] But, that doesn't mean you get to skimp on salaries.

Top performing companies conduct a full compensation review annually and have an in-house compensation team. These groups are wise to use compensation to promote exploration and learning, as opposed to a system designed to reward and punish individuals. Savvy companies no longer tie performance reviews to compensation and raises.

That said, all the pay in the world won't compensate for an abusive employer who creates a dangerous or threatening environment or withholds the tools employees need to do their job correctly. At their worst, compensation plans, especially in sales, can have diametrically opposed goals, harming both the business' bottom line and talent relationships.

In the scenarios below, one company finds a unique way to reward talent by involving them in the process. In addition to augmenting compensation, the employee input is a creative way to promote a workplace culture and, as a result, boost employer branding. Over at the McElroy Group, a dysfunctional compensation system remains in place years after it should have been reconfigured to align with a growing corporation's goals. The result gets physical.

## MASSAGING THE NUMBERS AT ELEVATE MORTGAGE

Kelsey observed the results of the vote on her computer with a wild look in her eyes. "Well, I'll be. It's a three-way tie."

Will gazed over her shoulder. "This is a disaster!"

"How is it even possible?" Kelsey asked.

"More importantly, what do we do?"

"Either someone casts a tie-breaking vote, or we ask everyone to vote again." Kelsey fired off a frantic text.

Gary ambled in three minutes later, all lanky limbs and chill attitude. "'Sup?"

"Get a load of this." Kelsey tapped her pen on the screen.

Gary contracted his body to get up close and personal with the data. He removed his glasses and took in the rows of identical numbers. He grunted, first with an air of incomprehension, then in measured astonishment. Looking at Kelsey and Will, he announced his verdict: "It's a black swan."

"A what?" Kelsey asked.

"A black swan," Gary said, pushing his glasses back up his nose. "A random event that is unexpected, difficult to predict, and creates lasting impact."

"We should have been prepared for this," Will said.

"You can't be. A black swan is obvious only in hindsight," Gary replied.

"Semantics aside," Will said, "what do we do?" The tension in the room was palpable.

Gary shrugged. "Choose the option you like the best and tell everyone it was the winner."

"I couldn't do that," Will said, "that would be dishonest."

Kelsey stared Gary down. "You're joking, right?"

Gary laughed nervously. "Of course."

"We got 555 votes with 185 for each option on how we should allocate our bonus—extra vacation days, cash bonus, or an onsite massage therapist."

"Only six of us are ineligible to vote," Will said. "That leaves nine people who didn't vote on how to distribute the quarterly profits."

"The poll was live for five days," Gary said. "That should have been plenty of time."

"Not for people that don't read their email when they're gone," Kelsey replied.

"What Neanderthal doesn't keep up with their email?" asked Gary.

"Maybe we should extend the deadline to include anyone who was gone last week," Kelsey suggested.

"No problem" Gary said. "I can find out who hasn't accessed the online poll yet and message them directly."

"Nine people," Kelsey said, "What if it's another tie?"

"Another black swan!"

"Freaky!" Gary said.

The final vote was 186 in favor of additional vacation days, 187 for a cash bonus, and 188 for an onsite massage therapist.

"Three people still didn't vote," Kelsey said. "How do you like that?"

"Less than a perfect democracy, but I'll take it," Will said. "A massage therapist it is."

Kelsey stood up, hands on hips. "Time to convert Bob's old office into a spa."

Will's next exchange with Kelsey was much less friendly and played against both their types. As the chief servant leader of Elevate Mortgage, Will was committed to making the company one of the region's best places to work. This entailed paying well above the industry average for all positions, among other things. Kelsey, as the chief people officer, objected to the company's ever-rising salaries and benefits, which was making it difficult for the income statement to remain in the black.

"When it comes to employer branding, we don't need these high salaries to prove ourselves. Our reputation speaks for itself," Kelsey argued.

"Good compensation ensures employee loyalty. I want to make sure we remain in the 70th to 80th percentile for all positions. What does the annual compensation study say?"

"I emailed you the report."

"Elevator pitch," Will said.

"You'll like what it says," Kelsey said.

Will sensed the frustration in her voice. "But you don't?"

"I'm always going to advocate for a strong benefits program, but I'm afraid we could get in real trouble if the economy turns south."

"I trust everyone at the company," Will said. "They receive a compensation report each year with salary and benefits ranked regionally and nationally. Our employer brand helps attract the right people, and our compensation system creates loyalty. This has been my ideal since the beginning: employee satisfaction through transparency."

"I agree with you in theory," Kelsey said. "But this is so far beyond the industry norm. People look forward to annual raises. That's how they know they're making progress. When they get a performance review and it's not followed by a salary increase, they send me nasty emails."

Will struck a conciliatory note. "I know it's hard to shift the paradigm, but paying for performance is a trap. It's much better to devote resources to providing ways for people to operate autonomously in the workplace."

Kelsey rolled her eyes. "It's a good thing I like you, because you drive me crazy."

"All the best CEOs drive people crazy. That's why they get fired so often."

"Better watch your back at the next board meeting." Kelsey smacked him on the shoulder with a file folder.

"Are you kidding, the Board loves me!"

"Let's keep it that way by staying in the black."

Just the title—chief servant leader—defined how Will spent his days. In his mind, a chief executive officer is a guy who schmoozes clients at the club or on the golf course, who then returns to the office for meetings where people point at charts peppered with zigzagging arrows. In contrast, a chief servant leader knows each employee's name, asks about their children, and listens—really listens—to what they say. He also listens for what they don't say.

For example, people complained for years that the Elevate office windows didn't open. Will had talked to the company that owned the building, but they refused to do anything about it, citing laws, ordinances, insurance liabilities, and what have you. But what Will really heard in people's complaints was, "We need fresh air." So, he worked with the property management company to create an outdoor space with tables and chairs. It gave people the option of working outside on nice days with Wi-Fi, a waterfall, and a koi pond. A few people hauled in their grills every now and then and had a cookout. Some joker always brought squirt guns.

When it came to the massage therapist thing, Will was cognizant of how close the vote had been and he prepared himself for a bit of backlash. Interestingly, many of the women in the office couldn't wait to book their appointments. They had a lot of opinions about hot stones and deep tissue techniques. It was the men who made jokes, uneasy on some level with the whole concept. Gil accosted Will in the café, confessing in hushed tones how he would feel weird getting semi-naked in the office, even in a private room with mood lighting and candles. Will listened, nodded. He didn't do anything to change the situation, but he let Gil know that he respected his opinion. Often that was enough. "With the way things are going," he told Gil, "we'll have another quarterly bonus decision to make before you know it."

Sometimes, Will liked to "catch people doing good." A particularly helpful customer service rep, staying calm through a DEFCON 1 phone call, for example, might be rewarded on the spot from his or her manager with a gift card to a restaurant. These unexpected perks brightened people's days more than an expected bonus. The biggest challenge was keeping things fresh. Tickets to concerts and sporting events were always popular, but Will liked to personalize things, too, with input from managers and supervisors.

One manager got a top sales associate tickets to a comic convention because he was really into cosplay. Another manager knew a team member's sisters, nieces, and nephews were visiting from Oklahoma and got all of them passes to the zoo.

Elevate's compensation system had evolved due to Will's penchant for investigation and need to do things differently from other companies. Conventional wisdom said that you pay your best people the most money. But Will had read the research. There was no evidence that incentives or a pay-for-performance system worked; in fact, there was data to suggest it could be counterproductive. Some people, like Kelsey, had trouble coming to terms with the fact that conventional wisdom could be wrong. "Money is an external motivator," Will explained to his incredulous detractors. "I want to support internal motivators instead." But internal motivators were tricky. That's why he created the Career Sculpting team. They found creative ways to engage the company's high performers by using their skills to foster innovation and growth. The initiative had nothing to do with compensation and everything to do with allowing talented professionals to live up to their potential.

Will knew, as did Kelsey and the rest of the HR team, that an entry-level customer service representative could have just as high job satisfaction as a director, even though one made $30,000 and the other made $130,000. Raises were useful only for obtaining temporary compliance. Creating a consistently engaged workforce required finding ways to help people live up to their potential and thrive.

Lesser minds would take this evidence as reason enough to skimp on salaries. If money isn't tied to performance, why not pay people as little as possible? To Will, that line of thinking was foolish. The whole idea of being the chief servant leader at Elevate is to give people what they need to help them excel at their jobs. It's a philosophy based on the theory of abundance, not scarcity; a growth instead of a fixed mindset. At Elevate, people are expected to constantly evolve with their job. They're rewarded with training and opportunities to achieve new goals. Will was doing his best to create an environment that energized people. Those who didn't take advantage of Elevate's opportunities were more or less self-selecting for a lesser career track. Some individuals were perfectly happy in their positions and deserved to make a sustainable living without feeling the need to climb the ladder.

"A decent salary looks like trust; a poor salary feels like control," Will told Kelsey. "Promising a reward to someone who is unmotivated is like offering a thirsty person a drink of salt water."

"You should go into the bumper sticker business," Kelsey said.

"I paid good money to Purdue to get this smart," he replied.

Kelsey considered Will's commitment to compensation transparency a dangerous tightrope act. Or maybe like being a lion tamer. Either way, it was a circus and it was dangerous. The American Dream relied on keeping money a mystery and not knowing how much your coworkers or parents made. It was impolite to discuss. No wonder so many people had problems managing it.

Still, Will's dedication to bucking the trend was admirable. While he didn't go as far as some businesses she'd heard about, where employees were publicly ranked by salary, he did more than most. Once a year, each employee received a report showing the nationwide salary range for their position so they could see where they ranked. This report also factored people's benefits—an incredibly important part of the equation.

Kelsey usually enjoyed compensation meetings with her team. They went something like this:

"Good afternoon, Sydney."

"Hi, Kelsey. How's it going?"

"Great. Have a look at your compensation package. You'll see that you're in the 80th percentile for what all human resources representatives make at similar sized companies throughout the country."

"Wow. That's fantastic."

"And you'll see that your benefits package brings that up to the 85th percentile. Do you have any questions?"

"What are you doing for lunch today?"

Okay, maybe this was a slight exaggeration, but the conversations were usually short and sweet and unrelated to longer, more complicated performance reviews. People appreciated knowing where they stood. Younger or newer employees saw how far they could go, more established employees sensed they had climbed the ladder, and everyone felt there was order in the universe.

Almost everyone, that is. Take Trevor, for example. When Kelsey presented his salary information to him a year ago, the fresh-out-of-college youngster couldn't understand why he wasn't near the top of his range for a human resources representative. Because you're 22, she said. He claimed he worked harder than his coworkers; came in early, went home late. Kelsey clarified this wasn't a performance review, but he persisted. She explained that this wasn't about comparing himself to his coworkers, it was about placing himself on a continuum for his position that took his experience into consideration.

He still didn't get it, and within a few months he was gone, having decided to become a whitewater rafting guide in Utah.

Of course, not everyone was thrilled with the massage therapist, but the appointments booked fast. The spots right before lunch were the most coveted. Even Kelsey, who thought it would be weird to take off half her clothes in Bob's old office, signed up for a fifteen-minute chair massage and later pronounced it one of the most exquisite experiences of her life. She didn't even have to remove her cardigan sweater. Will, in an adjoining chair on the other side of some potted palms, heard the stress melt from her voice and smiled broadly into his face rest as a therapist worked on a knot in his neck. He was always listening.

## OF HORSES AND BONUSES

Simon believed in compensating people for a job well done, and he was living proof that bonuses make people work harder. Simon was the CEO of the McElroy Group, a hospitality conglomerate comprised of mid-range hotel brands. The board of directors had rewarded him with a sizable bonus last year for a share price that had increased 12 percent in a challenging economic climate. He spent his windfall on an Aston Martin V12 Vantage S Roadster and a trip to Gaydon, England, to see it come off the line. But this big reward came with a big responsibility. The board expected Simon to maintain this level of growth, so he was looking into a hostile takeover of a down-on-its-luck competitor whose logo and color scheme hadn't been updated since 1985. He was working overtime trying to get the deal done.

As if the takeover wasn't stressful enough, his CFO busted into his office one morning to unload some bad numbers regarding their quarterly earnings. Nationwide, their occupancy rate was falling as their net unit growth increased. This was causing some cash flow issues and shareholders were spooked. Fickle investors were dumping their shares for no good reason, and Simon was in danger of having to announce a suspended dividend for the quarter.

Simon was incensed; he had already earmarked his next bonus for a yearling thoroughbred in Qatar with a top-notch pedigree. Race horses would give him an in with the Saudis, and who knows where that could lead. But his phone calls to those on the racing circuit kept getting interrupted by people giving him bad news he didn't want to hear. His temper became shorter as the threat to his bonus got greater.

Now Hillary, his VP of HR, was telling him that morale was low throughout the company. She sent out some kind of survey, and the results revealed that 80 percent of McElroy employees believed they were underpaid. Simon fumed—he had never approved such a survey! And he never would because of course morale was low. Half the McElroy workforce scrubbed bathtubs for a living! The other half had to deal with bombastic, entitled, and unreasonable business travelers and their reckless use of corporate credit cards.

HR needed to stress the generosity of the McElroy bonus program if they wanted to improve worker morale, Simon thought as he clicked on his brokerage account and checked his daily net worth. Any motivated individual could overcome perceived salary shortcomings and crank up their earnings by working harder than their coworkers. Many did—it was the American Way.

Simon grimaced as he observed how the overnight turmoil in the Asian markets affected his accounts. A loss in the high five figures! He reached for an antacid; little did he know it was just the beginning.

He opened his email and got to work deleting messages. It was the usual dreck, all meeting notes and CYA messages from his directors, until he saw an attached link from his VP of HR. He clicked, and a grainy video sprang to life showing Al Hedblad, the VP of Food and Beverage, in a shouting match with Ed Varney, the McElroy events director, at a fundraising event. The argument devolved into a shoving match, the two men knocking over furniture until they were separated by an ex-Marine bartender. The melee played out under a banner that read, "The McElroy Group: Working Together for a Cure." The video had 27,000 views.

Simon stormed out of his office and down the hall to HR. Hillary was just hanging up her coat.

"What the hell is this video all about?"

"I see you got my email," she said.

"Do you know how bad these optics are?"

"I'll get it taken down as soon as possible. It was just posted last night."

"This is a PR disaster."

"I'm on it."

"What were those idiots arguing about?"

"I'm going to have a talk with each of them and find out. But I know they have a history."

Ed and Al had both spent the night at the scene of the crime—the McElroy property in Sarasota, FL. Hillary reached Al first.

"It wasn't my fault," Al said. "Ed just doesn't understand business, that's all."

"Tell me, Al, were you drunk?"

"What? Of course not!"

"Glad to hear it."

It took Hillary a good five minutes to drill through Al's ego and get to the heart of the matter. It turns out that, Al, as head of Food and Beverage, was focused on negotiating lower costs with his current vendors. A lower cost structure would earn him a hefty annual bonus. Ed was trying to strong-arm him into switching to higher-priced vendors, for some stupid reason.

Hillary reached Ed on the phone after lunch. The video was history by then, but she still had to do damage control to soothe Simon. "Don't believe a word Al says," Ed told Hillary. "He's got these loser vendors. They're cheap, no one likes them, and they're ruining the brand. My goal is to increase event revenue, and I can't do that with the crappy products he keeps buying. He's jeopardizing my bonus."

Ah ha, Hillary thought. It was about money. Both men were worried that they wouldn't get their bonuses if they conceded to the other. Their goals were not aligned. Hillary wrote up their unprofessional behavior, making sure it went in their permanent files. Then, she tried to come up with a solution.

A week later, the video had become ancient history and the bruises had faded, so Simon didn't understand why Hillary wouldn't drop the issue. He vaguely listened as she stood and talked to him at his desk.

"The fight was caused by Al and Ed's conflict of interests. Al's bonus is tied to lowering costs, and Ed's is tied to maximizing event revenue," Hillary explained. "Ed feels Al's vendors have inferior products and services that will damage McElroy's reputation in key markets."

"Uh-huh," said Simon, glancing at his brokerage account. Thankfully it was ticking upward.

"We should eliminate bonuses with misaligned objectives and replace them with something that increases morale," Hillary suggested.

"There's no line item for morale on the balance sheet, so it's irrelevant," Simon replied. He had a three o'clock call with his horse dealer that could close the sale on a chestnut Arabian in Qatar, so he was hoping Hillary would lose interest and float back to her own office by then. But for some reason she kept talking.

"What I'd really like to do is conduct a comparative compensation study and have managers share the results with their teams. People might feel better about their jobs if they find out they make at- or above-market wages," Hillary said.

"Are you daft?" Simon bellowed. "What markets are you talking about? We don't need to arm people with information that makes us look bad." Simon pushed his chair back, exasperated that she was making him think about McElroy business. "What we need is a bonus program tied to performance. Like we have now. Who doesn't like incentives?" His thinking was rock solid. Incentives led to improvements, which led to a higher share price, which meant a happy payday for him. Visions of Triple Crown glory danced in his head.

Simon had to hand it to Hillary—she put up a good fight. In the end, he told her to do what she thought was best as long as they could show improvement by the end of the next quarter. That meant she only had a couple months to devise a program, roll it out, and start measuring results. She first assigned the VPs new bonus measurements that actually complemented each other. They looked like this:

| VP | Bonus Tied To |
| --- | --- |
| **Operations** | Cutting utility costs by 5 percent across the board |
| **Human Resources** | Keeping manager turnover under 8 percent and general staff under 18 percent |
| **Accounting and Finance** | Obtaining ROI of at least 4 percent on all investments |
| **Events** | Increasing event bookings company-wide by 10 percent |
| **Food and Beverage** | Supporting revenue growth of 10 percent with no erosion in Gross Margins |
| **Marketing** | 10 percent revenue growth |
| **Corporate Development** | Increasing midrange brand holdings by 25 percent |

Hillary's presentation was met with stunned silence for about five seconds, then everyone started talking at once. It sounded like a room full of children complaining that their younger sibling got a bigger slice of cake. The dam had burst, and resentment spilled forth.

The VP of Corporate Development said, "Simon, you know the takeover deal is fragile and requires SEC approval. It's not my fault if it doesn't pan out, so I shouldn't be punished for it. My bonus should be tied to how many deals I can bring to the table."

The VP of Operations made similar claims: "I don't dictate the cost of utilities. You know this is an energy-intense industry. I can swap out all the lightbulbs you want, but people hate compact fluorescent. They give off a cheap glow. People will kill us on Yelp."

"Can't you go solar or something? Turn down the heat in the swimming pools?" Simon asked. "Be creative. Use your expertise."

It soon became clear that despite Hillary's best intentions, the plan still pit the VPs against each other. The CFO's bonus was tied to maintaining low inventory levels, but the VP of Food and Beverage and VP of Events insisted on stockpiling to accommodate wild card requests. The VP of Marketing was cannibalizing Accounting and Finance by selling timeshares at fire-sale prices to make themselves look good.

Hillary realized too late that the bonus structure rewarded VPs, directors, and managers if they maximized their own departments—she had simply replaced one bad set of criteria with another. Simon stood with an evil grin as the room descended into chaos. He was loving it.

"I admire everyone's healthy spirit of competition. You're all incentivized to do your best. Our shareholders will reward us handsomely as soon as these goals are met. The sky's the limit."

Hillary wished she could disappear.

Life in HR felt like a siege. The complaints filtered in through backhanded compliments, petty rivalries, strongly-worded emails, and a minor car theft in the parking lot. Worse, the low morale at the top of the company filtered down to the rank-and-file, whose morale was already in the dumpster. Hillary was exhausted from all the listening:

"Why can't our salaries reflect industry standards?"

"I'm not in Sales. Why do I have to compete like I am?"

"These goals don't make any sense from a business standpoint."

"The CEO of WorldStay makes half of what Simon makes. Look it up!"

"I'm quitting if I don't get my bonus."

"The shareholders don't work here. Why do they have so much influence?"

"I haven't had a raise or a performance review in two years."

"No one pays attention to the innovations I've suggested."

"My department is being nickeled-and-dimed. It's short-sighted."

After eight months, the new strategy failed to move the company's numbers in any significant way. Hillary urged Simon to reconsider his compensation strategy, but he wouldn't budge. "We need to see this through," he said.

Hardly anyone had earned a bonus by the end of the fiscal year. The annual report was a disaster, the takeover deal had faltered, and Wall Street was watching. Simon was canned at the next board meeting.

The tickets were nonrefundable, so Simon still took a trip to Doha to visit that sleek, beautiful thoroughbred. However, a niggling thought entered from a small corner of his mind as he donned his eye mask and waited for the Ambien to kick in: maybe Hillary had a point.

## UNQUITTABLE

- Compensation is not limited to monetary payments. It includes intangibles that create a better workplace and impact overall employer branding.
- Perks like a meditation or exercise room, yoga classes, free meals, ergonomic chairs, better lighting, or modern/clean bathrooms collectively state that you care about people's well-being.
- Flexibility and modern PTO programs are part of the overall compensation package for all employees.
- Compensation adjustments occur annually, at a minimum.
- Compensation adjustments are not associated with performance reviews, and they are not discussed at those meetings.
- High performing employees are given bigger adjustments and/or bonuses.
- Bonuses or commissions are directly tied to the company's desired behaviors and outcomes.
- Market-based compensation analyses are conducted every one to three years.
- A clear compensation strategy exists.

## QUITTABLE

- Compensation adjustments are not made, or they are made unpredictably.
- Compensation adjustments are only made when asked for by employees.
- Bonuses and raises are split evenly among all employees.
- Pay ranges do not exist for various positions.

- Total compensation ranges are significantly below average, especially for lower-level employees.
- Incentive programs are focused on individual versus company-wide outcomes.

# CHAPTER 16

# Continuous Improvement

We're all familiar with continuous improvement (also known as CI or Kaizen) and the seemingly endless surveys it spawns. You can't make two clicks online these days without being asked to rate your experience with an app or website. We can stay ahead of the competition by gathering and analyzing data and fine-tuning our processes or products, but how can continuous improvement enrich your talent ecosystem? Well-intentioned organizations often have a structured CI program but only use it to fix processes or products.

Unquittable organizations expand their use of CI to identify and implement improvements in culture, engagement, morale, physical space, and employee development. The ultimate benefit of CI is that it both makes things better and empowers talent to fix what is wrong. Employees can feel helpless without a strong CI program. An inability to positively impact their work environment can lead to issues with morale and talent management.

Let's revisit Positive Electric and Super Cleaning Services. Even Scooter has his moments of doubt, feeling that some continuous improvement efforts go beyond his dedicated realm of human resources. Luckily, he's got a good guide in Oliver, his like-minded counterpart who came with the Positive Electric and Terra Lumen merger. Together, they explore Kaizen principles as they relate to talent issues. Over at Super Cleaning Services, Terry's running his business in accordance with his passé and unhelpful old-school beliefs. He puts an ambitious continuous improvement plan in motion when things come to a head, but his good intentions aren't enough—the talent can see how they don't benefit. Things don't go well.

## THE KAIZEN METAMORPHOSIS

Although few people knew it, Scooter's knack for organization extended to his bow tie collection, which he arranged in a bureau drawer according to color. The display sparked joy in his heart each morning as he prepared for his daily adventure at Positive Electric. Today he selected a periwinkle option, one of his favorite summer colors, to augment his taupe suit. Scooter's mind wandered to other forms of organization as continued his morning routine. Few things were as clear cut as a drawer full of neckwear. His efforts at strategic workforce planning in the office, while successful, could always be improved upon.

The issue at hand was the recent merger with Terra Lumen Systems. Terra Lumen was the bigger company, and this week Scooter was hosting Oliver Vrabel, an operations management expert, for a week-long, getting-to-know-you trip intended to "fix" Positive Electric's materials management issues. Scooter would dispute the fact that Positive Electric had any "materials management issues," but he was game to hear what Oliver had to say about Positive Electric's sophisticated enterprise.

Oliver burst into the lobby at 11:05 a.m., his bulky frame blocking the doorway. Scooter had been passing through at that very moment and was able to be the first person to greet him with a handshake.

"Scooter Johnson, head of HR," he said, shaking the gentleman's large hand and marveling at his cowboy hat and boots.

"Oliver Vrabel, Terra Lumen's VP of Operations, bringing greetings from Wichita, Kansas and the Great Plains of the United States." Scooter admired his skills of projection; his voice could gain the attention of a warehouse full of earbudded associates in an instant.

"Welcome to Positive Electric. Our team is looking forward to showcasing our strategic planning solutions and incorporating new measures to advance the goals of the merger."

"This is a fine company you got here, Scooter. Been looking over the data. Impressive. Got a few tweaks in mind."

"Oh?" The announcement gave Scooter the jitters, but the most important thing in HR was to hear people out. No need to get defensive…yet.

"Tell me, do you like Japanese food?"

Scooter's jitters turned to anticipation. "As a matter of fact, I consider myself a connoisseur of the regional cuisine of Osaka."

"Let's discuss this over noodles. That Wasabi House I passed on my way in any good?"

"They have a delightful edamame salad."

"I learned about Kaizen from Nakamura Haruki in Tokyo," Oliver said, slurping his soba noodles. "It was like learning to paint from Picasso in France."

Scooter was charmed and energized by this walking contradiction: the name, the vision, the cultural influences—it was all wonderfully disconcerting. He remembered hearing about the Japanese concept of continuous improvement from the bottom to the top of an organization. "Naturally, I'm familiar with Kaizen," Scooter said, "but only as a way to organize physical space and manufacturing processes. Tell me more about how to integrate it with strategic workforce planning."

"The theory is solid—it's change for better. The execution is where you find the artistry. We like to involve everyone in the process, from the CEO down to the summer interns. It's both local and global, macro and micro. Like a shark that dies when it stops swimming."

Oliver certainly likes his metaphors, Scooter thought.

"We're going to implement the Plan, Do, Check, Act Cycle."

"Fantastic!" Scooter said.

"Let's start with the facts. What can you tell me about the plunge in on-time deliveries and the surge in overtime since the merger?"

Scooter was brought up short as his face flushed; he didn't think anyone knew about those statistics. But it was true. Some things had gotten away from him while he was busy creating an enviable workplace. "We should sit down with the operations director and discuss these recent developments."

Oliver held up his hands. "No problemo, amigo. I'm looking forward to implementing solutions that will benefit both companies."

Scooter was generally amenable to change, but Oliver truly tested his limits over the following weeks, whether he was there in person or peppering his inbox with emails from afar. To start, Oliver didn't like Scooter's talent dashboard. Scooter was quite proud of both his dashboard and the PowerPoint presentation he crafted quarterly for the board with all the updated statistics. Oliver claimed it only showed positive statistics and didn't track things that were detrimental to the company, like cultural rifts between management and hourly workers. Scooter had always prided himself on being a good judge of character—it's what made him a natural in Human Resources. But he was starting to reconsider his initial rosy opinion of Oliver. Scooter was trying to remain impartial, but it was hard not to be defensive after enduring a torrent of emails insinuating that Positive Electric was not an enviable place to work!

Oliver had taken it upon himself to embark on a fact-finding mission to assess the landscape. Through a series of formal and informal interviews, Oliver helped Scooter ascertain that morale was low, as reflected in the 21 percent turnover rate and the average number of days required to fill an opening—fifty-three. That was almost two months, and in a region that had significantly higher unemployment than the national average no less!

It wasn't just that morale was low—the culture was toxic. How could Scooter have missed this? He made the rounds each morning, saying a warm "hello" to everyone he passed and receiving one in return. It was the best part of his day! How could he have missed the wafting green clouds of doom enveloping the entire company—office and warehouse? It was only when Oliver mentioned the miasmic lethargy that he began to notice them. Lethargy! Something Scooter had never experienced! He was a cheerful person, and it was hard for him to realize that not everyone viewed the world through his prism of optimism. With Oliver's help, however, he started to notice the little things: People took three-hour lunches or failed to come back from lunch at all. There were lots of jokes about sinking ships. Nobody seemed concerned about a serious ant infestation. Local kids had tagged the dumpsters with graffiti and management had no plans to erase it. People at all levels thought of meetings as a suggestion instead of a responsibility.

"How can all these be talent issues?" Scooter asked.

Oliver slipped his thumbs through his belt loops and rocked back on his heels. "When one tugs at a single thing in nature, he finds it attached to the rest of the world."

"Chief Seattle?"

"John Muir."

Scooter nodded in philosophical agreement.

Their furthered their exploration of the continuous improvement landscape. The inventory records were so muddled that they were barely legible, but Scooter had no idea—records had nothing to do with HR. But the Kaizen process involved everything. Oliver had access to all areas of the company and shepherded Scooter around, like the Ghost of Christmas Present giving Scrooge an eyeful. Whole shipments were missing, nothing was standardized, and the numbers that did exist didn't make sense. Oliver was told that the company didn't have a procedure in place for training new hires on the inventory system. Thus, many people had taken a stab at the records over the past eighteen months, with no training or quality control mechanism.

On-time, in-full deliveries were below 70 percent. Managers were largely unconcerned with this figure because Positive Electric was the only manufacturer of some of these parts in the country. Their customers weren't going to abandon them—there was no competition. Their supply chain was short and uncomplicated, but the same couldn't be said for their clients. "You're not helping your employer brand by irritating your customers," Oliver told Scooter. He had to confess he'd never thought of it like that.

The company was losing money. Scooter had discounted this fact earlier because the CFO always gave good reasons for being in the red. Oliver helped Scooter see that the CFO's "good" reasons were questionable at best.

Scooter tried not to become defensive, but he had to bite his tongue to prevent himself from lashing out at Oliver. What he wanted to say was, "You can't just amble in here with your spurs and chaps, quoting *The Art of War* and expecting to change a company that's been running smoothly for thirty-five years." What he actually said was, "I admire your unbiased opinion and welcome new strategies for how we can improve the culture here at Positive Electric." Then he smiled. Scooter believed that a smile is the start of opening your heart and being compassionate to others. At least, that's what the Dalai Lama said. If Oliver could quote Sun Tzu, he would quote his own guru.

At one meeting, several months into their working relationship, Oliver began to rattle off terms left and right—"organizational metrics," "geometrically disruptive turnover," "active disengagement." Scooter massaged his temples to stave off the inevitable migraine.

"Okay, okay, I get it. Don't bludgeon me with excessive vocabulary terms!"

"Sorry, partner," Oliver said. "I get a little overly enthusiastic sometimes."

"Enthusiasm is the yeast that makes your hopes shine to the stars," Scooter said.

"Confucius?"

"Henry Ford."

Oliver nodded knowingly. "I hear your frustration. If these were easy problems to solve, no business would have them."

"These problems are bigger than HR."

"The good news is that we've been given the resources to fix them."

"I do appreciate your positivity," Scooter said.

"You can't cross the sea merely by standing and staring at the water," Oliver said.

"Siddhartha?"

"Rabindranath Tagore."

Through a series of lunches infused with various strains of Eastern philosophy, Oliver and Scooter determined how to apply Kaizen to Positive Electric. Much of it sounded like good, old-fashioned common sense, which, as everyone knows, isn't so common. Scooter was on board with the 5S process of *seiri, seiton, seiso, seiketsu,* and *shitsuke* (otherwise known as sort, set in order, shine, standardize, and sustain), but he wasn't sure how to adapt it to human resources. A 5S Kaizen event was a natural fit for the warehouse, however, where there were plenty of boxes, inventory, shelving, people, and heavy equipment scattered about. Scooter found the idea of everything having its place and being inspected and cleaned regularly intensely appealing, as proven by his bow tie drawer.

Oliver served as Scooter's sensei as they explored Kaizen as a long-term approach to continuous improvement. They agreed to pilot some Kaizen events with HR first and gather data that would convince other departments at Positive Electric to follow suit. Together they came up with the following HR issues to address:

1. Lack of organizational/cultural metrics
2. Departments in dysfunction due to high turnover
3. Departments that are inefficient due to being under staffed
4. Overall dissatisfaction of the workforce
5. An "us" versus "them" mentality between hourly workers and management

The first Kaizen event addressed the turnover rate. While many processes were already part of Scooter's strategic workforce planning, Oliver encouraged a new method of collecting and using data that was easier to act upon. It was more data-driven than people-driven, something that initially made Scooter feel uncomfortable. They implemented exit interviews to ascertain the primary causes of turnover, and then analyzed the amount, types, and primary causes of turnover. Scooter wasn't used to looking at information with a more data-driven approach.

Luckily, Terra Lumen encouraged the process because they had minimized hurdles that would have been more monumental before the merger. Scooter doubted that the CEO of Positive Electric would have hired a consultant to conduct a SWOT analysis, but now the decision was made for him. Scooter, who had previously considered himself a deft hand at obtaining useful feedback, was amazed at the darn good data the consultants collected from a wave of interviews on how people categorized the strengths, weaknesses, opportunities, and threats to the company.

This first series of Kaizen events and SWOT interviews took the entire summer. People got used to seeing Oliver around the office. The outfit of his first impression—John Wayne minus the badge and spurs—was modified to suggest less horseback riding and more Midwestern can-do optimism. Many people (though certainly not everyone) had let down their guard a bit, having been assured that their jobs were secure. The consultants revealed that the company, while not necessarily profitable, wasn't in debt, and it had little competition in the local market. If it could get its weaknesses under control, like the turnover and lack of standardized processes, they could gain a lot from investing in new equipment and expanding its product line.

The data revealed truths that Scooter couldn't believe he'd been blind to before. 80 percent of the company's turnover came from the warehousing, shipping, and logistics departments. An even deeper dive into the data revealed that much of the toxicity in the warehouses could be traced directly to Carl McLaren, the director of operations. The less said about him, the better.

Oliver and Scooter spent hours consulting and deciding what to do with this information. It was clear that Carl needed to be moved, but to where and replaced by whom? The answers revealed themselves in time: Carl became the new transport logistician (a new title), and the previous supply and receiving supervisor got a bump up to director of operations. Carl's ego needed significant soothing, requiring a remodeled office and new company phone. However, he knew he could have been let go, so his typical blustery shower of invectives remained muted. He had never been a people person.

Conversely, the new director of operations, Jake, had been with Positive Electric for only two years. He was young but qualified. Most importantly, the guys in the warehouse liked him because he started there as a supervisor. He *was* a people person—a bridge-builder instead of a bridge-burner. One of the first things Jake did in his new position was institute skip-level meetings. Turns out the rank and file in both the warehouse and manufacturing had some good ideas. There was an uptick in spontaneous social events, like happy hours and bowling nights. Lunch hours reverted to normal lengths.

Scooter commissioned his niece to create two decorative wooden signs saying, "If you do not change direction, you may end up where you are headed. –Lao Tzu." He hung one in his office and gifted the other to Oliver. They looked upon the changes they had wrought across Positive Electric and Terra Lumen over the past year and were pleased.

The next Kaizen event was creating a talent dashboard to track vital HR stats: turnover rate, number of open positions, average days to fill open positions, number of job applications received, morale, and engagement. Scooter was under the impression he was already doing this and was nonplussed to discover that his data was "corrupted," as Oliver said. Different HR reps were using questionable calculations to make themselves look good, so the duo instituted a system of checks and balances. Unsurprisingly, concepts like morale and engagement, obtained through surveys and calculated via an employee Net Promoter Score (eNPS), were skewed in favor of optics rather than truth.

Retooling the talent dashboard wasn't really that hard. A small, cross-functional team attended a webinar and were guided through the process by the consultants. They kept the existing software but changed how they gathered data. When Scooter voiced his concern about backsliding into the old ways, Oliver added a few new, one-time steps to the process by having the new data procedures enshrined in the company's quality management system. This meant that anyone learning the system in the future would encounter only the new guidelines. The new procedure also made the dashboard a splash page on the company's intranet, helping increase transparency. Scooter noticed that the new format "gamified" the data somewhat, with everyone in HR competing to see how they could beneficially impact the numbers.

Scooter took the wheel for the third major Kaizen event while Oliver worked intensely with Operations on other issues. The task was reducing the time it took to fill vacant positions. Scooter's goal was to cut the fifty-three days down to twenty-five. It would be a stretch, but he was up for the challenge. He and his staff eagerly analyzed the process. They made many changes, some small and some ambitious, and the average number of days to fill a position fell to thirty-one within eight months. Equally as important, the number of open positions was reduced by almost half. This change alone was significantly appreciated by employees who'd been carrying the weight for understaffed departments. Scooter treated the entire HR department to a steak dinner. They had earned it.

A year later, the management team, along with the consultants and Oliver, gathered for a presentation on the entire continuous improvement program. Turnover in the warehouse was still too high, but it was down significantly and moving in the right direction. Engagement had also improved, as evidenced by a substantial hike from the first eNPS score of -57 to a whopping +3. Morale went up after managers took leadership training and instituted a new review process. An unexpected byproduct of the process was that two new initiatives had risen organically. First, the manufacturing managers took it upon themselves to organize a local volunteer day. Forty-nine employees at Positive Electric signed up for the city's annual "Paint the Town" effort to beautify several community parks. They worked until the sun went down, collecting trash, planting flowers, and slapping a fresh coat of paint on benches and playground equipment. Second, a small Logistics team wrote an app that allowed customers to track each order's real time progress on its route from raw materials to shipping. No one had asked them to do it, but they were encouraged by the CEO when they proposed the idea. It was being released on a trial basis, and early feedback indicated that customers appreciated the sneak peek into logistics. When the customer's watching, everyone tends to be on their best behavior.

Oliver and Scooter made a point of having lunch together at Wasabi House whenever Oliver was in town. On one such visit, Oliver presented Scooter with a small box.

He was taken by surprise. "What's this?"

"Just a little thank you for taking the Kaizen process seriously. Go ahead—open it."

Scooter lifted the lid and gasped. "It's perfect!" He held up a new bow tie patterned with light bulbs that he could add to his collection.

"Remember what Thomas Edison said when he invented the light—"

"I haven't failed. I've just found 10,000 ways that won't work."

## THE DIRTY DEEDS OF SUPER CLEANING SERVICES

Greg's hair was standing on end he was so mad. He was about to leap over that metaphorical line in the sand and be fired for insubordination: "Don't stick your nose where it doesn't belong, Terry."

"You don't know what you're talking about." Terry was worked up as well, sweat glistening at his temples.

"Yesterday you said that only dieting housewives eat Greek yogurt."

Terry chuckled.

"I don't need your opinion about my breakfast!"

The floodgates had opened. Greg had been the sales manager at SCS for nine long, miserable months. What he had originally envisioned as a cushy position that would allow him to explore his more libertine pursuits had become a millstone that he dragged through each part of his life. He was now the opposite of fun: haggard, overworked, riddled with anxiety, and suffering bouts of insomnia. Something had to give.

"The real issue here is that the Sales department has missed every single one of its targets. That's on you!" Terry said, with a sharply pointed finger.

"You haven't given me the tools or the time to turn things around."

"I gave you six months. That was the deal."

"I don't even have access to all the sales data. Plus, you keep shifting the goal posts. One day it's 5 percent, then it's 7 percent. I can't work with that."

"Sales are supposed to go up, not down. That's the only data you need."

"Look, I tell my team to work hard and sell more. It's not my fault if they don't."

"Yes it is!"

"You can't expect sales to go up when salespeople keep quitting."

"It's your job to keep them from quitting." Terry raised his fists to the sky. "How do you not understand this?"

Greg's hatred for Terry grew each time he opened his mouth. "They would stay if you stopped skulking around like a spy, trying to catch them in some lurid act of malfeasance."

"I'm protecting my investment." Terry's eyes were bulging in a manner that suggested a medical emergency. "Or have you forgotten I own this operation?"

"That's all we are to you—numbers on a page, not real people deserving real respect."

"You'll get my respect when you earn it."

Greg placed his hands on the back of the chair, clenched his fingers until they turned white, and flung the chair against the wall in one adrenaline-fueled motion. It crashed against a cheaply framed motivational poster so old the colors of the sunset had faded to pastel. The poster and the chair thumped to the floor. Greg didn't stop to inspect the damage.

"I quit." He stormed out, not waiting for Terry's response. He didn't even stop to collect his coffee cup and remaining containers of yogurt in the refrigerator. He stabbed his finger on the elevator down button and felt a weight lifted off his shoulders for the first time in months.

Terry's nostrils flared with each breath. His jaw clenched. He stood there, amid an empty office. The salespeople were out. Who knows where the receptionist was. Why had he ever agreed to manage this this ill-conceived business venture? It was supposed to be an easy way to pad the investors' retirement accounts, but it had brought him nothing but headaches. He'd been in sales his whole life and would have never imagined talking to a superior the way Greg had spoken to him. No sense of decency or respect.

But Greg got the last word in. A few days later, when he had finally calmed down and felt he had gained perspective, he drafted an email to Terry, compelled by his sadness and lingering sense of responsibility for those who were still stuck at SCS. He listed what he saw as the company's flaws:

- **Lack of autonomy:** Everyone feels micromanaged, like they can't even go to the bathroom without a critique.
- **No flexibility:** Salespeople require trust that they're out doing their jobs when they aren't in the office. Having to report back at certain times disrespects the way that people go about their work.
- **Poisonous office culture:** Fueled by lack of trust, everyone suspects everyone else for everything from stealing their food from the fridge to talking about them behind their backs. Every outburst of laughter ends with someone thinking that others are talking about him.
- **No confidence in the product:** Our prices are high, and our service is average to poor—nothing distinguishes it from any other company. We have no specialty which makes it hard to sell.
- **Lack of standard processes:** Everyone does their own thing, and everyone does it differently. We don't even have a template for reporting and managing sales data. This gives rise to inefficiencies.
- **Lack of competency:** The crews vary by competency and are too hampered by a lack of standardized processes.

- **Lack of training for office staff and crew members:** No one sees this as an investment in lowering the turnover rate. People want to feel like they know how to do their jobs.
- **Bad reputation:** If we're lucky, people haven't heard of us. The problems start when they have.
- **Dismal finances:** Everybody knows it.
- **No raises for two years.**
- **I repeat:** No raises for two years.
- **Everyone's looking for another job:** No one's five-year plan involves still being at SCS.
- **HR stopped listening to people eons ago:** They're just trying to get bodies in the door.
- **Accounts payable processes suck:** Trying to track something through purchasing or accounts payable is practically impossible. How does anyone even know where the money is going? More importantly, did anyone care?

Greg hit send.

Terry fumed. His fingers pounded the keyboard as he replied, flinging invectives onto a glowing screen. Two minutes later he stopped, overcome by a wave of discomfiture. Everything Greg wrote was true, and deep down it scared him to death. Terry deleted his diatribe and took out a legal pad and pen. It was time to get back to the basics.

The other partners had entrusted this operation to him because of his business acumen. It was their money he was losing, and he'd have to answer for it. He knew it was time to get serious about an improvement plan.

He wrote well into the night and even used a whiteboard to map out some of his ideas. His plan was bold, multifaceted, intended to shock a dying company back to life. He had vision, goals, a three-phase outline that would increase sales and net income. He made everyone in the company a stakeholder of an action plan for new processes. The transformation was designed to be nothing short of miraculous—the kind of case study they'd be talking about in business school for years to come. Maybe *Fortune* would even do a profile story. Eventually, Terry got it uploaded to a computer and had the receptionist draw up the slides for the presentation. He rolled it out two weeks after Greg left, with a goal of seeing concrete improvements by the end of the next month. He called it "SCS Force Majeure: A New Beginning." It was playful, and yet deadly serious. The top initiatives included:

- Drafting new HR policies regarding flexibility and a new compensation structure
- Hiring for a new position: quality control director
- Creating a task force charged with developing a new training program for salespeople and cleaning staff
- Hiring an outside consultant to redefine the corporate culture
- Implementing functional improvement teams to define standardized processes for purchasing, accounting, data entry, sales, advertising, human resources, and operations.

Terry couldn't help but marvel at his brilliance. It was the most ambitious continuous improvement initiative he'd seen in his entire career. The staff seemed a little awestruck at first. But they'd come around and figure out how to climb aboard the Change Train. SCS was going places.

Terry put in late nights. He followed up with people. He emailed, scheduled meetings, and tried to layoff his knee-jerk reaction for bad puns. He went at full throttle, going so far as to treat the whole company to a pizza lunch. And not cheap pizza, either—it was the good stuff from Romero's.

He had a spring in his step for a couple of weeks, but soon he was brought up short by Cynthia, the receptionist. "How's it going with that presentation for the partner meeting next week?" he asked.

She sighed heavily and looked up at him. "Do you want a new employee handbook, or do you want this presentation? Because you're only getting one of them today."

He did not like the tone of her voice *at all*. He lapsed into his old ways: "I want you to manage your time so you can get all your work done."

She glared at him.

"And I want you to take this company's success as seriously as I do."

"You can't just demand that people drop everything and do what you want," she said.

*Yes I can,* he thought. "Look, we have to make the partners happy," he said. "We all have to learn new ways of doing things, and being able to pivot to new processes is an important way to show you're a team player."

She mumbled something about being a team player under her breath.

"Speak up, why don't you?"

"It's not important."

"Your main priority today is the presentation."

It was time for lunch. Terry grabbed his jacket and headed out for a sandwich. When he got back, Cynthia was gone. Her bag, her coat—gone. Computer powered down. He checked his email to see if she had decided to work at home and finish the presentation, but there was nothing. In fact, practically the whole office was empty. Didn't any of them realize they were in jeopardy? Didn't they care?

Terry was in a panic. He was meeting with the partners in three days and the numbers were dismal: 26 percent of their positions were unfilled. Sales are down 18 percent each year. They had a net loss of 5.6 percent, or $1.1 million.

The partners were nonplussed. Terry explained his continuous improvement initiatives and bought himself six months. But they were very clear: If things don't turn around, they'll pull the plug.

He took the news back to the rank and file, but they failed to see the urgency of the situation. Instead of banding together to save their livelihoods, the staff appeared defeated. Nine more people left within the next month. The numbers never turned around, landing dead on arrival six months later with an additional loss of $820,000.

The scene in the conference room was brutal, and Terry felt like he was in a dream watching someone else be eviscerated in slow motion. The partners voted to liquidate the company and oust Terry from the partnership. His shares were bought out and all remaining employees were laid off. "That wasn't a continuous improvement plan," Dale said. "That was a Hail Mary, and it fell short." They never played golf together again.

The sting lasted for days, weeks even. His wife couldn't console him. He'd lost his friendships with the other partners and his career had ended on a dark note. He went over it endlessly in his mind—where had he gone wrong?

He didn't know why, exactly, but he contacted Greg, and they met at Houlihan's for what turned out to be an autopsy of SCS over a few rounds of scotch. Greg was now working for a software developer and seemed to be happy.

"What do they do differently from SCS?"

"Everything. It's just so different."

"You're still in sales?"

"It's more of a camaraderie instead of a competition. We get farther when we work together."

"That's just not how it was when I was your age."

"Plus, you can't beat the benefits."

"They give you a free gym membership or something?"

"I'm going to Aspen next week for a conference."

"They must be loaded to be throwing their money around like that."

"I'm more than a salesperson to them. I'm an asset."

Terry stared at the bottom of his empty glass. "An asset, huh? All this time I thought I was the asset."

"Continuous improvement is a cycle that's driven by the organization. Not something that can be imposed from the top at the last minute. I told you that years ago, but you didn't listen."

"We didn't need it years ago."

"Yes, you did."

## UNQUITTABLE

- Your company constantly strives to improve.
- A structured continuous improvement/Kaizen program is utilized.
- Kaizen events are not limited to process improvements. They include improvement opportunities for morale, culture, engagement, and employee development.
- Employees at all levels participate in Kaizen events.

## QUITTABLE

- Your company thinks it does everything right.
- Your company has no formal method for identifying and implementing improvements.
- Cultural improvements are not identified and focused upon.

# CHAPTER 17

# Leadership Buy-In

Let's say you don't have the ear of upper management. How do you put any of these talent tools to work? It helps if your organization has a vision, mission statement, and a good handle on strategic planning. By now, you probably know whether you're working at Big John's or FarmBerry—that alone should tell you how to proceed. That said, the best way to get buy-in is through data. Do what you can with the resources you have at hand to make your case. Explain the benefits of an initiative in terms of what problem it solves: lowering turnover, raising engagement, attracting more qualified candidates, reducing recruiting costs, reducing the cost of quality, etc. Then link it to an existing mandate—promoting good customer service, increasing market share, or differentiating the brand. Finally, connect all this to a clear financial result: boosting profits, lowering overhead, or decreasing product returns. Give them a realistic time frame to see results, but don't tell them that "it's an investment in the future." Too vague. Have a plan with dates and deliverables. Take ownership. If it's a good plan, you'll be willing to stand behind it.

Without strong leadership buy-in, your endeavor is doomed to fail, no matter how well-crafted or intentioned it may be. A friend of mine recently relayed the following story. Her first job out of college involved working in a division of about one hundred people at a 300-person company. The director of her division spent ten months rolling out an incredibly detailed reorganization that upended all one hundred people, shuffling everyone into newly created departments and splitting up well-functioning teams that were meeting all their goals. The CEO was invited to give a few words at the culminating launch event. He stood in front of the group and simply said, "I don't know why I'm here." He hadn't been involved in the reorganization in

223

any way. Needless to say, within months, that same CEO wanted a different structure that reflected his own vision. He took another ten months to set a big reorganization involving the entire company in motion; everything the division director had spent so much time and money on was undone. Needless to say, nearly two years of constant disruption and endless meetings about work flow didn't do much for morale. Turnover went up, engagement went down, and financial results languished.

At FarmBerry, a long history of good communication, mentoring, and talent development has led to an ecosystem of trust and confidence in individuals at all levels. Leadership buy-in means management acts with transparency and never gets mired in negativity. It also means empowering talented individuals and giving them opportunities to live up to their potential and advance the company at the same time. The result is a vibrant and thriving corporate culture. Conversely, at Delicious Foods, a merger has resulted in a corporate culture without focus. Leaders are more interested in their own advancement than listening to those who have the best interest of the company in mind. This mentality stymies growth and creates an "us vs. them" environment, benefiting no one.

## KUMBAYA AT FARMBERRY, INC.

Everybody kept telling Kelly that millennials were different, but she wasn't buying it. Young people of every generation want the same things. A good job with opportunities for advancement; decent pay that reflected their talent and worth to a company; and an acknowledgment from management that they are human beings with families, dogs, and plans to visit Machu Picchu. Perhaps the only thing that had changed in the past twenty years was what millennials spent their cash on—hip restaurants instead of a down payment on a four-bedroom colonial. Many were still paying off student loans rather than maxing out their 401(k) contributions, but the concept of going to work and earning a paycheck hadn't changed.

Kelly had been at FarmBerry, Inc. for seven years and had just recently been promoted to chief human resources officer, filling the spot that opened when Jan became CEO. So far, Kelly's career had been a fairy tale. She believed in the company's products—organic, fruit-based foods—and loved her coworkers. She was excited to be part of a growing company that operated ethically and created a work environment that encouraged people to thrive.

However, there was still room for improvement. The average number of days to fill an open position used to be less than twenty, but it had been steadily increasing and was now up to twenty-nine. Turnover had increased from 3 percent to 5 percent. Some employers would kill for 5 percent, but Kelly wanted that 3 percent back—it was a bragging point, proof that FarmBerry's corporate culture was admired. Kelly suspected that these increases reflected a slight dip in their employer brand, and her goal was to give it a spit shine. FarmBerry had a corporate university, annual training for all employees, and a strong commitment to teambuilding, but the specifics hadn't changed much in ten years.

She picked up the phone and called Jan. "I need your opinion."

"Is it about the new pepper jam? Because I recommend it with cream cheese and crackers."

"That sounds delicious, but it's about our numbers."

"Oh?"

"The 5 percent turnover and the twenty-nine days to fill a position."

"Yeah. We're keeping an eye on that." Jan always had an eye on the monthly talent dashboard.

"Attracting and retaining talent. We're good, but we need to be great."

"I've looked at the data upside down and backwards," Jan said. "What's your take on it?"

"We've got more competition both in our industry and in the region. Not to mention, many of our competitors are focusing on creating a great talent ecosystem. They're becoming better at fighting for talent."

Jan cut to the chase. "It's that upstart Green Grocer and their amazing guava juice."

Green Grocer was their biggest competitor nationwide. Like FarmBerry, they had their own organic farms and enviable, state-of-the-art production facilities. Their line was broader than FarmBerry's, but there was a lot of overlap. Worst of all, they were located just fifty miles away, taking advantage of the same great farmland and talent pool.

Kelly sighed. "We have lots of job applicants who also apply to Green Grocer. Their employer branding is strong. Ours needs to be stronger."

"I couldn't agree more, Kelly. Our program needs to be reimagined. Got any ideas?"

"Is there money in the budget for retooling?"

"Come up with a plan and I'll let you know."

"Give me a month."

"Thanks, Kel."

Jan trusted Kelly. In fact, Jan had been the one to hire her in an effort to improve the company's diversity, a constant issue due to FarmBerry's rural Midwest location. Kelly had been tasked with revamping their employer brand strategy to attract more diversity to the company. Kelly may have been the first person of color in the C-suite, but she surely wouldn't be the last.

Likewise, Kelly knew she had Jan's support. It wasn't just that they were friends as well as colleagues. As CEO, Jan supported all the departments at FarmBerry. It was just her style. With good people in management, Jan was free to focus on her own goals—her "Big Rocks," as she called them:

1. Maintain a great talent ecosystem to increase employee engagement and satisfaction
2. Foster innovation
3. Maintain the company's focus on healthy, organic, and delicious products

She focused on one of these Big Rocks in her monthly column for the company newsletter. Each employee defined their own Big Rocks, and both Kelly and Jan saw the concept as a useful tool for focusing on what really mattered.

Kelly's Big Rocks evinced the same philosophy as Jan's:

1. Foster a positive environment conducive to the company's growth and success
2. Foster innovation
3. Work with employees to maximize their personal and professional success

Kelly enjoyed a challenge, and she wasted no time assembling a small task force of HR associates who felt the same way. Devon and Talia were like-minded millennials, well-educated, enthusiastic, and committed to the company. Talia rode her bike to work every day, and Devon was known to launch into Motown songs when things got quiet around the office. Kelly suspected they were a couple, but it was really hard to tell—and anyway, it was none of her business as long as they remained professional, which they always did.

Thanks to an abundance of analytics and historical talent dashboards, Kelly had no problem gathering a plethora of up-to-date data. But it was Devon and Talia who headed the cross-functional group that created the revamped employer branding program outline. They prepared a presentation for company leaders at their quarterly meeting and unveiled a seven-point plan for reinvigorating the FarmBerry employer brand:

1. Update the corporate university content and delivery, including a more aggressive transition from class-based instruction to online learning. They also advocated for a speaker series open to everyone that would address topics relating to business and ideation.
2. Update their flexibility programs. Green Grocer had copied FarmBerry's significantly. Flex hours and work at home options needed to be expanded.
3. Upgrade onboarding to address millennial learning styles by developing more apps and self-paced learning programs.
4. Provide all new employees with an assigned mentor on day one.
5. Increase the tuition reimbursement program. Millennials had enough debt, but nearly all of them recognized the value of ongoing education.
6. Institute "personal project time" to increase innovation. This included an interesting "farmer's internship" with their closest organic supplier and "open hours" at the company's test kitchens.
7. Create a knowledge-capture and transfer program for all departing baby boomers that would extend beyond the typical exit interview. It would rely heavily on taped interviews and a document management system.

Kelly saw her role in the task force as that of a mentor, which was a double-edged sword. She was free to focus on her other duties, but she missed being a part of the action and the energizing brainstorming that was bonding the group together. They seemed to have a lot of inside jokes about popular culture that were lost on her, and she couldn't help but feel that the fabled generation gap was real.

Devon and Talia did a great job with the presentation. They had great communication and technical skills that allowed them to present a concise PowerPoint slide deck like the smooth operators they are. Kelly was proud of them.

When the lights went back on in the conference room, the first question was from the controller: "About the costs here on page eight…"

Kelly was ready to jump in and answer, but Devon stepped up and handled the question with aplomb: "There will be some new costs, but we also plan to roll the effort into our existing internship program this summer, leveraging one program for another and maximizing resources."

Talia chimed in, "The investment cost is recouped on the other end in terms of lower turnover rates. I invite you to check out some of our citations listed on the last page of the handout. You'll see some great statistics that reinforce our suggestions."

The controller nodded, satisfied. The conversation continued, with a few individuals diving into the weeds of the tuition reimbursement program and batting around some hypotheticals. Before too long, however, Jan weighed in.

"Great presentation, Devon and Talia. You've given us lots to think about. I see how you've taken what we do now and updated it to keep us competitive. I like that you started with specific metrics you'd like to see change and developed the program with an end goal in mind. That will help us gauge our success."

"I'd like to point out," Kelly interjected, "it was their idea to create the synergy between this program and the internship program. Not only will that keep development costs down, but also it enables us to launch the new program in a well-defined timeframe."

"I agree," Jan said. "Kelly, I'll entrust ownership of this project to your area. I know you can manage the financial aspects. However, I'd like a more formal work plan with deliverables and dates prior to launch."

"We'd be happy to help with that," Devon said.

"Oh—before I forget, I've got some resources you could use," Jan said, indicating Devon and Talia. "Stop by my office after 3:00 p.m."

It was a regular FarmBerry lovefest, the kind that Kelly knew would make more cynical executives roll their eyes and feel sick to their stomach. Kelly had worked at places like that before and knew that some leaders valued their ability to steamroll over subordinates more than their ability to create consensus. But Jan had never operated that way.

As Kelly headed back to her office, she mused that once again her theory about millennials had proven to be correct. Conventional wisdom held that their communications skills were atrocious due to an upbringing devoid of face-to-face conversation. While it was true that millennials were more adept with hashtags and tweets than she would ever be, the millennials Kelly knew were as conversant as anyone in the generations ahead of them, even if they appeared to have an unquenchable thirst for tattoos.

## THE DEVIL AT DELICIOUS FOODS

Not many men looked good in a bloodred dress shirt, but Richard wasn't just any man. Paired with a pinstripe jacket and an enviable head of hair, his shirt underscored his savvy style and branded him as a maverick in the snack food business, where most guys were considered overdressed if their shoes were tied. Richard's finely tuned, bespoke European sedan was his favorite accessory, and it was a sign of respect for the craftsmen who designed it that he donned leather driving gloves for his daily commute. Richard considered it his duty to be an aspirational figure in his employees' lives. Someone to look up to.

Richard, a former investment banker, had landed at Apple Private Equity (APE) two years ago after his marriage fell apart and he needed a fresh start. He not only gave his ex-wife the house, but also shelled out a considerable sum each month for her to raise his children. He bought a condo, a motor-cycle, and a timeshare in Bermuda. He wasn't the type to dwell on the past. Then again, he wished he could go back in time and short Steel Worth stock. He might still be dining at Peter Luger.

Through a series of inexplicable events (he didn't quite know how it happened, because he was spending all his time with lawyers and real estate agents), Richard had landed in this godforsaken, Midwest hellhole, heading a dying mom-and-pop business called Delicious Foods. The name alone drove him crazy, but it was beyond his power to change it. He knew, because he had tried.

APE acquired Delicious Foods a while ago, because that's what they did: buy and restructure failing companies, merge them with similar companies, then sell them at a profit. Mergers and Acquisitions 101. Richard had expected to stay with APE as a segment CFO, but apparently, he ticked off the wrong partner, so they sent him to fix Delicious Foods or die trying. He suspected it was Rutherford, who still held a grudge against Richard for winning the March Madness pool. Now Richard had to drive three counties over just to get his car serviced.

APE bought three other food distributors shortly after they acquired Delicious Foods. Richard was in charge of all of them from his wood-paneled office at the end of Loser Lane. All told, there were 410 employees with an annual revenue of $210 million. That's a lot of Cracker Jack and MoonPies.

It's no secret why Delicious Foods was in such bad shape when APE stepped in. Doug, the founder's son and previous president, had no idea what he was doing. He didn't have a formal business education or even a mentor, and here he was, thinking he could run a multimillion-dollar company. It's a miracle it lasted as long as it did.

A year after Richard's arrival, Delicious Foods was still limping along under the transition team. Frankly, Richard had done all the cost cutting he could, and the employees needed to step up their game if they wanted to keep their jobs. Then again, Richard didn't understand why they even wanted these jobs in the first place. If he'd been born here, he would have escaped the first chance he got. Even the municipal golf course was a joke.

Richard was surprisingly still in the office on a Friday afternoon (his tee time had been cancelled on account of rain) when he got blindsided by the HR manager. He had been successfully avoiding her and her meeting requests for months. But, at 3:07 p.m., just as he was catching up on his social media, she knocked on his door.

"Mr. Wendell, do you have a moment?"

"Hmm?" He continued scrolling through Twitter.

"I want to run a few ideas by you."

He glanced up. He didn't know her name, but he recognized her blast-from-the-past earrings. She was the third HR manager since he'd been there. "I was just getting ready to leave."

Remarkably, she took this as an invitation to enter his office.

"I prepared a report you might be interested in." She handed him a modest stack of papers, stapled in the corner.

He tossed it on the edge of his desk. "Give me the elevator pitch."

He listened to her with seriously compromised attention as he considered the following, in no particular order: Would he be able to reschedule his tee time? Should he grill steak for dinner? When could he fit a car detailing into his schedule? Nevertheless, he caught the gist of her speech: high turnover rate, unfilled job positions, yadda yadda.

"There's so much we don't know about these trends," he heard her say, after deciding on bratwurst instead of steak. "We could use analytics software and some metrics training to really get a handle on the talent issue."

*The talent issue.* It was an odd phrase. Richard was a numbers guy, and he knew the numbers didn't look so hot. But *talent* sounded like a group of high school theater kids who wanted to put on a play. It didn't seem relevant to the company's situation.

The HR manager finally stopped speaking, and Richard looked up. "Thanks for your insight. We'll look into it."

"Would you like me to forward the report to anyone else?"

"This is good," he said, nodding at the hard copy on his desk.

"I'd be happy to talk about it at the next APE conference call," she offered.

"That's generous of you. I'll let you know." Richard nodded his head to indicate that he was done with her. She still stood there. "Thanks for your time."

"Okay." She looked like she was gearing up for another spiel.

"Bye now." He picked up the phone, as if he had an important call to make.

"I'll follow up later." Then she turned and left.

Richard stood up from behind his desk and shut the door. It should never have been open in the first place.

*Sweetie…Candy…Petunia…*her name was on the tip of his tongue. He glanced at the papers she left as he swept them into the trash. *Cookie!* That was it.

People like Cookie never understood that business was a numbers game. Her kind were always yammering about how "people are our best assets," but that wasn't how things really worked. Delicious Foods had managed to temporarily stay afloat due to APE's acquisitions strategy, but they were deep in the red now. People could talk about "low morale" all they wanted, but Richard guaranteed that morale would go through the roof once the company started turning a profit again. When the company makes money, everyone's happy. That's just how business worked.

Richard was pulling into the parking lot the following Monday when he saw an ambulance and a police car near the loading dock, lights flashing. He pulled over immediately and called the receptionist. He didn't want to get any closer to the building in case it was an active shooter.

"Good morning, Mr. Wendell," the receptionist greeted him, as per usual.

"What's going on over there? I see an ambulance and a police car."

"There's a situation in the warehouse. I believe it's under control."

"Thanks." Click. Must be those Neanderthals in shipping, he thought. He never went back there if he could avoid it, and he usually could.

Turns out a supervisor and one of his direct reports had settled a disagreement the old-fashioned way—in the parking lot. One man went to grab a rifle from his truck after a couple of blows, when the other body slammed him against the vehicle. There was blood, a concussion, and loss of consciousness. Cookie's email to Richard included a full report, assurance that both idiots (she didn't use the term) had been fired, and a guarantee that there would be no legal action against Delicious Foods or APE.

But Cookie kept sending emails, with subject lines like "Sensitivity Training" and "How to De-escalate Situations." Richard had to humor her because the brass at APE had caught wind of the situation and demanded he address it. Cookie scheduled separate trainings for general employees and managers. The cost of the consultants made Richard livid. Why couldn't those guys have just saved it for a bar like normal people?

Now, Cookie was pestering him with emails about the consequences of low morale when all she should really be doing is hiring less pugnacious people.

Cookie was in an awful dilemma—she'd hit a brick wall with Richard Wendell. The numbers were alarming: It now took her department an average of sixty-seven days to fill a job opening. Turnover was through the roof. No one had received a raise in four years. Everyone was working overtime whether they wanted to or not, and everyone was frazzled. Should she go over Richard's head to the APE executives? On one hand, Cookie wanted the resources to change such a desperate situation; on the other, she couldn't sufficiently quantify the issues and clarify what she needed. Richard wouldn't like it if she went over his head, but she felt a duty to fight for everyone she knew at Delicious Foods. She was literally sick to her stomach and losing sleep.

Cookie had tried reason and statistics. Materials management was a sham and resulted in expensive errors that made customers angry. Back orders were at record numbers. And now, one concussion later, the VP of Warehousing was getting on her to fill the supervisor position pronto. She knew several perfect candidates for the position in her own family, but she would never recommend they apply. In fact, she wanted to tell the candidates who interviewed for any position to turn around, run, and never look back.

The final straw was when Colin quit without even having another job lined up. Her most trusted HR manager was out the door without even giving a two weeks' notice, embarking on a new adventure as the primary caregiver for his two children. Cookie was so envious she considered not even making him a cake for his going away party, but she finally relented because it was only fair that he have fond memories of his final moments at Delicious Foods.

The following Monday morning, she flicked on the light in her office only to find Richard sitting in her chair. "I looked through that plan you left on my desk a couple weeks ago."

She placed her coat over her visitor's chair. "And?"

"You know we don't have the money for any of those initiatives."

At this point, Cookie was both livid and tired of the struggle. She threw her keys on the desk. "It feels like I'm the only one trying to save this company. You want it to fail."

Richard's face morphed into an expression of surprise. "You need to hire better people."

Anger bubbled up inside Cookie, and she stepped toward his stupid feet on her desk. "You need to give me something to work with!"

"You've had plenty of time to make things work."

"You really expect me to work miracles? You're paying below-market wages in an area with nearly full employment."

"I expect you to work harder," said the man whose feet were still on her desk.

"I have a full agenda today, between meetings, and interviews, and listening to people tell me they need extra time off for their grandmothers' funerals. I'm working plenty hard. What I don't have are the resources to offer people what they deserve."

It didn't matter what she said—Richard was never going to bend. He stood up slowly, hands in his pockets, and made his way out the door. He paused and turned around. "You're on notice."

Cookie wanted to scream! A bloodcurdling cry that would unleash the fury locked in her gut. Instead, she pounded her desk and counted to five. Then fifteen. She took deep breaths and paced, her mind racing.

When her heart rate was back down in the normal range, Cookie reached for the phone. It was time to do what she should have done a long time ago—find a new job. She dialed her friend Kelly at FarmBerry, Inc. It would be a pleasure to trade junk food for something more wholesome.

## UNQUITTABLE

- Corporate culture starts at the top. If you're trying to change culture, leadership must be bought-in. The desired changes will not take hold otherwise.
- The CEO must genuinely value an aspirational culture.
- Gain leadership buy-in by speaking a leader's language. It helps to relate an initiative to a financial impact on sales or profitability. Find out what leadership wants and frame your discussion in those terms.

- The CHRO thinks strategically and is considered one of the key leaders within the organization.
- The CHRO actively promotes a high-quality talent ecosystem to all other corporate leaders.

## QUITTABLE

- The CEO doesn't understand the power of a strong, engaged team and/ or maintains power by isolating individuals and ruling through fear.
- Leaders are not intentional about the design and implementation of the organization's culture or talent ecosystem.
- Leaders do not reinforce the organization's core values through words or actions.

# Conclusion

## PUTTING IT ALL TOGETHER: THE TALENT ECOSYSTEM

The unquittable organization is constantly evolving. It's a dynamic system that welcomes input, adapts to new situations, and generates ideas. Talented individuals use their existing abilities, develop new skills, and are recognized for the value they bring to the customers, bottom line, organization's culture, and each other.

The tools in each of these chapters are useful on their own for addressing a specific need. Taken together, they become something more powerful—a talent ecosystem. It's tempting to dip into your toolbox, select the right tool for the right job, and then pack it away again. But the intelligent organization constantly uses these tools to create a vibrant workplace that attracts, retains, and develops top talent.

In the talent ecosystem, all the elements work together to create a functioning whole. Some elements may be more robust than others, but all are present and accounted for in a significant way. For example, using attraction tools without also using retention tools won't make you an unquittable organization. You can't have great compensation and benefits with outdated policies and think you're winning the war for talent.

The talent ecosystem needs to be measured. What are you going to do, invest in these techniques and then hope for the best? No—you're going to monitor the situation and make sure the ecosystem is nourished and remains healthy. Good metrics include morale and engagement scores, retention rates, number of days to fill a job, etc. Regular measurements mean you'll know where the trouble spots are before they even appear. Think about when you go to the doctor and get your vital signs checked. They're compared to a baseline and provide crucial diagnostic information. Without good statistics, the talent ecosystem is just a feeling.

If you're creating your talent ecosystem from scratch by drafting a framework and finding new ways to manage talent, you're going to need people and time. Broad-based efforts create buy-in, and they take time, usually two to five years. Keep the faith.

## CORE COMPETENCIES

A vigorous talent ecosystem goes hand in hand with a suite of core competencies. A core competency is a skill you've creatively approached and mastered, something you consider your area of expertise. Each organization should have a well-defined array of core competencies, things you do extremely well that, in some cases, distinguish you from your competitors: sales, operations, financial reporting. Anything you do deliberately, intentionally, and skillfully. This collection will obviously include your organization's product or service, but it also needs to include an internal core competency for talent management. I believe that this will be critical in the future war for talent. Companies that lack this core competency will struggle to survive.

## ONE FINAL STORY

As a talent strategy consultant, I was tasked with helping a company (let's call it Kenwall Construction) turn their marginally performing business around. More specifically, the company was unable to grow due to issues with attracting and retaining talent. Without the necessary personnel, the company was stuck in the doldrums. Kenwall was typical of the industry—its workforce was overwhelmingly comprised of young men with lots of testosterone. Foul language hung in the air, and incentives and respect were in short supply. People would come and go quickly due to a lack of career paths, so management was unable to gain any traction in growing the company. They were always scrambling for entry-level talent. Where would you start?

We knew we needed to create a great place to work, one with an employer brand and culture. My team first assessed the current situation, and then started with intentionally designing core values. We worked with the CEO to create a vision for the company. Think about it—most construction companies are focused on building things. It's simple. But we had to go against the mold and get a bit touchy-feely to expand the corporate culture.

The resulting core values were threefold. First, the CEO became determined to "do what's right for the employees." This was his single core value that he owned. Next, the employees were entrusted to "do what's right for the customer," and finally, to "take care of each other." These core values became the backbone of an intentionally designed culture.

The CEO implemented Monday morning staff meetings early on in the process. This was his opportunity to share information and successes with the team and foster a group dynamic. Staff members could also nominate each other as "cultural champions" at the meetings and recognize those who exemplified their new core values or performed a good deed the previous week. These champions were awarded $50 gift cards. More than once, a team member nominated someone for calling out an unsafe practice, thereby keeping their coworkers out of harm's way. Rewarding positive behaviors makes it more likely they'll be repeated in the future. Little by little, this trickle-down accountability and reinforcement created a positive corporate culture that had a long-term impact on attracting and retaining talent.

## ONE FINAL, FINAL STORY

We were consulting for a company that was a parts supplier, and many of its positions were in the warehouse. The turnover rate for those jobs was through the roof. You might think: Who wants to work in a warehouse their whole life? And that was the point. The company wasn't presenting these employees with viable career paths (ladders and lattices), so if they weren't interested in working in the warehouse, they left for greener pastures. We worked with leadership to create and promote career lattices that allowed individuals starting out in the warehouse to move onward and upward to other areas of the company. The key was making sure that new hires were aware of their long-term options from the start. Once the career paths were implemented and communicated, turnover levels began to drop considerably.

It was also crucial to work with people to determine their skills and interests. Those who liked numbers were encouraged to join the Inventory team, while people-oriented individuals were recommended sales positions. A career sculpting program improved both retention and engagement, and over time, more employees were working within positions they enjoyed. Everyone benefited! The company's leadership might have thought that making job and career transitions was obvious, but it wasn't to the young people starting out.

We also worked with the CEO to devise a plan for reinforcing adaptive, constructive behavior and discouraging unwanted behaviors. This resulted in a safer, more productive warehouse, and those on the team were then well-positioned to become productive, long-term employees throughout the company. Each of the minor changes improved the company's overall talent ecosystem. Today, this company is on its way to becoming a great place to work, and maybe someday it'll be considered unquittable!

## GO FORTH AND BECOME UNQUITTABLE!

Reading this book already makes you part of the solution and an asset for your organization. As you move through your career, it helps to always think of people in terms of their talents and untapped potential. Include yourself in that, and you'll become an integral part of a thriving talent ecosystem.

# Endnotes

## INTRODUCTION

1. "Company History," Toyota USA Newsroom, accessed December 2, 2019, https://pressroom.toyota.com/company-history/.
2. "1974 Toyota Corolla TE Prices and Values," NADAguides, accessed December 2, 2019, https://www.nadaguides.com/Cars/1974/Toyota/Corolla-TE/2-Door-Sedan/Values; Dan Neil, "The 50 Worst Cars of All Time," Time, Time Inc., September 7, 2007, http://content.time.com/time/specials/2007/article/0,28804,1658545_1658498_1657866,00.html.
3. "Volvo," Consumer Reports, accessed December 2, 2019, https://www.consumerreports.org/cars/volvo/.
4. "Baldrige FAQs: Baldrige Award Recipients," NIST, last modified November 15, 2019, https://www.nist.gov/baldrige/baldrige-faqs-baldrige-award-recipients.
5. "History," Singer Sewing Company, accessed December 2, 2019, https://www.singer.com/history.
6. "The Tale Of How Blockbuster Turned Down An Offer To Buy Netflix For Just $50M," GQ, September 19, 2019, https://www.gq.com.au/entertainment/film-tv/the-tale-of-how-blockbuster-turned-down-an-offer-to-buy-netflix-for-just-50m/news-story/72a55db245e4d7f70f099ef6a0ea2ad9; Christopher Harress, "The Sad End Of Blockbuster Video: The Onetime $5 Billion Company Is Being Liquidated As Competition From Online Giants Netflix And Hulu Prove All Too Much For The Iconic Brand," International Business Times, December 5, 2013, https://www.ibtimes.com/sad-end-blockbuster-video-onetime-5-billion-company-being-liquidated-competition-1496962.
7. Heather Long, "America Has a Record 7.1 Million Job Openings, Making It an Especially Advantageous Time to Ask for a Raise," The Washington Post, October 16, 2018, https://www.washingtonpost.com/business/2018/10/16/america-has-record-million-job-openings-making-it-an-especially-advantageous-time-ask-raise/; Associated Press, "The U.S. Now Has More Open Jobs Than Job Seekers," CBS News, June 5, 2018, https://www.cbsnews.com/news/the-u-s-now-has-more-open-jobs-than-job-seekers/.
8. Mitra Toossi, "Labor force projections to 2024: the labor force is growing, but slowly," Monthly Labor Review, U.S. Bureau of Labor Statistics, December 2015, https://doi.org/10.21916/mlr.2015.48; Associated Press, "The U.S. Has 1 Million More Job Openings Than Unemployed Workers," CBS News, March 15, 2019, https://www.cbsnews.com/news/the-u-s-has-1-million-more-job-openings-than-unemployed-workers/; Eric Morath, "U.S. Job Openings Topped 7 Million for the First Time," The Wall Street Journal, October 16, 2018, https://www.wsj.com/articles/u-s-job-openings-topped-7-million-this-summer-1539702755.

9. Áine Cain, "Costco employees share the 7 best parts of working at the retail chain with a cult-like following," Business Insider, April 3, 2018, https://www.businessinsider.com/costco-jobs-best-part-2018-4#the-majority-of-workers-said-that-pay-benefits-and-job-security-are-a-huge-draw-1; Abigail Hess, "McDonald's Is Tripling Its College Tuition Benefit for Employees," CNBC make it, CNBC, April 4, 2018, https://www.cnbc.com/2018/04/03/mcdonalds-is-tripling-its-college-tuition-benefit-for-employees.html; Michael Stallard, "Why Culture Makes Costco America's Best Employer," ATD, October 12, 2017, https://www.td.org/insights/why-culture-makes-costco-americas-best-employer; "McDonald's Sets Global Goal to Reduce Barriers to Employment for Two Million Youth," The Aspen Institute, August 22, 2018, https://www.aspeninstitute.org/of-interest/mcdonalds-sets-global-goal-to-reduce-barriers-to-employment-for-two-million-youth/; Liza Featherstone, "Wage Against the Machine: If Costco's Worker Generosity Is So Great, Why Doesn't Wal-Mart Imitate It?" Slate, June 27, 2008, http://www.slate.com/articles/business/moneybox/2008/06/wage_against_the_machine.html.

# CHAPTER 1

1. Eric Morath, "U.S. Job Openings Topped 7 Million for the First Time," The Wall Street Journal, October 16, 2018, https://www.wsj.com/articles/u-s-job-openings-topped-7-million-this-summer-1539702755.

# CHAPTER 10

1. "Majority of U.S. Employers Support Workplace Flexibility," WorldatWork, October 5, 2015, https://www.worldatwork.org/docs/worldatworkpressreleases/2015/majority-of-us-employers-support.html.

2. Jessica Howington, "80% of Companies Offer Flexible Work Options," FlexJobs, October 27, 2015, https://www.flexjobs.com/blog/post/80-companies-offer-flexible-work-options/.

3. Howington.

# CHAPTER 15

1. Tomas Chamorro-Premuzic, "Does Money Really Affect Motivation? A Review of the Research," Harvard Business Review, April 10, 2013, https://hbr.org/2013/04/does-money-really-affect-motiv.

2. Chamorro-Premuzic.

3. Chamorro-Premuzic.

# Index

## Symbols

5S process  210
360-degree review  141, 151
401(k) plans  6, 45

## A

absences  140
  unscheduled  128
absenteeism  7
abundance, philosophy of  158, 194
accountants  3, 31
accounting  76, 179
  system  146
accounts payable  217
accusations  101
acquisitions  187, 232
action plans  157, 182
  individual  150, 157
adjustments in compensation  202
advancement
  career  137
  opportunities  11, 98
advertising  17, 36, 83
agriculture  42
Airbnb  61
American Dream  195
analytics with people. See people analytics;
  talent dashboard
annual reviews  84, 88, 138
Apple  113
apprenticeships  7
Arizona  104
The Art of War  209
Aruba  63, 66
aspirational employer brand. See employer
  branding
assets  84
attracting talent  1, 69, 136
  career development  16, 18

mission statements  20
recruiting  24
auditors  159
autonomy  56, 69, 216

## B

baby boomer  xvii
Back Bay  63
background checks  51
back orders  233
balance sheet  199
balance, work-life  2, 7
  exit interviews regarding  119
  flexibility and  125, 127
banking, mortgage  14
bankruptcy  177
base pay  62, 111
  incentives and  57
behavior
  correction  151
  desired  56
benefits, employment. See employee benefits
black swan  190
Blockbuster  xv
Blue Grotto  86
Bonneville Salt Flats  86
bonuses  198
  attracting talent using  11, 101
  compensation systems  118, 189
  performance management  143
  referral  55, 57, 66
  signing  11
Boston  64, 66
bottom line  183, 237
  employer branding and  22
  internships and  27
  mentoring and  155
  people analytics and  181
brand
  corporate  173
  reputation  116

branding. *See also* employer branding
  product 11, 19
break room 48
budgets 49, 87, 176
  corporate universities and 123
  mentoring and 153
Buick 86
Bureau of Labor Statistics 189
business
  development 89
  family owned 49
  margins 181
  model 24
  plan 135
  strategy 146
  trajectory 150
buy-in leadership 223, 224–236, 238
  quittable 235
  unquittable 234

# C

California 35, 63
Camus, Albert 12
candidate
  attraction 113
  database 14
capitalism 55
career development 103
  attracting talent and 16, 18
  employee performance and 137
  flexibility and 130
  internships and 27
  pathways 75
career ladders 43
  onboarding and 49
  pathways and 69
career pathways 52, 80, 98
  corporate universities 113
  incentive systems and 56
  lattices and ladders 69, 80
  quittable 81
  sculpting and 83
  strategic workforce planning and 171
  turnover and 239
  unquittable 80
career sculpting 83–96
  coaching vs. 83, 95
  mission statements and 87
  pathways and 83
  quittable 95
  retention and 239

retirement and 90
  strategic workforce planning 171
  unquittable 95
Caribbean 64
cash cow 145
cash flow 197
CFO (chief financial officer) 197, 209
chief financial officer (CFO) 197, 209
chief servant leader 193
childcare 125, 189
CI. *See* continuous improvement (CI)
citizenship 15
clients 38
climate. *See* economic climate
coaching 141, 151
  career sculpting vs. 83, 95
  mentoring and 156
  performance management and 137, 140
collaboration 144
  mentoring and 163
  performance management and 137
commission 57, 62, 65
  compensation systems and 189
  incentives and 55, 56
communication(s) 38, 69
  corporate universities 123
  flexibility 136
  improving 80
  mentoring 153
  techniques 129
community 15
  outreach 12
company
  car 189
  culture 11. *See also* corporate culture
  diversity 226
  dress policies 140
  goals 113
  growth 29
  loyalty 58, 74, 80
  systems 42
  trust within 126
compensation 237. *See also* base pay; bonuses; perks; raises
  commission and 189
  comparative study 199
  decisions 138
  employer branding and 190, 192
  goals and 199

quittable 202
salaries and 189
systems 189–190
unquittable 202
competencies, core 238
competition 34, 201
amongst coworkers 67
incentives and 65
noncompete clauses 135
performance management and 137,
144
computer science 179
conflict of interest 135
continuous improvement (CI) 140, 205
plan 25
program 25, 220
quittable 221
teams 19
unquittable 220
contractors 159
contract terms 141
control 136
copywriters 83
core competencies 238
core values 87, 239
corporate universities and 123
employer branding and 13, 15
incentives for 56, 59
mentoring and 157
onboarding and 41, 42, 52
performance management of 147, 151
corporate brand 173. *See also* branding
corporate culture 119, 224, 237. *See
also* culture; trust, culture of
corporate universities and 122
employer branding and 20, 24
exit interviews and 112
flexibility within 125
onboarding and 41, 42, 52
toxic 118, 208
corporate universities 113, 113–124
career pathways and 113
communications 123
core values and 123
customer service and 123
goals and 113
leadership buy-in 225
millennials and 113
people analytics 182
quittable 123
strategic workforce planning 171

unquittable 122
corporations
multinational 167
shareholders 197
stockholders 167
Cost Competition Failwave xiv–xv
costs 175
COVID-19 xviii
coworkers 67, 141
Cozumel 13
cross-training 121, 127
culture 190, 216. *See also* corporate culture;
trust, culture of
aspirational 113
corporate 52, 125, 208
destination 169
*The Curious Leader* 86
customers
internal 12
needs 125
customer service 62, 64, 193
corporate universities and 123
employer branding and 15
exit interviews and 98
flexibility and 133
incentive systems 57, 59

# D

damages 71
dashboard, talent 171, 173, 181, 183
data, qualifiable 213
DDOS attack 16
deadlines 128
delegation 163
deliverables 34, 171, 228
Deloitte 113
desired behavior 56
destination culture 169
development
business 89
career 137. *See also* career
development
employee 9, 158
professional 95, 113
direct deposit form 51
directing, management style 163
discussing, management style 163
Disney World 5, 7

disruptions in production 167
diversification 171
diversity 226
dividend, suspended 197
documentation 136
dress policies 140
drug use 48

**E**

earnings 197
economic climate 11
    downturns in 167
economics 37
    free market 55
ecosystem, talent 187, 205, 237
education 7. *See also* corporate universities
    class-based instruction 227
    ongoing 227. *See also* learning
    teachers 125
EEOC (Equal Employment Opportunity
    Commission) 5, 134
efficiency 142
electricians 7
elevator pitch 23, 231
employee benefits 6, 195, 237
    compensation systems 189, 195
    fringe 56, 77
    incentives 55–56
    onboarding 41
employee handbook 50, 218
employee Net Promoter Score (eNPS).
    *See* eNPS
employees
    development of 9, 103, 158
    engagement 136, 180, 212, 213, 239
    evaluation 138
    experience 24
    full-time 103, 180
    goals 113
    performance 137
    recognition 19–20, 43, 55
    satisfaction 192
    talent vs. xiii
employer branding 8, 11–25, 202, 225, 226
    aspirational 25
    bottom line 22
    career paths and 80
    compensation and 190, 192
    continuous improvement and 209

corporate universities and 113
customer service 15
exit interviews and 97
incentives and 56
internships and 27
people analytics and 187
problems 17–23
quittable 25
strategic workforce planning 169
successful 12–16
unquittable 24–25
employers 1
    promotion 25
employment benefits. *See* benefits,
    employment
empowerment 43, 153, 224
engagement. *See* employees, engagement
engineering 79, 179
engineers 3, 170
eNPS (employee Net Promoter Score) 19,
    114, 187, 213
entry level positions 49, 118
Equal Employment Opportunity
    Commission (EEOC) 5, 134
error, margin of 130
evaluation, employee 138
exit interviews 97–112, 145, 227
    continuous improvement and 211
    corporate universities and 119
    customer service 98
    growth 103
    performance management and 145
    quittable 112
    recruiting 104, 110
    unquittable 112
expansion 170
expectations 137
expenses 42, 65, 146
experience 27
external motivators 194

**F**

facilities 6
failwaves xiv–xvi
Farrell, Colin 105
feedback 55, 137
FIFA World Cup 104
FIT (Functional Improvement Team) 43
five-year plan 217

flat management structure  83
flex hours  227
flexibility  125, 136, 181, 216
    career development  130
    communication  136
    customer service  133
    program  227
    programs  136
    quittable  136
    in scheduling  11, 12, 189
    unquittable  136
flow, cash  197
flow charts  139
Ford Motor Company  xiv
*Fortune*  3, 217
foundation, organizational  153
full-time employees  103, 180
Functional Improvement Team (FIT)  43
futurists  3

**G**

gaps
    generation  228
    skills  173
General Electric (GE)  113
General Motors (GM)  11
gift, parting  112
GM (General Motors)  11
goals  13
    compensation and  199
    corporate universities  113
    expansion  170
    mentoring  157
    sales  134
Google  11, 87
graphic designers  14
group involvement  14
growth  133, 169
    career paths and  69
    employee  9
    exit interviews and  103
    performance management  150
    potential  47
    sculpting and  83, 95
    strategic workforce planning  168
grunt work  39

**H**

hands-on management style  143

harassment  101
health insurance  75
hierarchy  44
    flattened  43
high-level summary  142
hiring  104, 110. *See also* quotas
    people analytics and  183
    process  22, 49
    strategic workforce planning and  167
holiday bonuses  11, 118. *See
        also* compensation
hospitality  46, 50
    career pathways and  74–75
hostile takeover  197
hours
    lunch  212
    recording  41
    time tracking  42
Houston  88
HR
    department  47
    industry  6
    management  5, 7
    sensitivity training  103
    stats, vital  212

**I**

IBM  11
improvement, continuous. *See* continuous
        improvement (CI)
incentives  55–68, 62. *See also* bonuses;
        compensation
    career pathways and  56
    commission and  55
    compensation systems  194, 200, 203
    competition and  65
    motivators  194
    performance management  146
    programs  58
    recruiting and  51, 66
    salaries and  62
    successful  56–60, 66–67
    systems  55–56
    unsuccessful  60, 67
income statement  192
Indiana  88
Indianapolis Motor Speedway  38
individual action plans  150, 157
informal work arrangements  125
infractions  140, 151

innovation 10, 227
    career pathways 78
    compensation 194
    employer branding 14
    onboarding 43
    strategic workforce planning 169
in-office staff 125
institutional knowledge 153
    mentoring and 166
insubordination 214
insurance 193
    unemployment 186
intangibles 202
internal customers 12
internships 3, 27–40, 37, 228
    attracting talent 15
    bottom line and 27
    career development and 27
    incentive systems 56
    onboarding and 35
    quittable 39
    strategic workforce planning 171
    unquittable 39
interpersonal skills 142
interviews 4, 30. *See also* exit interviews
    onboarding 47
    people analytics 183
    prescreen 14
    strategic workforce planning 176
inventory 71, 99
investigations, workplace 101
invoicing 41
Italy 86

**J**
job
    applicants 8, 183
    applications 50, 212
    blue-collar 129
    descriptions 83, 94, 95, 168, 173
    evolution 194
    full-time 44
    market 1, 8
    offer 41
    openings 49, 118, 183
    people-oriented 179
    postings 11, 49
    requirements 125
    satisfaction 83, 180
    security 211
    seekers 1, 8, 11, 12

justifiable termination 141

**K**
Kaizen 205
knowledge
    capture 227
    transfer 170, 181

**L**
labor market 49, 177
ladder, career 49, 69, 80, 239
lattice, career 69, 80, 239
lawsuits 5, 71
layoffs 178
leadership 12, 34, 142. *See also* buy-in
    leadership
    quittable 235
    unquittable 234
leadership, buy-in 224–235
leads 146, 150
learning. *See also* education; corporate
    universities
    curve 44
    online 227
    self-paced 227
    styles 227
leisure 125. *See also* work-life balance
line item 199
living wages 19, 55. *See also* pay; salaries
logistics 72
losses 177. *See also* damages
loyalty 74, 80, 137, 192

**M**
mail carriers 125
management 48, 129, 167. *See
    also* performance management
    hands-on 143
    materials 206, 233
    structure, flat 83
    styles 163
    training 110
manuals, policy 1
manufacturing 10, 79
margins 99, 104, 148, 181
    of error 130
market
    demands 63

job 1
marketing 23, 36, 37, 41, 43, 168. *See also* employer branding
materials management 206, 233
system 185
maternity leave 154
McDonalds 113
meaningful work 39
medical coverage 118
meetings 128
skip-level 109, 212
mental and physical well-being 136
mentoring
bottom line 155
budgets and 153
coaching vs. 156
collaboration because of 163
core values 157
mission statements and 157
mentorship 153–166, 156, 227
career paths and 79
incentives and 59
institutional knowledge 166
internships and 39
onboarding and 44, 52
people analytics 182
performance management and 142, 146
quittable 166
sculpting and 83
successful 154
unquittable 165
unsuccessful 171
mergers 179, 206, 224, 230
millennials xix, 88, 224
attracting 12
corporate universities 113
education and 7
minimum wage 49, 51
corporate universities 118
Minnesota 36
mission statements 104
attracting talent 20
career sculpting 87
exit interviews and 100
mentoring 157
onboarding 42, 46
performance management and 147, 150
morale 212, 213

compensation and 197
continuous improvement and 205
people analytics and 179, 182, 185
performance management and 148
mortgage banking 14
motivation 189. *See also* compensation; incentives
internal 194
types of motivators 194
Muir, John 209
multinational corporations 167

**N**
needs, customer 125
Netflix xv
networking 38, 89
new hires 21, 43
New York 35
noncompete clause 135
nurses 125

**O**
objectives, SMART 157, 158
occupancy rate 197
office work 8
Oklahoma 86, 88
onboarding 41–54
attracting talent and 11
career ladders and 49
core values 41–42
core values and 52
innovation 43
internships and 35
interviews 47
mission statements 42, 46
quittable 52
recruiting and 41, 49
unquittable 52
onsite childcare 189
openings, job 49, 118, 183
optics 213
ordinances 193
organizational foundations 153
Orlando, FL 2
outreach, community 12
overhead 65
overtime 49, 104, 207. *See also* compensation

# P

paid time off (PTO) 134, 202. *See also* compensation
pandemic xviii
paperwork 42
part-time
  employees 103, 180
  jobs 3, 49
pay
  ceiling 84
  cuts 48
  grades 115
  scale 175
  structure 94, 110
paychecks 71, 189
payday 12, 144
pay-for-performance 194
payroll 5, 50
  time tracking 42
PDCA (plan, do, check, act) cycle 207
people analytics 179–188, 183
  corporate universities and 182
  employer branding and 187
  hiring and 183
  interviews 183
  quittable 188
  recruiting 183
  retirement 181
  unquittable 187
people problems 185
performance
  attraction 69
  awards 55
  improvement 140
  reviews 145, 147, 171, 189, 202
performance management 137, 137–152, 147
  coaching 137, 140
  core values 147, 151
  growth 150
  incentives and 146
  mission statements and 147, 150
  promotions 139
  quittable 151–152
  salaries and 151
  system 137
  unquittable 151
perks 11, 15, 193, 202. *See also* compensation
  unexpected 193
personality tests 44, 157

personnel
  files 94
  issues 101
philosophy
  of abundance 158, 194
  of scarcity 158, 194
physical well-being 136
pitching 36, 56
  elevator 23, 231
Pixar 113
plan, do, check, act (PDCA) cycle 207
planning
  financial 178
  strategic 139
  succession 172
  workforce 206
plans
  continuous improvement 205
  five-year 217
  individual action 150, 157, 182
plumbers 1, 7
poaching 98, 136
policy
  dress 140
  manuals 1
  violations of 140
pool of talent 11, 225
positive reinforcement 158
prescreening 13–14
pricing 63
problems
  people 185
  solving 142
product
  branding 11, 19
  safety 46
production 167
productivity 8, 125, 136
professional development 95, 113
profits 177
promotions 119, 144
  career pathways 78, 81
  corporate universities and 114
  exit interviews and 98
  flexibility and 130
  performance management 139
  related failures 113
PTO (paid time off) 134, 202. *See also* compensation

punctuation  83

## Q

quality control  41, 44, 213
Quality Failwave  xiv
quarterly reports  42
quittable organizations. *See also* unquittable
    organizations
    career pathways  81
    career sculpting  95
    compensation systems  202
    continuous improvement  221
    corporate universities  123
    employer branding  25
    exit interviews  112
    flexibility  136
    incentives  67
    internships  39
    leadership buy-in  235
    mentoring  166
    onboarding  52
    people management  188
    performance management  151–152
    strategic workforce planning  178
quotas  7, 66, 134. *See also* hiring

## R

raises  57, 137, 144
ranking, salary  195
recession  xix
recognition, employee  19–20, 43, 55
recruiting  175
    attracting talent and  24
    exit interviews and  104, 110
    incentives and  57, 66
    mentoring and  153
    onboarding and  41, 49
    people analytics and  183
    strategic workforce planning and  168
referral program  59, 66
reimbursements  146
    tuition  172
relationships, cross-departmental  159
release to the market  151
reorganization  223
replacement  170
reporting  42
reputation  9, 217
    attracting talent and  11

effect of  18
research
    and development  69
    internal and external  24
restructuring  212
results-orientation  137
resumes  12, 18
retention  1, 237, 239. *See also* turnover
    career pathways and  81
    corporate universities and  113
    flexibility and  130, 136
    incentives and  55, 58
    mentoring and  158
    people analytics  179, 180
    sculpting and  239
    strategic workforce planning and  167
retirement  6, 8
    career sculpting and  90
    people analytics and  181
    strategic workforce planning and  170,
        172
retooling  226
retraining  104
return on investment  56
revenue  177, 199
reviews  84, 88
    360-degree  141
    annual  138
    check-ins vs.  138
right to self-expression  140
rollout  153
rotational opportunities  80
roundtable talks  20

## S

safety violations  141
salaries  6. *See also* compensation
    compensation and  189
    corporate universities and  122
    incentives and  62
    performance management and  151
    ranking  195
    starting  19
sales  8, 33
    goals  134
    incentives and  56, 59, 61
sales, outside  78, 132
San Francisco  66
satisfaction, employee  192

scarcity, philosophy of 158, 194
scheduling 74, 121
    flexible 11, 12
sculpting, career 83, 239
    career pathways and 83
    growth 83, 95
secretaries 4
self-determination 55
self-expression, right to 140
self-paced learning 227
self-starters 27, 62
seniority 71, 72
service 56
shadowing 121. *See also* mentoring
shipping and receiving 70
sick leave 103, 131, 136
Silicon Valley 61, 63
sink or swim mentality 42
skills. *See also* corporate universities
    assessment 121
    development 81
    gaps 170, 173
    interpersonal 142
skillsets 8
skip-level meetings 109, 212
SMART objectives 157, 158
social events 212
social media 37, 38, 56
    employer branding and 25, 117
    internships and 33, 36
    mentoring and 159
    sculpting and 88
software developers 3
sous chefs 3
speaker
    guest 3
    series 227
splash page 213
staffing 129
    in-office 125
standardization 216
start date 41
starting salary 19. *See also* compensation
statistics, importance of 237
stocks, daytrading of 64
strategic
    management 163

planning 139. *See also* strategic
    workforce planning (SWP)
    thinking 139
strategic workforce planning (SWP) 167,
    170, 182
    career pathways 171
    corporate universities 171
    growth 168
    hiring and 167
    internships 171
    interviews 176
    quittable 178
    retention and 167
    retirement 167
    unquittable 178
strategy 146, 174
    acquisitions 232
    compensation 202
    performance management and 137,
        150
    talent 153
    talent development 155
    talent management 69
    workforce planning 167, 178. *See
        also* strategic workforce planning
        (SWP)
strengths, weaknesses, opportunities, and
    threats (SWOT) analysis 211
structure 170
substance abuse 50
succession planning 172, 178
summary, high-level 142
Super Bowl 75
suppliers 181
supply chain 209
suspended dividend 197
SWOT analysis 211
SWP (strategic workforce planning).
    *See* strategic workforce planning
system, performance management 137

## T

takeover, hostile 197
talent 2, 7, 81, 205, 231. *See also* attracting
    talent; talent dashboard
    corporate universities and 113, 123
    development 147, 174
    ecosystem 187, 205, 237
    employees vs. xiii
    flexibility and 136

incentives 55
management 69, 205
management strategies 69, 167
mentoring 153, 155
pipeline 27, 121
pool 11, 225
retaining 1
sculpting 83
training 170
turnover and 56
war 2, 237
workers vs. 8
workforce planning and 167
talent dashboard 171, 173, 181, 183
continuous improvement 207
quittable 188
unquittable 187, 188
Talent Failwave xiii, xvi
teambuilding 14, 80, 225
teamwork 43
Technology Failwave xv–xvi
telecommuters 125
tenure 22, 121, 178
termination, justifiable 141
territoriality 163
thinking, strategic 139
Timbuktu 86
time off 11, 103. *See also* vacations
incentives 55, 66
paid 134, 202
toxic culture 118, 208. *See also* corporate culture
Toyota xiv
trading 64
training 119, 146, 232
annual 225
career pathways 79
communications 129
continuous improvement 217
corporate universities 117
cross-training 80, 121
incentives 58
lack of 119
management 110
onboarding 41, 52
performance management and 144
retraining 104
sensitivity 103
workforce planning 167, 170, 194
transitions 123, 144, 160

transparency 213
compensation 195
culture of 141
flexibility and 129
satisfaction and 192
travel 41
trust, culture of 126, 130, 132. *See also* corporate culture; culture
compensation and 195
importance of 216
leadership buy-in and 224
performance management and 141
truth 213
tuition reimbursement 158. *See also* corporate universities
compensation and 189
incentives 55
leadership buy-in 227
workforce planning and 172
Turks and Caicos 64, 65
turnover 8, 175, 217. *See also* retention
attracting talent and 21
career pathways and 69
corporate universities and 113, 119
exit interviews and 103, 104
flexibility and 128, 133, 134, 136
generational 153
incentives and 56
people analytics and 180, 187
performance management and 144

**U**

underperformance 151
understaffing 213
unemployment 177, 186, 208
unexcused absences 140
unit growth, net 197
universities, corporate 113. *See also* corporate universities
unlimited vacation 125. *See also* time off
unquittable organizations 24, 153. *See also* quittable organizations
career pathways 80
career sculpting 95
compensation systems 202
continuous improvement 220–221
corporate universities 122–123
employer branding 24–25
exit interviews 112
flexibility 136
incentives 66

unquittable organizations (*continued*)
    internships 39
    leadership buy-in 234
    mentoring 165–166
    onboarding 52
    people analytics 187–188
    performance management 151
    strategic workforce planning 178
unscheduled absences 128
us-vs.-them mindset 129, 211, 224

**V**

vacancies 185, 213
vacations 55, 125, 132, 134
values 239
    attracting talent and 13, 15
    career sculpting and 87
    corporate universities and 123
    incentives and 56, 59
    onboarding and 41, 42, 52
    performance management and 147,
        151
vendors 198
    relations 42
venture capital firms 61
visions 12, 157, 164
vital HR stats 212
voluntary leave 112
voluntary separations 97
volunteers 43, 77

**W**

W-4 form 41
wages, living 55. *See also* compensation
war for talent 2, 237

welcome packet 51
well-being 136
    health and 13
wellness programs 13, 14
work 125
    arrangements, flexible 125
    environment 6, 55
    history 8
    from home 189, 227
    hours 6, 41, 49
    meaningful 39
    plan, formal 228
workers xiii, 8
    hourly 208
workflow 39
workforce 170, 174
    aging 174
    career sculpting 84
    development 27
    growth 1
    innovative 43
    planning 206. *See also* strategic
        workforce planning
    skills assessment 121
working
    conditions 11
    hours 183
    styles 44, 157
work-life balance 2, 7, 89
    attracting talent 11, 14
    flexibility and 125, 127
    reasons for leaving 119
workplace
    culture 190. *See also* corporate culture
    investigations 101
work plan, formal 228
worst case scenario exercises 160

# ADDITIONAL SHRM-PUBLISHED BOOKS

*Preventing Workplace Harassment in a #MeToo World: A Guide to Cultivating a Harassment-Free Culture*
Bobbi K. Dominick, Esq.

*California Employment Law: An Employer's Guide, Revised & Updated for 2020*
James J. McDonald, Jr.

*The SHRM Essential Guide to Employment Law: A Handbook for HR Professionals, Managers, Businesses, and Organizations*
Charles H. Fleischer

*Developing Business Acumen SHRM Competency Series: Making an Impact in Small Business HR*
Jennifer Currence

*Applying Critical Evaluation SHRM Competency Series: Making an Impact in Small Business HR*
Jennifer Currence

*Mastering Consultation as an HR Practitioner*
Jennifer Currence

*From Hello to Goodbye: Proactive Tips for Maintaining Positive Employee Relations, Second Edition*
Christine V. Walters

*The Practical Guide to HR Analytics: Using Data to Inform, Transform & Empower HR Decisions*
Shonna D. Waters, Valerie N. Streets, Lindsay A. McFarlane, and Rachael Johnson-Murray

*HR on Purpose: Developing Deliberate People Passion*
Steve Browne

*The Price of Pettiness: Bad Behavior in the Workplace and How to Stomp it Out*
Alex Alonso

*A Manager's Guide to Developing Competencies in HR Staff*
Phyllis G. Hartman

*Extinguish Burnout: A Practical Guide to Prevention and Recovery*
Rob & Terri Bogue

*The HR Career Guide: Great Answers to Tough Career Questions*
Martin Yate

*Ace Your SHRM Certification Exam: A Guide to Success on the SHRM-CP® and SHRM-SCP® Exams*
Nancy A. Woolever, editor

*The Talent Fix: A Leader's Guide to Recruiting Great Talent*
Tim Sackett

*Motivation-Based Interviewing: A Revolutionary Approach to Hiring the Best*
Carol Quinn

*The Recruiter's Handbook: A Complete Guide for Sourcing, Selecting, and Engaging the Best Talent*
Sharlyn Lauby

*The Power of Stay Interviews for Engagement and Retention, Second Edition*
Richard P. Finnegan

*Predicting Business Success: Using Smarter Analytics to Drive Results*
Scott Mondore, Hannah Spell, Matt Betts, and Shane Douthitt

*From WE WILL to AT WILL: A Handbook for Veteran Hiring, Transitioning, and Thriving in the Workplace*
Justin Constantine

*Investing in People: Financial Impact of Human Resource Initiatives, Third Edition*
Wayne F. Cascio, John W. Boudreau, and Alexis A. Fink

*Solve Employee Problems Before They Start: Resolving Conflict in the Real World*
Scott Warrick

*Actualized Leadership: Meeting Your Shadow & Maximizing Your Potential*
William L. Sparks

*The 9 Faces of HR: A Disruptor's Guide to Mastering Innovation and Driving Real Change*
Kris Dunn

*Digital HR: A Guide to Technology-Enabled Human Resources*
Deborah D. Waddill

# SHRMSTORE BOOKS APPROVED FOR RECERTIFICATION CREDIT

*107 FAQs About Staffing Management*/Fiester, 9781586443733 (2016)

*47 FAQs About the Family and Medical Leave Act*/Fiester, 9781586443801 (2016)

*Manager's Guide to Developing Competencies in HR*/Hartman, 9781586444365 (2017)

*Ace Your SHRM Certification Exam*/Woolever, 9781586446147 (2019)

*Actualized Leadership*/Sparks, 9781586445683 (2019)

*Applying Critical Evaluation*/Currence, 9781586444426 (2017)

*Black Holes and White Spaces*/Boudreau, 9781586444624 (2018)

*California Employment Law*/McDonald, 9781586446390 (2020)

*Compensation Sense 101*/Faurote, 9781732663503 (2018)

*Defining HR Success*/Strobel 9781586443825 (2015)

*Destination Innovation*/Buhler, 9781586443832 (2015)

*Developing Business Acumen*/Currence, 9781586444143 (2016)

*Developing Management Proficiency*/Cohen, 9780367253103 (2020)

*Developing Proficiency in HR*/Cohen, 9781586444167 (2016)

*Digital HR*/Waddill, 9781586445423 (2018)

*EmployER Engagement*/Mahan, 9781950906253 (2020)

*Erasing Institutional Bias*/Jana, 9781523097579 (2018)

*The Essential HR Guide*/Carasco, 9781586445898 (2020)

*Extinguish Burnout*/Bogue, 9781586446345 (2019)

*From Hello to Goodbye, 2nd ed.*/Walters, 9781586444471 (2017)

*From WE WILL to AT WILL: Veteran Hiring*/Constantine, 9781586445072 (2018)

*Give Your Company a Fighting Chance*/Danaher, 9781586443658 (2015)

*Go Beyond the Job Description*/Lesko, 9781586445171 (2018)

*Good People, Bad Managers*/Culbert, 9780190652395 (2017)

*HR on Purpose*/Browne, 9781586444259 (2017)

*HR Rising*/Browne, 9781586446444 (2020)

*HR's Greatest Challenge*/Finnegan, 9781586443795 (2015)

*Human Resource Management*/Bauer, 9781506363127 (2019)

*Humanity Works*/Levit, 9780749483456 (2018)

*Investing in People, 3rd ed.*/Cascio, 9781586446093 (2019)

*Leadership from the Mission Control Room*/Hill, 9780998634319 (2017)

*Leading an HR Transformation*/Anderson, 9781586444860 (2018)

*Leading the Unleadable*/Willett, 9780814437605 (2017)

*Leading with Dignity*/Hicks, 9780300229639 (2018)

*Manager Onboarding*/Lauby, 9781586444075 (2016)

*Mastering Consultation as an HR Practitioner*/Currence, 9781586445027 (2018)

*Motivation-Based Interviewing*/Quinn, 9781586445478 (2018)

*New Power: How Power Works*/Heimans, 9780385541114 (2018)

*One Life: Leverage Work-Life Integration*/Uhereczky, 9782874035180 (2018)

*Organizational Design that Sticks*/Albrecht, 9781948699006 (2018)

*Overcoming Bias*/Jana, 9781626567252 (2016)

*Peer Coaching at Work*/Parker, 9780804797092 (2018)

*Perils and Pitfalls of California Employment Law*/Effland, 9781586443634 (2014)

*Point Counterpoint II: People & Strategy*/Vosburgh, 9781586444181 (2017)

*Practices for Engaging the 21st Century Workforce*/Castellano, 9780133086379 (2014)

*Predicting Business Success*/Mondore, 9781586445379 (2018)

*Preventing Workplace Harassment*/Dominick, 9781586445539 (2018)

*Reinventing Jobs: Applying Automation to Work*/Jesuthasan, 9781633694071 (2018)

*Solve Employee Problems Before They Start*/Warrick, 9781586446291 (2019)

*StandOut 2.0*/Buckingham, 9781633690745 (2015)

*Stop Bullying at Work*/Daniel, 9781586443856 (2016)

*Strategic HR*/Krow, 9781734223705 (2020)

*The 9 Faces of HR*/Dunn, 9781586445737 (2019)

*The Big Book of HR, Revised*/Mitchell, 9781632650894 (2017)

*The Circle Blueprint*/Skeen, 9781119434856 (2017)

*The HardTalk Handbook*/Metcalfe, 9781727046205 (2018)

*The HR Career Guide*/Yate, 9781586444761 (2018)

*The HR Insider: Land Your Dream Job and Keep It!*/Jeshani, 9781717475565 (2018)

*The Non-Obvious Guide To Employee Engagement*/Grant, 9781940858746 (2019)

*The Power of Stay Interviews, 2nd ed.*/Finnegan, 9781586445126 (2018)

*The Practical Guide to HR Analytics*/Waters, 9781586445324 (2018)

*The Price of Pettiness*/Alonso, 9781586446192 (2019)

*The Recruiter's Handbook*/Lauby, 9781586444655 (2018)

*The Self Determined Manager*/Deacon, 9781628655827 (2019)

*The SHRM Essential Guide to Employment Law*/Fleischer, 9781586444709 (2018)

*The Square and the Triangle*/Stevens, 9781612061474 (2018)

*The Surprising Science of Meetings*/Rogelberg, 9780190689216 (2019)

*The Talent Fix*/Sackett, 9781586445225 (2018)

*Thinking in Bets*/Duke, 9780735216358 (2018)

*Thrive By Design*/Rheem, 9781946633064 (2017)

*Touching People's Lives*/Losey, 9781586444310 (2017)

*Type R: Transformative Resilience*/Marston, 9781610398060 (2018)

*View from the Top*/Wright, 9781586444006 (2016)

*WE: Men, Women, and at Work*/Anderson, 9781119524694 (2018)

*Work Rules!*/Bock, 9781455554799 (2015)